Tutorial

To Accompany

Marketing Engineering
Computer-Assisted Marketing Analysis and Planning

Gary L. Lilien
The Pennsylvania State University

Arvind Rangaswamy
The Pennsylvania State University

Tutorial

To Accompany

Marketing Engineering
Computer-Assisted Marketing Analysis and Planning

Gary L. Lilien
The Pennsylvania State University

Arvind Rangaswamy
The Pennsylvania State University

 **ADDISON-WESLEY**

An imprint of Addison Wesley Longman, Inc.

Reading, Massachusetts • Menlo Park, California • New York • Harlow, England
Don Mills, Ontario • Sydney • Mexico City • Madrid • Amsterdam

A portion of the material in this Tutorial is subject to permissions cited in the main text.

Jenny's Gelato Case
AN ANALYTICAL APPROACH TO MARKETING DECISIONS by Dyer/Forman, ©1991.
Reprinted by permission of Prentice-Hall, Inc., Upper Saddle River, NJ.

Zenith High Definition TV Case
Copyright © 1990 by the President and Fellows of Harvard College.
Harvard Business School Case 591-025.
This case was prepared by F. Sultan as the basis for class discussion rather than to illustrate either effective or ineffective handling of an administrative situation. Reprinted by permission of Harvard Business School.

Johnson's Wax/Enhance Case
Copyright © 1982 by the President and Fellows of Harvard College.
Harvard Business School Case 583-046.
This case was prepared by Darral G. Clarke and revised in 1986 by Robert J. Dolan as the basis for class discussion rather than to illustrate either effective or ineffective handling of an administrative situation. Reprinted by permission of Harvard Business School.

Blue Mountain Coffee Company Case
From Marketing Management: Analytical Exercises for Spreadsheets, 2/e by Lilien. Copyright © 1993
By permission of South-Western College Publishing, a division of International Thomson Publishing Inc., Cincinnati, Ohio 45227.

Syntex Laboratories Case
Copyright ©1983 by the President and Fellows of Harvard College.
Harvard Business School Case 584-033.
This case was prepared by Darral G. Clarke as the basis for class discussion rather than to illustrate either effective or ineffective handling of an administrative situation. Reprinted by permission of Harvard Business School.

Tutorial to accompany Lilien/Rangaswamy: *Marketing Engineering:Computer Assisted Marketing Analysis and Planning*

Copyright © 1998 Addison Wesley Longman, Inc.

ISBN: 0-321-00195-8

12345678910-CRS-00999897

CONTENTS

PREFACE

This volume contains exercises, cases, and tutorials organized according to the same chapter sequence as volume 1. The primary purpose of this volume is to facilitate hands-on learning of the concepts and models described in volume 1. The exercises and cases describe management decision situations and the tutorials give step-by-step instructions for using the software. Typically, cases are more complex, and offer more details about the context for the marketing decision problems. Except for the "How Many Draft Commercials?" exercise (Chapter 1), every exercise or case has associated software.

To learn effectively from these materials, you must have some knowledge of marketing and familiarity with the Windows operating system and the Excel spreadsheet program. Although there is often strong temptation to get going with the software, we urge you to first read the accompanying exercise or case carefully before you work with the software. The "point and click" nature of this software belies the sophistication of the underlying models. So, take time to understand model outputs and experiments with alternative inputs as you try to resolve the decision situations presented to you.

Many of the software modules will accept new data sets that you provide. However, before you input your own data, use the software with the accompanying exercise or case to understand its capabilities and limitations. Remember also that all the software are educational versions that have limits on the problem sizes they will accept.

To get software tips and updates, please visit our web site, http://www.hepg.awl.com/lilien-rangaswamy/mktgeng. You can also send us your comments and suggestions about the software by using the e-mail facility available at this site.

Acknowledgments

This volume evolved over the past three years and represents a major undertaking. Mary Haight ably (and cheerfully) coordinated the development and production of this volume ensuring consistency in its structure and presentation. Katrin Starke helped us put these materials together. Vickie Schlegel and Andrew "Nuke" Stollak helped in producing the camera-ready copy. This trio worked as a team, often into the wee hours. We thank them for their extraordinary efforts. Finally, Penn State's ISBM generously supported this work, allowing us sometimes to take over the entire office space after hours for the production of these tutorials.

Gary L. Lilien
Arvind Rangaswamy
The Mary Jean and Frank P. Smeal
College of Business Administration
The Pennsylvania State University
June 1997

INTRODUCTION TO MARKETING ENGINEERING SOFTWARE (VERSION 1.0)

Installing *Marketing Engineering*

Installing the Marketing Engineering Software onto your computer's hard disk is an easy process, but you should still read through the entire installation instructions before you start.

A. This software is supplied to you on a CD-ROM. Before you start, make sure that you have the proper hardware and operating system:

Minimum configuration: IBM-compatible PCs running the 486 processor (33 MHz), 8 MB RAM, 55 MB available hard disk space, and a CD-ROM drive. Several applications (e.g., some Excel spreadsheet models and ADCAD: Ad Copy Design) will not run reliably under the minimum configuration.

Recommended configuration: IBM-compatible PCs running the Pentium or equivalent processor (60 MHz or better), 16MB RAM, 55 MB available hard disk space, and a 4× or better CD-ROM drive.

Operating system: Windows 3.1, Windows for Workgroups 3.11, Windows 95, and Windows NT.

Microsoft Excel: Parts of this software require the availability of Excel 5.0c or Excel 7.0. If you have not installed Excel on your system, you may still be able to use the non-Excel models included in this package. Marketing Engineering does not support Excel 97.

B. *Installing the Software*

1. Start Windows.

2. Insert the Marketing Engineering CD-ROM into your CD-ROM drive.

3. Run the install.exe application in drive x:\, where x is the letter of your CD-ROM drive.

4. Follow the instructions on the screen to complete the installation. We recommend that you install this program in the default directory c:\mktgeng, although it will work on any non-network drive.

> **NOTE**: *If you are installing Marketing Engineering under the Windows 3.1 or Windows for Workgroups 3.11, you **may** need to install additional files as described below.*

Check your windows and windows\system directories to see if you a have a file called win32s.ini. If you don't have this file you need to download and install a free patch file called pw1118.exe from Microsoft's ftp site:

ftp://ftp.microsoft.com/Softlib/MSLFILES/

Place the self-extracting file pw1118.exe in a directory of its own, because it expands into many files. (Alternatively you can copy the file into a temporary directory that gets cleaned out regularly.) First execute pw1118 which will generate a set of installation files including Setup.exe file. Next execute setup.exe.

Required add-ins for running Excel applications

For most Excel applications, you need the Solver tool. In addition, the Promotional Spending Analysis (MassMart) worksheet requires the Analysis ToolPak. These add-ins are not part of the default configuration when you install Microsoft Excel. Under the **Tools** menu on your version of Excel, check the list of **Add-Ins** to see whether they are included. If not run the Excel (or MS Office) setup procedure (with the original installation disks or CD) and select the respective options to install these add-ins.

Setting up Marketing Engineering after installation

Setting preferences: If you wish to customize the location of the files used by the program, go to the **Help** menu and select **Preferences**. In particular, make sure that the path to Excel.exe is correctly specified.

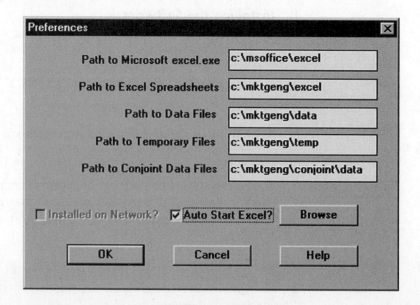

You can install the software on a network only with the network version of Marketing Engineering. If you check **Auto Start Excel,** the program will automatically start Excel every time you open Marketing Engineering. If you turn off this option, you can still open Excel whenever you want to by going to the **File** menu and choosing **Open Excel**.

Opening applications: When you start Marketing Engineering, you will briefly see the following screen:

On the **Model** menu select a model, e.g., **Positioning Analysis**.

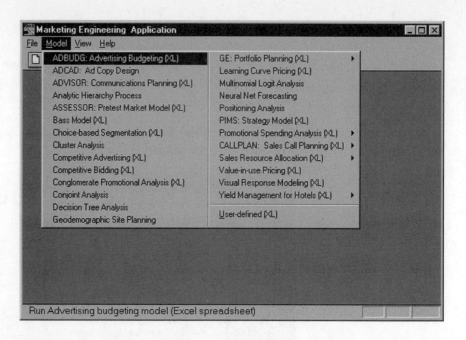

Tips for using the software

Marketing Engineering consists of three different types of software modules:

1. Windows-based programs that will run directly off the Marketing Engineering main menu:

    Cluster Analysis
    Multinomial Logit Analysis
    Positioning Analysis

2. Spreadsheet models that will be loaded under Excel:

    ADBUDG: Advertising Budgeting
    ADVISOR: Communications Planning
    ASSESSOR: Pretest Market Model
    Bass Model
    Choice-based Segmentation
    Competitive Advertising
    Competitive Bidding
    Conglomerate Promotional Analysis
    GE: Portfolio Planning
    Learning Curve Pricing
    PIMS: Strategy Model
    Promotional Spending Analysis
    CALLPLAN: Sales Call Planning
    Sales Resource Allocation
    Value-in-use Pricing
    Visual Response Modeling

Yield Management for Hotels

3. Stand-alone applications that are "loosely" connected to the main menu and are simply executed when invoked:

ADCAD: Ad Copy Design
Analytic Hierarchy Process
Conjoint Analysis
Decision Tree Analysis
Geodemographic Site Planning
Neural Net Forecasting

Select **Index** under the **Help** menu to get information about individual models and how to run them.

NOTE: *The following tips apply only to software modules that are **Microsoft Excel applications***.

Opening Excel models directly: You can open Excel models directly by clicking on *.xls files located in the (default) directory, c:\mktgeng\excel. This can be helpful if you have limited memory on your computer system to load the marketing engineering program. If you move the Excel files to a new directory, make sure that the file modgen.ind is also located in the new directory.

Moving between the main marketing engineering window and an Excel application: To move back and forth between the Marketing Engineering main window and an Excel application you can use the ALT+TAB key combination. You can also get back to the Marketing Engineering main window from an Excel application by going to the **Model** menu and clicking **Back to Mktg. Eng.**

Entering data into a Excel spreadsheet: After you enter data in a cell, press the Enter key to ensure that the data gets registered within the spreadsheet.

Using Solver: In some cases the Solver runs in Excel will not converge. You may then have to provide Solver with new starting values. See the appendix in Chapter 2 of the textbook.

Unprotecting locked cells: If you want to make changes to locked cells or if you want to unprotect the spreadsheet for certain Solver runs, go to the **Tools** menu, select **Protection**, and click **Unprotect**.

Saving Excel files. If you want to save any of the Excel spreadsheets that you modify, save it in the same directory (default: c:\mktgeng\excel) in which the other Excel files are located.

NOTE: *The following tips apply only to software modules that run directly off the main menu. These include Cluster Analysis, Multinomial Logit Analysis, and Positioning Analysis.*

Incorporating your own data sets: There are three ways to create new data sets for Cluster Analysis, Multinomial Logit Analysis, and Positioning Analysis.

1. ***Load an ascii file containing the data in the appropriate format*** : Use a standard word processing program to generate a text file that can be directly read by the program. The format for the file follows:

Perceptual Mapping	Line 1
3 4	Line 2
5.6 6.0 4.6 3.6	Section 1
4.4 3.6 5.2 2.2	
2.9 6.4 2.7 2.6	
Sprint	Section 2
MCI	
AT&T	
Other	
Value	Section 3
Service	
Special Programs	

Line 1: Enter title of data set
Line 2: Enter the number of rows and the number of columns of data
Section 1: Enter the data (separate by comma or space)
Section 2: Enter column headings
Section 3: Enter row headings

You can load this file into Marketing Engineering by selecting **File**, followed by **Open**. You will be prompted for the file name.

2. ***Import data from Excel*** : First, open the Marketing Engineering program. From the **File** menu, select **New**.

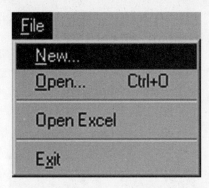

Enter a file name and click **OK** to see the following screen.

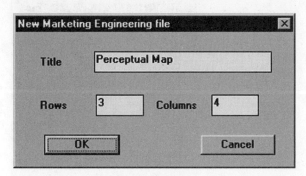

Enter a title for the data and the number of rows and columns. Next, enter or import a data set into Excel (just the data, no labels):

You can now import the data from Excel into Marketing Engineering in one of the following two ways:

Copy and paste the data directly into Marketing Engineering. In Excel, select the data range you want to import into Marketing Engineering. From the **Edit** menu use **Copy** or **Cut** to paste the data to Windows clipboard. Use the ALT+TAB key combination to get to the Marketing Engineering window. Place the cursor on the first row and first column of the blank spreadsheet and paste the data from Excel onto the Marketing Engineering worksheet. If you want to override the default column and row headings, enter the new names by selecting

Marketing Engineering's **Edit** menu and then **Edit Row Labels** or **Edit Column Labels**.

   Import as an Excel 4.0 file. Save the data as an Excel 4.0 worksheet. Go to the **File** menu in Marketing Engineering and select **Import Excel**. You will be prompted for the file name.

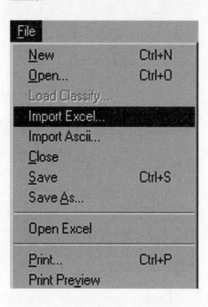

3. ***Import just data from an Ascii*** *file*: First open the Marketing Engineering program. From the **File** menu, select **New**. You will be prompted to provide a title for the data and the number of rows and columns. Load a text file that contains just the data (the 3×4 data set above), one record per line with data separated by a space or tab. Position the cursor on the first row and first column of the spreadsheet. On the **File** menu, select **Import ASCII**. You will prompted for the file name.

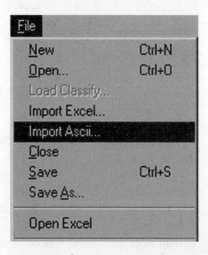

   If you wish to override the default column and row headings, enter the new names directly on the spreadsheet by going to the

Edit menu and selecting **Edit Row Labels** or **Edit Column Labels**.

4. ***Enter the data manually*** : On the **File** menu click **New**. You will be prompted to provide a title for the data and the number of rows and columns. Next you can enter data in the blank spreadsheet starting with the first column of the first row.

Viewing the data: Once you have entered or imported data into Marketing Engineering, you will see a graphical display of the data.

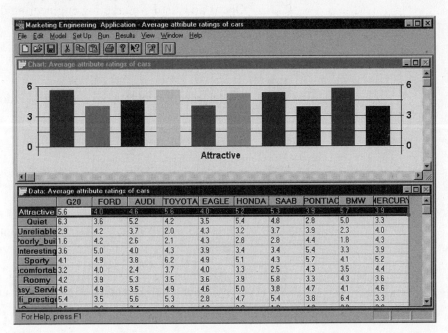

By clicking on a column or row header on the spreadsheet you can obtain a graphical display of the data in that column or row. You can also simultaneously display any subset of the data by dragging the mouse over the desired cells. On the **Edit** menu, you can use **Insert** and **Delete** to make changes to the data.

Changing row and column labels: On the Edit menu use **Edit Row Labels** and **Edit Column Labels** to make changes.

Modifying data: You can make changes to the data directly on the spreadsheet. These changes will be incorporated the next time you run the model. However the changes will not be saved for the future unless you specifically save them by going to the **File** menu and choosing **Save** or **Save As**.

Description of the Icons on Marketing Engineering toolbar. On the main window of Marketing Engineering, you will see the following toolbar.

Below is a short description of the each of the items on the toolbar:

Tool	Description
	Creates a new marketing engineering data worksheet.
	Opens an existing marketing engineering data worksheet.
	Saves the currently loaded file.
	Cuts a selection and places it on the Windows clipboard.
	Copies a selection to the clipboard.
	Pastes the contents of the clipboard.
	Prints the active data worksheet according to the current print settings.
	Displays marketing engineering version and copyright information.
	Opens the main help file for marketing engineering.
	Runs the selected program (Cluster Analysis, Multinomial Logit Analysis, or Positioning Analysis).
	Displays next chart in Multinomial Logit Analysis and Positioning Analysis.

HOW MANY DRAFT COMMERCIALS?*

Your boss directs TV advertising for a large corporation. Currently, the corporation's outside advertising agency creates a draft commercial and, after getting your boss's approval, completes production and arranges for it to be aired.

Your company's advertising budget is divided between creating and airing commercials. Your boss is considering increasing the proportion of the budget devoted to the first "creative" part of the process. He would do this by commissioning multiple ad agencies to each independently develop a draft commercial. He would then select the one for completion and airing that he determines would be most effective for promoting sales.

The standard technique for evaluating a draft commercial involves showing it to a trial audience and asking what they remembered about it later ("day after recall"). Both the effectiveness of a commercial and the exposure it receives will influence sales.

Your boss wants you to develop a marketing engineering approach for determining the "optimum" number of draft commercials to commission.

TEAM EXERCISE

Assemble your marketing engineering team in a room. Identify one member of the group to serve as an observer/reporter. The selected observer is not permitted to say anything during the modeling session.

Your team must deliver a model capable of answering your boss's question. You do not have to answer the question; just develop a model that can be used to do so.

Use a combination of equations, words, diagrams, flowcharts or graphs to express your model. Remember that someone else has to make sense of the model you develop.

In the class, each team will present its model and the observer for the team will then report on one admirable aspect of the team's process.

References

O' Connor, Gina Colarelli; Willemain, Thomas R.; and MacLachlan, James 1996, "The value of competition among agencies in developing ad campaigns: Revisiting Gross's model," *Journal of Advertising*, Vol. 25, No. 1 (Spring), pp. 51-62.

Gross, Irwin 1972, "The creative aspects of advertising," *Sloan Management Review*, Vol. 14 (Fall), pp. 83-109.

---

* This exercise is adapted from an exercise developed by Professor Thomas R. Willemain of Rensselaer Polytechnic Institute for classroom use, and is used here with his permission.

TUTORIAL FOR CONGLOMERATE INC. PROMOTIONAL ANALYSIS (CONGLOM)

The CONGLOM spreadsheet and the associated exercise is intended to familiarize you with building formulas in Excel, to teach you to use Excel's Solver function, and to introduce the concept of response functions.

On the **Model** menu, select **Conglomerate Promotional Analysis** (conglom.xls) to see the **Introduction** screen.

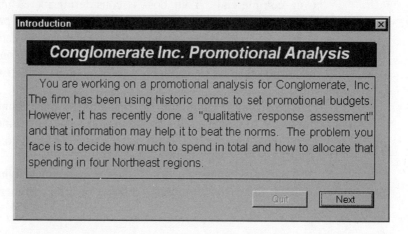

Click **Next** to see the main spreadsheet.

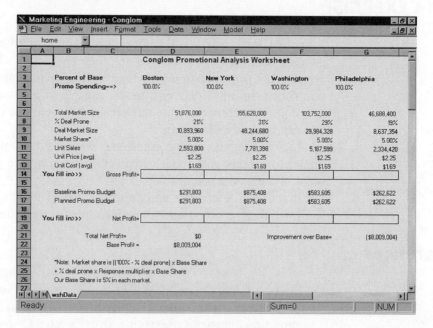

If you fill in the gross-profit and net-profit cells correctly your screen will look like this:

NOTE: *You must fill in the gross profit and net profit cells using Excel formulas that you develop.*

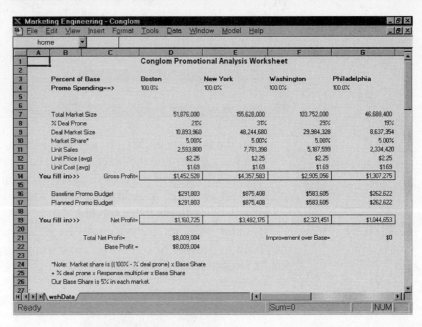

Next, you must determine the "optimal" spending level that maximizes Total Net Profit (cell D21). (Your spending level for each of the four regions must be greater than or equal to zero.)

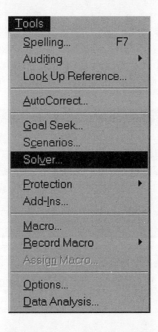

On the **Tools** menu, select **Solver** to perform this task.

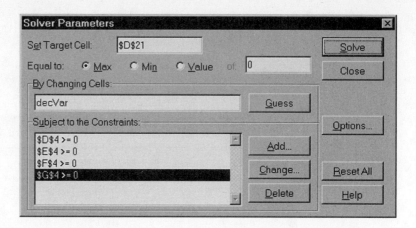

Enter the target cell, D21, the one you want to maximize.

You must determine the percent of the base promotional expenditure that will be allotted to each area (i.e., the decision variables are cells D4 to G4). And you need to **Add** constraints to be sure the values in D4 to G4 are ≥ 0. Click **Solve** to try solving.

In some cases, the Solver run in Excel will not converge. You may then have to provide Solver with new starting values. Please see the appendix to Chapter 2 of the text.

For other options, go to the **Model** menu and select **Main Menu**. The main menu offers the following options:

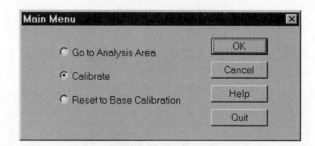

To modify the built-in response functions, select **Calibrate**. Choose one of the regions to pull up the base data for calibration and to change those data.

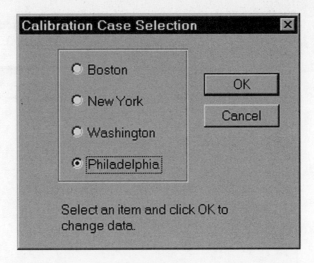

If you select Philadelphia, you will see the current values for the Philadelphia promotional response function. These are given as fractions of base response compared to fractions of base spending. These values are used to estimate the parameters of an Adbudg function (see Chapter 2).

In this case, you are asked to estimate and enter the sales level that you think would be realized if Conglomerate had

- No promotional budget
- Half of the current promotional budget (0.5 × $262,622)
- 50 percent more than the current promotional budget (1.5 × $262,622)
- An unlimited promotional budget

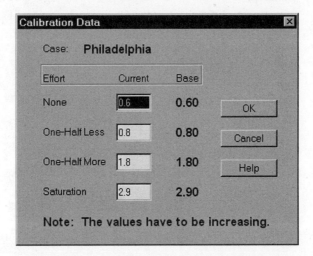

The base values for these four levels (0.6, 0.8, 1.8, and 2.9, respectively) are normalized relative to base sales level ($2,334,420). Thus the value 0.6 means: "If we cut our promotional budget to 0, we expect to sell 60 percent of $2,334,420."

If you make Philadelphia much less responsive to promotional effort by entering lower values in the **Current** column and click **OK**, you will see the new promotional response curve compared to the old one (you can thus verify that the new input data make sense).

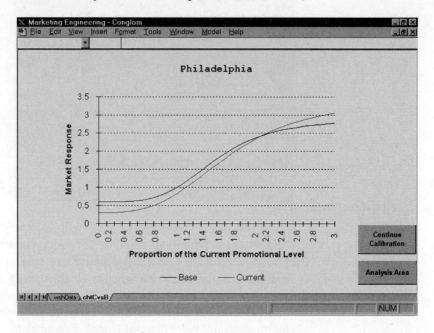

Click **Analysis Area** to do other analyses with different assumptions about market response. For example, by changing the values in cells D4 to G4 (multipliers of the current or base spending level) you can see the impact of changing spending levels and allocations on total net profit. You can recover the original base calibration at any time by going to the **Model** menu, selecting **Main Menu**, and selecting **Reset to Base Calibration**.

CONGLOMERATE, INC. PROMOTIONAL ANALYSIS

UBC (Unsweetened Breakfast Cereals) is one of Conglomerate, Inc.'s oldest divisions, competing heavily with Kellogg Co. and General Mills. Historically the division has been setting its own annual promotional budgets (across all six brands in the market) based on managerial judgment and rules of thumb.

UBC recently began to develop promotional response model tools to help it decide the level and allocation of promotional spending. It started with a prototype spreadsheet. The spreadsheet is intended to encourage discussion about the appropriate level of consumer promotions for four of its markets and to familiarize brand managers with *marketing engineering* and the related software tools and ideas. In this case, they were to learn about response modeling and optimization with Excel's Solver tool.

To get feedback on the value of the prototype, UBC purposely left the software incomplete. It is asking you (as a brand manager) to complete the missing cells in the spreadsheet (gross and net profit) using Excel formulas.

In addition, the brand group has been through a judgmental calibration exercise as background for promotional-response modeling. In essence, UBC asked the group to say what would happen to sales response for UBC brands as a whole if UBC spent $0? Fifty percent of the base level of promotional spending? One hundred and fifty percent of the base? An unlimited amount?

Using the brand managers' answers to these four questions, the software constructs a response model, which relates the amount of promotional spending to the sales that result from that spending.

The training session is designed to accomplish several goals:

- Familiarize you with building formulas in Excel
- Introduce you to the functionality of Excel's Solver tool
- Introduce the concepts of response functions and judgmental calibration
- Produce a preliminary promotional budget (and some sensitivity analysis) for these four Northeast regional markets
- Provide design feedback for a more complete, operational decisionsupport tool

NOTE: *The only cells you should change when running Solver are Cells D4 to G4—the percent of base promotional spending. The program updates the actual spending in cells D17 through G17 automatically.*

In your analysis, consider several scenarios:

Scenario 1: Optimal budget and allocation with no constraints.

Scenario 2: Optimal allocation with the same, planned (base) level of promotional spending.

Scenario 3: Optimal budget and allocation if promotional spending must be increased or decreased proportionally in all markets. (Hint: Set cells E4, F4, and G4 equal to cell D4 and change only D4 in the optimization.)

Scenario 4: Optimal budget and allocation as in scenario 1 but with the saturation spending response for Philadelphia set lower than that in the base calibration (say 2.0 versus the current level of 2.9). (An outside consultant says that Philadelphia is not nearly as sensitive to promotions as the brand group had originally guessed.)

After running through these scenarios, make suggestions to the marketing-engineering software designers about the uses and limitations of the tool (including enhanced versions) for the UBC division. The following issues have come up in earlier discussions: use at the brand level versus the SBU level, dynamics of market response, competition, other (missing) marketing-mix elements, model validation, and the like. What are the most critical characteristics to include in such a tool to ensure its broad use?

TUTORIAL FOR VISUAL RESPONSE MODELING (MODELER)

Modeler is an Excel spreadsheet that analyzes graphs designed to help you understand the results of market-response models with a single independent variable. Modeler has two modes of analysis: forecasting (where the independent variable refers to time) and response (where the independent variable refers to the marketing-mix element of interest).

The program allows you to

- Select a model form from a library of common response models
- Build a custom or user-defined model (with up to four parameters)
- Estimate model parameters (if data are available)
- Develop a profit function to explore the profit implications of the model (in response mode only)
- Explore how changes in response model parameters (such as elasticities) and profit parameters (such as production cost) affect market response

This tutorial is divided into three sections: In section 1, we describe how to develop a market response model and calibrate it with data. In section 2, we develop a user-defined function and apply it to the same data. Section 3 concerns the forecast model.

Section 1—Response curve for built-in model

From the **Model** menu select **Visual Response Modeling** (modeler.xls) to see the **Introduction** screen.

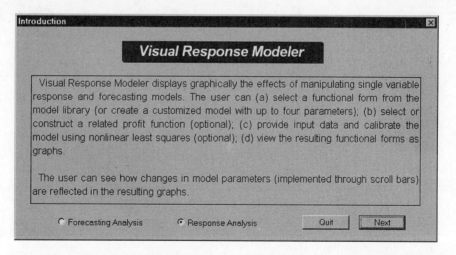

In the **Introduction** dialog box select **Response Analysis,** and click **Next** to go to the **Main Menu**.

From the **Main Menu**, choose the form of the response function and, optionally, the form of the profit function. For example, click the built-in ADBUDG response function from the drop-down menu and Marketing

Effort from the drop-down **Profit Function** menu to examine the effect of advertising expenditure.

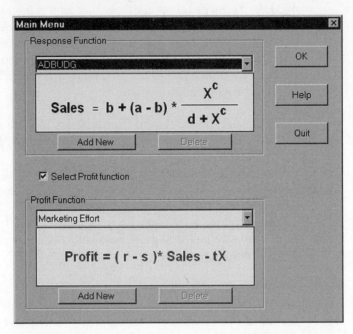

Click **OK** to get to the **Data Maintenance** sheet. The example screen below shows a short data series for marketing effort level (X) and the corresponding sales level (Y). These are data that you provide.

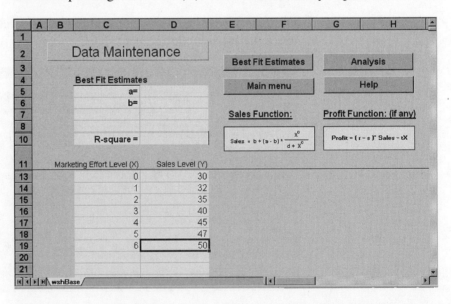

If you click **Analysis** without first selecting **Best-Fit Estimates**, you get the warning **No Best-Fit**. Even though calibrating the function takes time, it is generally a good idea to ask for the best-fit estimates—if only to get a benchmark.

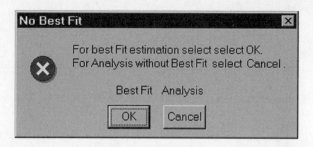

If you run **Best Fit Estimates**, you will get the **Curve Fitting** dialog box. You can specify constraints on the coefficients or provide initial guesses to be used in estimating coefficients. In the example below, we have entered initial estimates for the ADBUDG coefficients.

NOTE: *To obtain the best-fit estimates, the model minimizes a squared error objective function using Excel's Solver. As this involves a nonlinear least-squares estimation procedure, the algorithm may converge to a local (nonoptimal) solution or not converge at all. However, if you have reasonable initial estimates (and, in some cases, if you impose constraints, e.g., c>1) for the parameter coefficients, you can improve the chances that the algorithm will converge to a good solution. See Chapter 2 in the textbook for some insight into what parameter values may be reasonable.*

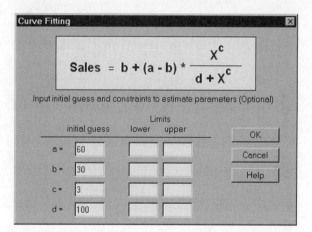

The program displays the results of the estimation procedure on a new sheet. If the procedure fails to converge on a solution, click **Retry** to get back to the **Curve Fitting** dialog box. Click **Discard** to start over. If the parameter estimates make sense and seem to provide a good fit (e.g., as indicated by a high R-square value), keep them and click **OK**.

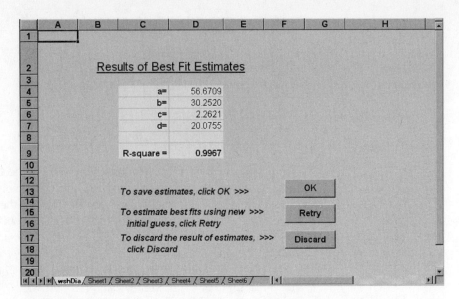

The **Data Maintenance** sheet shows the calculated estimates.

Once you have completed the data maintenance part of the analysis, click **Analysis.**

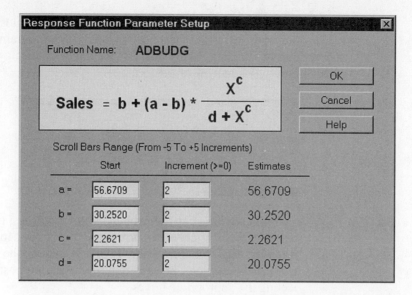

You will see the **Response Function Parameter Setup** dialog box. Specify the "tracking" ranges for each of the parameters. This will enable you to explore visually how the response curve changes as you vary the parameter values around the starting values. Specifically, the parameters can be varied from -5 increment to +5 increment around the start values. The program lists previously determined best-fit estimates to provide you with some guidance about what ranges to plot.

Click **OK**. You will get the **Profit Function Parameter Setup** dialog box if you previously checked this option in the **Main Menu**. In the example shown below, the increments have been given values of zero, which fixes the parameter values for the profit function.

Note that the parameters for the profit function are denoted as

> r = unit price,
> s = unit cost,
> t = unit cost of marketing mix variable.

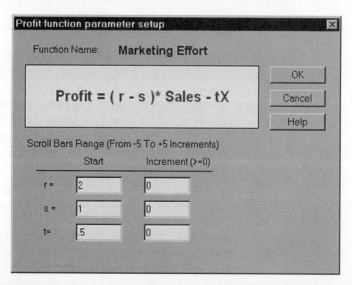

Next, specify the plotting range along the category axis (x-axis). To help you to specify a suitable range, the program informs you of the number of data points that are available for display. You can choose to plot over a narrow or broad range.

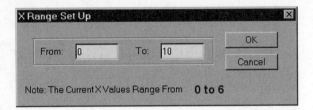

Finally, you can investigate your functions graphically. The first curve plotted reflects the current starting values for the parameters you provided earlier. Select **Show Profit** to include the profit function in the chart. You can look at your input data or the best fitting curve, by selecting the appropriate boxes.

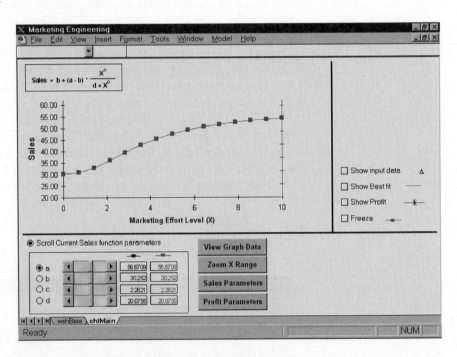

Select **Scroll Current Sales Function Parameters** to gain control of the scroll boxes linked to the response curve coefficient values. You can move the slider to change the values of the respective parameters and observe the effects on the curve. You can also try a graphical parameter calibration on the original data.

If you like a curve, check **Freeze** and the program will save the current parameter values as a reference. As you continue changing the parameter values, the changing curve will separate from the reference curve. You can have up to four curves, i.e., current, best fit, frozen, and profit, plotted on the screen at the same time.

Choose **Scroll Profit Function Parameters** to gain control of the scroll boxes linked to the profit-function coefficients. You can investigate the impact that parameter changes have on profitability, e.g., what happens if costs go down.

To modify the parameter setup for the visual tracking, e.g., the "tracking ranges," click **Sales Parameter** or **Profit Parameter**. To focus on smaller areas by defining finer ranges, click **Zoom X Range**.

Click **View Graph Data** to see the data behind the graphs as shown below.

	A	B	C	D	
1					
2			**Current Graph Data**		Back
3					
4					
5		*Marketing Effort Level (X)*	*Current Estimated Sales (Y)*	*Profit*	
6		0.00	30.252		
7		0.71	30.853		
8		1.43	32.905		
9		2.14	36.020		
10		2.86	39.465		
11		3.57	42.670		
12		4.29	45.380		
13		5.00	47.557		
14		5.71	49.267		
15		6.43	50.601		
16		7.14	51.643		
17		7.86	52.463		
18		8.57	53.114		
19		9.29	53.635		
20		10.00	54.057		
21					
22					

wshBase \ wshGraph

Section 2—Response curve for custom model

You can set up models with functional forms other than those provided by Modeler. To do this, access the **Main Menu** and click **Add New**.

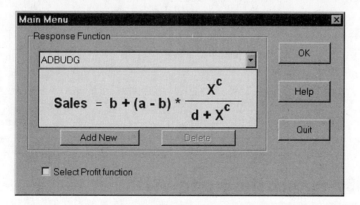

You can specify functions with up to four parameters. Input the formulas in Excel fashion (start your formula with the "="). Use X as the independent variable and a, b, c, and d (in alphabetical order) as parameters.

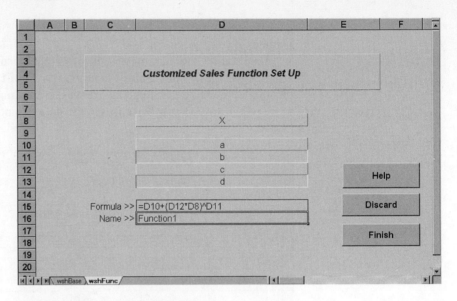

Click **Finish,** and your formula is displayed.

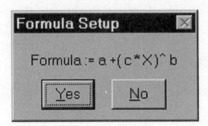

Click **Yes** if you want to retain the formula. Now, you can go back and reanalyze your old data with the new formula.

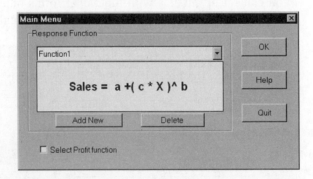

Section 3—Forecasting analysis

Modeler can also be used as a forecasting tool. From the **Model** menu, click **Introduction**. In the **Introduction** dialog box, select **Forecasting Analysis** and click **Next**.

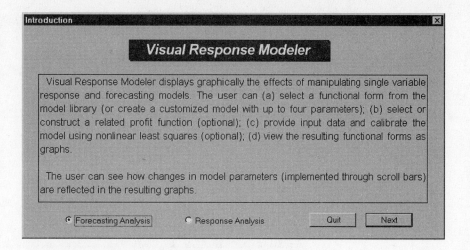

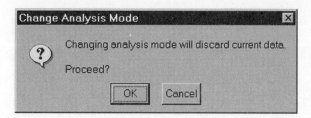

You will get a message warning you that all the data originating from previous analysis in the response mode will be discarded. Click **OK** to get to the **Main Menu**.

As before, you can select a functional form from the built-in model bank or design your own models. As an example, choose the **Bass** model.

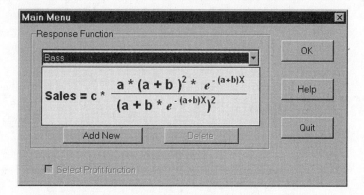

Click **OK**. On the **Data Maintenance** sheet click **Analysis** (no new data input) to get to the **Response Function Parameter Setup**. Provide parameter coefficients, values for the increments as well as for the range along the category axis (x-axis) to be plotted.

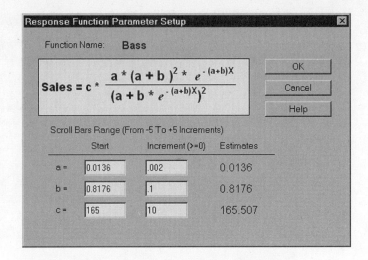

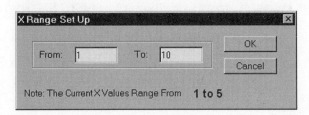

Subsequently, the program charts the resulting graph. You can do an analyses similar to that in the response function example; however, since X now refers to time, you cannot perform profit analyses.

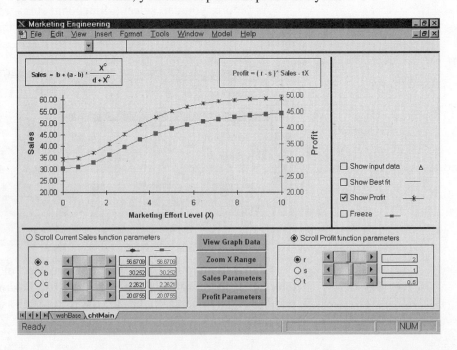

CONGLOMERATE, INC. RESPONSE MODEL EXERCISE

As part of the promotional resource allocation exercise that UBC's managers performed (see Conglomerate Inc. Promotional Analysis), they had to construct a response model. A response model relates a variable under the control of management (promotional spending in this case) with an important output (such as sales, the variable we focus on here). The result is a relationship between promotional spending and sales that can be linked to profit through a formula such as, for example,

Profit = Sales(Promotional $) × (Unit price - Unit cost) - Promotional $

Marketing Engineering provides a tool called Visual Response Modeler to develop and explore both response models and related profit functions.

In conjunction with the Conglomerate Inc. Promotional Analysis exercise, we will explore the promotional spending response analysis for New York.

Input information (drawn from the Conglomerate Inc. Promotional Analysis spreadsheet):

Promotional Spending ($MM)	Sales (MM units)
$0.00	6.3
$0.44	6.7
$0.87	8.0
$1.31	9.3
$5.00 (very large amount)	11.8

Price (to the trade) = $2.25
Cost to deliver to the trade = $1.69
(including manufacturing, shipping, and allocated overhead)

EXERCISES

1. Use Modeler to estimate the parameters of the response function and set up the associated profit function. Use ADBUDG for this purpose, as well as the associated profit function that has the form above. (You will have to go through the **Data Maintenance** step—inputting and calibrating the model.)

   a) Analyze the associated function (look at small variations around the parameter estimates) and variations in the parameters for the profit function.
   b) What does the model suggest as the best level of promotional spending? (Does this correspond with what you saw in the Conglomerate Inc. Promotional Analysis Exercise?)
   c) What happens to that optimal spending level if

- The market saturates at 13.8MM units rather than the 11.8MM above?
- Improvements in logistics allow us to reduce the cost of delivered goods to New York to $1.39/unit from $1.69/unit?

2. Comment on the strengths and weaknesses of Visual Response Modeling software as an aid to exploring and building models of market response to marketing effort.

TUTORIAL FOR CLUSTER ANALYSIS

The Cluster Analysis program is a sophisticated software tool for conducting segmentation studies. It also enables users to develop marketing programs for targeted segments by using characteristics that maximally discriminate between customers in different segments.

The program implements two cluster-analysis procedures: Ward's (hierarchical) method and a K-Means (nonhierarchical) procedure as well as an associated factor analysis procedure to preprocess input data and a discriminant analysis procedure to identify the variables that best discriminate between the clusters.

To run Cluster Analysis, you must have a data file structured so that the rows are customers and the columns are the variables that reflect the preferences or needs of those customers (the segmentation basis variables. If you select the discriminant analysis option, you must identify a second separate data file with the same number of rows (referring to the customers) but possibly with a different number of columns (which reflect the segment descriptors). The needs data and the descriptor data are kept in two separate files to ensure that segmentation criteria and targeting criteria need not and often will not be the same.

We illustrate the use of the program below, referring to the exercise on Conglomerate's new PDA. The exercise concerns identifying need-based segments for a new type of personal digital assistant (PDA) and finding a way to target the selected segments. The data for this exercise are in two files:

- PDA.DAT contains information on the needs of sampled customers.
- PDA_DIS.DAT contains information on demographics and other variables relevant to developing a program for targeting a PDA to these customers.

From the **Model** menu, select **Cluster Analysis**. You will be prompted to choose the file containing input data. Use the file PDA.DAT for the exercise. This will load the data into the program.

NOTE: *If you make changes to the data to evaluate alternative solutions, the program will not automatically save these changes. Save the changes (under a separate file name if necessary) by going to the **File** menu and clicking **Save As**.*

Go to the **Set Up** menu to select the parameters for your analysis as shown in the following example:

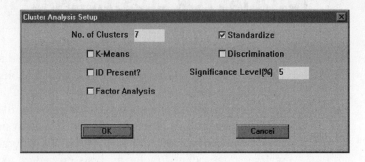

In the area for **No. of Clusters,** you can choose between two and nine clusters (segments) for analysis. If you choose **Standardize**, all variables will be standardized to 0 mean and unit variance before analysis. Choosing this option is a good idea if the variables are measured on different scales, as is the price variable in this example. **Discrimination** allows you to maximally discriminate among the resulting segments using the demographic variables available in PDA_DIS.DAT (the program will prompt you to indicate this file name when needed). **ID Present** allows you to label a case in the data. Such identification is useful in developing segment-specific marketing programs.

NOTE: *The ID Present option is disabled in this educational version of the software.*

As a default, this program uses the Ward's minimum-variance hierarchical-clustering analysis. By selecting **K-Means,** you can run a K-Means clustering algorithm. In this case, the output of hierarchical clustering provides the initial configuration for the K-Means clustering. After you select the options for the run, click **OK**.

If you check **Factor Analysis,** the program will preprocess your input data to identify a set of factors (see the appendix of Chapter 4 of the text), which it then uses in the cluster analysis procedure. Factor analysis will standardize the variables before finding the underlying factors. However the resulting factor scores, which are then used for factor analysis, are not standardized. We recommend that you use unstandardized factor scores in the cluster analysis procedure. Thus, you should not check **Standardize** in the setup box.

Next go to the **Run** menu and select **Run Model**. If you selected **Factor Analysis,** you will see the following dialog box that asks you to select the number of factors you want to retain for the cluster analysis procedure (this allows you to override the number of factors recommended by the program).

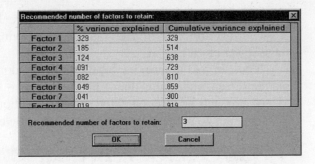

Recommended number of factors to retain:

	% variance explained	Cumulative variance explained
Factor 1	.329	.329
Factor 2	.185	.514
Factor 3	.124	.638
Factor 4	.091	.729
Factor 5	.082	.810
Factor 6	.049	.859
Factor 7	.041	.900
Factor 8	.019	.919

Recommended number of factors to retain: 3

OK   Cancel

After the program runs, you will see the results of the analysis displayed in the top window. To see the output more clearly, you can maximize this window. In this example, the resulting screen displays the members of the five segments.

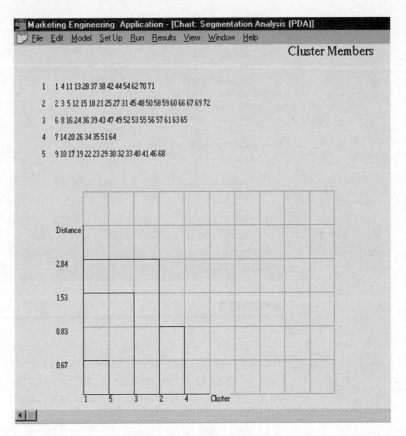

If you scroll down the window, you will see a dendogram showing the distances between the clusters. If you want to remove the grids from the dendogram, go to the **View** menu, choose **View Options**, and clear the check box for **Grid**. (The dendogram is displayed only if you did not choose the K-Means clustering option.)

In this example, clusters 1 and 5 are the closest clusters, separated by a distance of 0.67 units; clusters 2 and 4 are separated by 0.83 units; and clusters 1 and 3 are separated by 1.53 units. If you decide on a four-cluster solution, the two nearest clusters (1 and 5) will be merged into one cluster. Use the dendogram to select an appropriate number of clusters. (One way to determine the number of clusters is to look for a solution in which the clusters are separated evenly). You can combine clusters that are close to each other by specifying a solution that contains fewer clusters.

You can add descriptive labels to the dendogram. Click anywhere on the screen, and a label dialog box will appear. What you enter in this dialog box will be inserted at the selected location. To delete the labels you entered, go to the **Edit** menu and choose **Delete Labels**.

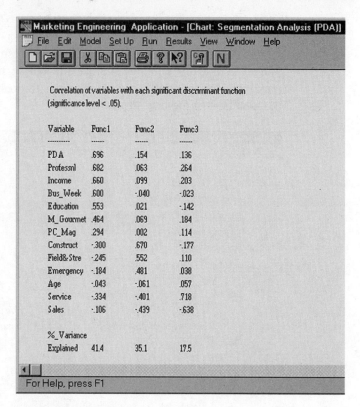

EXHIBIT 1

Exhibit 1 shows the correlation between each variable and the statistically significant discriminant functions. (This is displayed only if you selected **Discrimination** in the **Set Up** box.) The *absolute magnitude* of this correlation indicates the extent to which a variable discriminates between the clusters. In this example, whether someone is a professional is an important descriptor of the cluster to which that person belongs. The "Professional" variable correlates highly with a discriminant function (Function 1) that explains 41.4 percent of the variation among the respondents included in the study.

To print a copy of the summary results to an attached printer, go to **File** and choose **Print**. To cut and paste these results as an object in another Windows application (e.g., Word for Windows), bring the display window to the foreground, go to the **Edit** menu and select **Cut** or **Copy** and then paste into another Windows application.

You can view an extensive set of associated diagnostics (means of variables in each segment, hit rate, etc.) by going to the **Results** menu and selecting **View Diagnostics**.

If you selected **Factor Analysis,** the first set of diagnostics that you would see is the following table showing variance explained by each factor and the factor score matrix.

Diagnostics for factor analysis

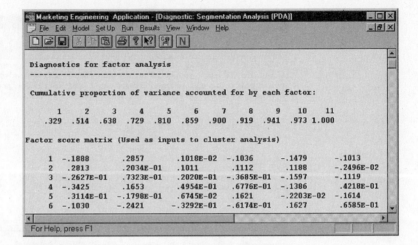

EXHIBIT 2

Diagnostics for cluster analysis

If you did not select **K-Means** in the **Set Up** box, you will see the table shown below for the hierarchical-clustering procedure (Ward's method).

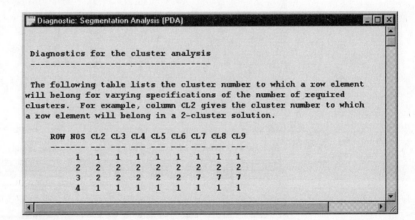

EXHIBIT 3

Exhibit 3 lists the cluster number to which a row element (case) will belong for varying numbers of clusters. For example, row 3 will belong to cluster 2 as long as you specify fewer than seven clusters. If you specify more than seven clusters, this respondent will be assigned to cluster 7.

If you selected **K-Means** in the **Set Up** box, you will see the table shown in exhibit 4 giving the probabilities of each row element belonging to each cluster. The probabilities are in inverse proportion to the distance between a respondent's characteristics and cluster centroids.

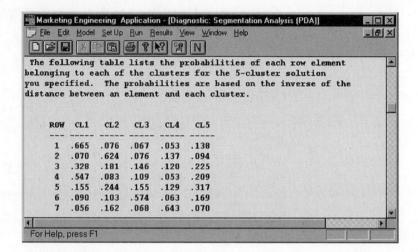

EXHIBIT 4

Marketing Engineering Application - [Diagnostic: Segmentation Analysis (PDA)]
File Edit Model Set Up Run Results View Window Help

Actual Cluster	# of cases	Predicted cluster				
		CL1	CL2	CL3	CL4	CL5
CL1	13	6	1	1	2	3
		46.2%	7.7%	7.7%	15.4%	23.1%
CL2	20	2	11	0	2	5
		10.0%	55.0%	.0%	10.0%	25.0%
CL3	17	2	0	13	1	1
		11.8%	.0%	76.5%	5.9%	5.9%
CL4	8	0	0	0	8	0
		.0%	.0%	.0%	100.0%	.0%
CL5	14	4	3	0	1	6
		28.6%	21.4%	.0%	7.1%	42.9%

Hit rate: Percent of total cases correctly classified: 61.11

For Help, press F1

EXHIBIT 5

Exhibit 5 presents a summary of the predictive validity of the discriminant analysis. The overall hit rate is the proportion of all individuals who are correctly assigned by the discriminant functions. The matrix indicates the predictive ability of the discriminant functions with respect to each cluster.

You can also see the mean of each needs variable in each cluster and the mean of each descriptor variable (if you had selected **Discrimination** in the **Set Up** box).

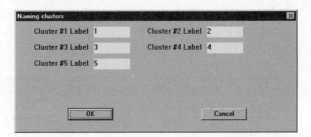

EXHIBIT 6

Once you settle on a cluster solution you may wish to name the clusters for identification and for generating reports. Choose names that seem to best characterize those clusters. On the **Edit** menu click **Edit Cluster Labels** and enter the appropriate names in the boxes provided.

Once you complete cluster analysis, you can use the results of the completed analysis to classify any number of new cases according to the discriminant functions. This ability to assign a large database of customers to selected target segments based on a smaller study sample enhances the implementability of the segmentation study. First, load a file containing demographic information about the new cases. For the purposes of this tutorial you may use PDA_DIS.DAT for classification. Go to the **File** menu and click **Load Classify**.

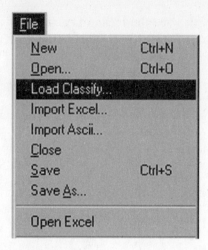

Next, go to the **Run** menu and click **Classify**.

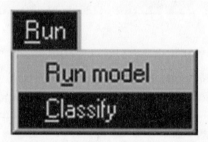

This will display the results of the classification analysis on the spreadsheet, showing the segment to which each new case was assigned. Here case 1 is assigned to cluster 1, case 3 to cluster 2, etc.

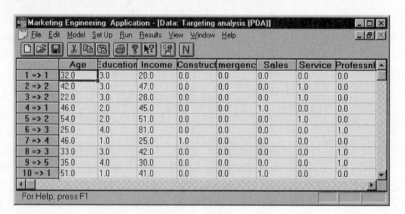

Limitations of the educational version of the software

Maximum number of variables:	15
Maximum number of observations:	200
Maximum number of clusters:	9
Nominal variables:	Cannot use nominal data in cluster analysis, but you could use nominal variables (dummy coded) in discriminant analysis.

References

Dillon, William R. and Goldstein, Matthew 1984, *Multivariate Analysis: Methods and Applications*, John Wiley & Sons, New York.

Hartigan, J.A. and Wong, M.A. 1979, "K-Means Algorithm", *Applied Statistics*, Vol. 28, No. 1, pp. 100-108.

Moriarty, Rowland T. and Reibstein, David J. 1982, *Benefit Segmentation: An Industrial Application*, Report No. 82-110.

Murtagh, F. 1985, *Multidimensional Clustering Algorithms*, (CompStat Lectures 4). Physica-Verlag, Würzburg/Wien.

CONGLOMERATE INC.'S NEW PDA CASE

Conglomerate Inc.'s new PDA (1995)

The cellular phone division of Conglomerate Inc. has teamed up with a PC manufacturer to develop, produce, and market a novel hybrid combination of a personal digital assistant (PDA) and a "smart" cellular phone. They have tentatively named it **ConneCtor**. It transmits and receives both data and voice (unlike competing PDAs which focus on data).

ConneCtor
Another Conglomerate Success Story?

ConneCtor is lightweight and is shaped like a portable phone with a small backlit LCD touch screen along the handset. Its (open) operating system performs standard cellphone functions and such personal information management (PIM) functions as a calendar, calculator, and address book. It can send and receive faxes, voice messages, and e-mail. Users can input data in four ways:

- By typing on the screen keyboard
- By using a numerical keyboard
- By writing on the screen in "digital ink"

■ By speaking into the phone (it includes voice recognition software)

The voice recognition feature is based on a neural network that is trained to recognize a particular user's voice patterns. An additional feature unique to **ConneCtor** is linkage via wireless local area networks to other PDA's.

In summary, the features of Conglomerate's handheld device are

■ Instant communication from PDA to PDA
■ Cellular phone and pager, fax and e-mail
■ Calendar, scheduler, calculator, and address book
■ An open system for customized applications
■ A paperless note pad
■ Voice recognition

Conglomerate is now trying to identify segments within the market for PDAs, target appropriate segment(s) for **ConneCtor,** and position **ConneCtor** in the chosen segments.

Background on the PDA market

In August 1993, Apple introduced its Newton PDA. The broad acceptance that Apple had anticipated did not materialize, and Apple sold only 80,000 Newtons that year. In 1995, the PDA appeared to be on the verge of greater growth and development. The PDA market had grown in four areas: specialized vertical applications (e.g., physician scheduling), PIM (personal information management), mobile communications, and as a supplementary gateway into the Internet.

Even though it has four main applications, the PDA is primarily targeted at "road warriors" or "mobile professionals." This group consists of approximately 25 million people in the United States, of whom about 5 million travel with a computer notebook. Many of these individuals already have cellular phones and must send and receive a large number of messages and data. The standard PDA cannot handle their needs.

The survey

Conglomerate, Inc. hired a market research firm to survey the market across a broad range of occupation types. The survey includes a screening item asking respondents if they had or would consider a PDA. Only those respondents who answered affirmatively to that question were retained for further analysis.

The questionnaire

The questionnaire asked the respondents to provide data on two kinds of variables: segmentation basis or needs variables and variables that could be used in describing or targeting the clusters using discriminant analysis.

Questions for determining segmentation-basis variables

X1   Whenever new technologies emerge in my field, I am among the first to adopt them.
(1 = Strongly disagree......7 = Strongly agree)

How often do you use the following:
(1 = never......7 = always)

X2   a) Pager?

X3   b) Phone or voice mail?

X4   c)Scheduling or contact-management tools, i.e., filofax or similar devices?

X5   How often do others send you time-sensitive information (e.g., work orders)?
(1 = never......7 = daily)

X6   How often do you have to send time-sensitive information while away from your office?
(1 = never ...... 7 = daily)

X7   How much of your time do you spend away from your office location?
(1 = 0 %......7 = 70% or more)

X8   How important is wireless communication to you?
(1 = Not at all important.....7 = very important)

X9   How important is it for you to share information rapidly with colleagues while away from an office location?
(1 = not at all important......7 = very important)
How much would you be willing to pay for a personal digital assistant (PDA) with the following features: instant communication from PDA to PDA, cellular phone and pager, fax and e-mail, calendar, scheduler, calculator, address book, open system for customized applications, paperless note pad, and voice recognition?

X10   a) Monthly (for all services that you use)?

X11   b) Invoice price for the PDA device with all features?

Questions for determining variables for discriminant analysis

Z1   Age

Z2   Education (1 = high school, 2 = some college, 3 = college, 4 = graduate degree)

Z3   Income

Type of industry or occupation: (0 = no, 1 = yes)

Z4   Construction

Z5   Emergency (fire, police, ambulance, etc.)

Z6   Sales (insurance, pharmacy, etc.)

Z7   Maintenance and service

Z8   Professional (e.g., lawyers, consultants, etc.)

Z9   Do you own a PDA?

Media consumption (Readership of magazines): (0 = no, 1 = yes)

Z10   *Businessweek*

Z11   *PC Magazine*

Z12   *Field & Stream*

Z13   *Modern Gourmet*

EXERCISES

1. Run only cluster analysis (without **Discrimination**) on the data to try to identify the number of distinct segments present in this market. Consider both the distances separating the segments and the characteristics of the resulting segments.

2. Identify and profile (name) the clusters that you select. Given the attributes of **ConneCtor**, which cluster would you target for your marketing campaign?

3. Go back to **Set Up**, check **Discrimination**, and rerun the analysis. How would you go about targeting the segment(s) you picked in question 2?

4. How has this analysis helped you to segment the market for **ConneCtor?**

5. What other data analyses would you do to develop a marketing program for **ConneCtor**?

TUTORIAL FOR CHOICE-BASED SEGMENTATION (ABB)

The ABB spreadsheet illustrates the use of choice-based segmentation as applied at ABB Electric. It is designed to accompany the ABB Electric segmentation case.

On the **Model** menu, select **Choice-based Segmentation** (abb.xls) to see the **Introduction** screen.

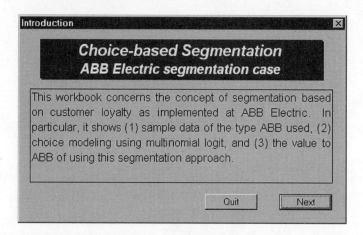

Click **Next** to get to the **Main Menu**.

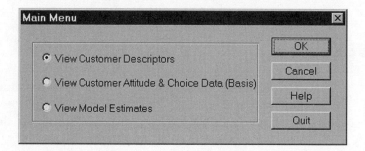

On the **Main Menu** select **View Customer Descriptors** and click **OK**. This will bring you to the main worksheet containing customer descriptor data on 88 customer firms.

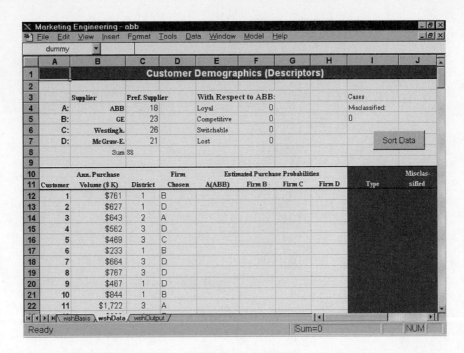

Click the **Sort Data** button to unprotect the spreadsheet if you want to use Excel's sort function on this database. Sorting can be helpful for answering the first question in the exercise.

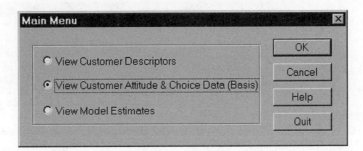

Next go to the **Model Menu**, choose **Main Menu**, and then select **View Customer Attitude and Choice Data** to view a list of the ratings of the suppliers by the same 88 customers whose descriptor information you saw earlier.

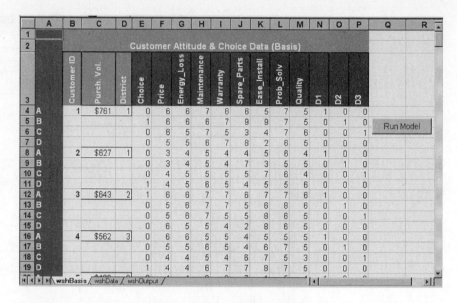

Click the **Run Model** button to develop choice-model estimates from the selected data. A dialog box will prompt you to specify the data range for the choice model. The column titled "Choice" contains data values that are either 0 or 1. A "1" means that the customer chose the corresponding supplier (A, B, C, or D).

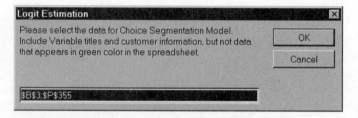

When you select the data range, please include the "Customer ID," "Purchase Volume," "District," and "Choice" columns as well as the title bars for the variables selected for analysis.

NOTE: *Although you must select contiguous areas for processing, you can trim the input data beforehand. For example you can delete outliers or discard variables from the set. We recommend that you set the calculation mode to manual on the* **Tools** *menu, choose* **Options**, *then* **Calculation**, *and then choose* **Manual** *if you wish to make several modifications to the data at once.*

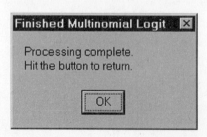

Message boxes may pop up to indicate the status of the processing. When a message box appears, click **OK** to continue.

After the program executes the choice model, it will calculate each customer's probability of purchasing from each of the suppliers. In addition, it computes MNL (multinominal logit) coefficient estimates for all the variables included in the model.

You will now see a table showing the coefficient estimates for each independent variable and the associated statistics. The three dummy variables, D1, D2, and D3, capture the impact of suppliers' overall reputations. In addition columns Prob{1} through Prob{4} summarize the choice probabilities of each supplier for each customer.

| | X Marketing Engineering – abb | | | | | | | | _ | 6 | X |

| | File | Edit | View | Insert | Format | Tools | Data | Window | Model | Help | | |
| | A1 | | | MNL Estimation Result | | | | | | | | |

	A	B	C	D	E	F	G	H	I	J
1					MNL Estimation Result					
2		Coefficient	Standard E	t stat					p-value (2-tailed)	
3	Price	2.180582	0.586579	3.71746					0.00038	
4	Energy_Loss	2.65561	0.673706	3.94179					0.00018	
5	Maintenance	0.593692	0.437028	1.35847					0.17828	
6	Warranty	1.140702	0.330995	3.44629					0.00092	
7	Spare_Parts	-0.13262	0.21757	-0.60955					0.54395	
8	Ease_Install	0.520023	0.172875	3.00808					0.00355	
9	Prob_Solv	2.032181	0.549676	3.69705					0.00041	
10	Quality	2.639413	0.687749	3.83775					0.00025	
11	D1	-0.123791	0.678549	-0.18244					0.85572	
12	D2	-0.671218	0.71941	-0.93301					0.35373	
13	D3	-0.687235	0.715046	-0.96111					0.33951	
14	CustomerID	Purchase V	District	Choice	Prob{1}	Prob{2}	Prob{3}	Prob{4}		
15	1	761	1	B	15.30%	82.27%	2.42%	0.01%	Paste	
16	2	627	1	D	0.00%	0.00%	2.61%	97.39%	Data	
17	3	643	2	A	74.70%	25.29%	0.01%	0.00%		
18	4	562	3	D	48.79%	39.73%	0.00%	11.48%		
19	5	469	3	C	1.97%	0.01%	98.02%	0.00%		
20	6	233	1	B	0.01%	96.85%	3.09%	0.04%		
21	7	664	3	D	40.47%	7.69%	0.08%	51.76%		

wshBasis / wshData \ wshOutput /

Ready   Sum=0   NUM

Click **Paste Data** to pass the estimated purchase probabilities for all customers on to the descriptor sheet.

	X Marketing Engineering – Abb.xls
	File Edit View Insert Format Tools Data Window Model Help
	M41

	A	B	C	D	E	F	G	H	I	J
1				Customer Demographics (Descriptors)						
2										
3		Supplier	Pref. Supplier		With Respect to ABB:				Cases	
4	A:	ABB	18		Loyal	9			Misclassified:	
5	B:	GE	23		Competitive	9			14	
6	C:	Westingh.	26		Switchable	13				
7	D:	McGraw-E.	21		Lost	57			Sort Data	
8		Sum	88							
9										

	Ann. Purchase		Firm	Estimated Purchase Probabilities					Misclas-
11	ustomer	Volume ($ K)	District	Chosen	A(ABB)	Firm B	Firm C	Firm D	Type	sified
12	1	$761	1	B	15.3%	82.3%	2.4%	0.0%	4_Lost	
13	2	$627	1	D	0.0%	0.0%	2.6%	97.4%	4_Lost	
14	3	$643	2	A	74.7%	25.3%	0.0%	0.0%	2_Competitive	
15	4	$562	3	D	48.8%	39.7%	0.0%	11.5%	1_Switchable	@
16	5	$469	3	C	2.0%	0.0%	98.0%	0.0%	4_Lost	
17	6	$233	1	B	0.0%	96.8%	3.1%	0.0%	4_Lost	
18	7	$664	3	D	40.5%	7.7%	0.1%	51.8%	1_Switchable	

The column labeled "Type" indicates the loyalty segment to which a customer belongs. The column labeled "Misclassified" indicates whether, on the immediately previous occasion, a customer purchased from a supplier who did not have the highest choice probability.

We assign customer firms to one of the four segment types (loyal, competitive, lost, and switchable) using a simple heuristic:

Loyal if the firm is a current customer of ABB (i.e., purchased from ABB on the immediate previous purchase occasion) and its probability of choosing ABB is greater than 0.80.

Competitive if the firm is a current customer of ABB and its choice probability is less than 0.80.

Lost if the firm is: (1) not a current customer, and (2) its probability of buying from one of the competitors is greater than 0.80, or its probability of buying from ABB is less than 0.15.

Switchable if none of the above applies.

Professor Gensch used a formal model and statistically tested for the significance of the differences in probabilities between individual firms in the analysis (see Gensch 1987).

Use this information to develop a segmentation and targeting strategy for ABB Electric by sorting the database on several criteria to explore which customers it should target and what marketing strategies may be appropriate.

Reference

Gensch, Dennis H. 1987, "A two-stage disaggregate attribute choice model," *Marketing Science*, 6 (Summer), pp. 223-239.

Gensch, Dennis H. 1990, "A choice-modeling market information system that enabled ABB Electric to expand its market share," *Interfaces*, Vol. 20, No. 1 (January-February), pp. 6-25.

ABB ELECTRIC SEGMENTATION CASE*

History

In March 1970, ABB Electric was incorporated as a Wisconsin-chartered corporation with initial capital provided by ASEA-ABB Sweden and RTE Corporation. The new firm's management was to operate independently of the parent company. The company mission was to design and manufacture a line of medium-sized power transformers to market in North America. The firm produced such electrical equipment as transformers, breakers, switchgears, and relays used in distributing and transmitting electrical energy. Four main types of customers buy this electrical equipment: (1) investor-owner electrical utilities (IOUs), the largest segment; (2) rural electrification cooperatives (RECs); (3) municipalities; and (4) industrial firms. Most of ABB Electric's customers were electrical utilities.

Situation in 1974

After three years of operation, ABB Electric was approaching the breakeven point when it encountered a serious problem. Its market share in 1974 was around six percent. In 1974, total industry sales of electrical equipment dropped 50 percent compared to 1973. Further ABB Electric was a small player in an industry dominated by large competitors such as General Electric, Westinghouse, and McGraw-Edison.

ABB Electric faced several other issues at this time. The sales force relied on traditional methods of selling and was not well focused. The salespeople acted independently and did whatever they thought they needed to do to close sales quickly. At the same time, the board of directors was pushing for standardization of products and cost reduction. The board felt that to compete effectively against the larger companies and to improve its current position of marginal profitability, ABB Electric would need a cost advantage. The directors thought this particularly important because all the major competitors made good quality products that were similar to ABB Electric's. ABB Electric would have to find some way to differentiate itself in the marketplace.

Virtually all of ABB Electric's sales were to one type of customer, the investor-owned electrical utilities. Because these utilities already had substantial inventories, sales to this group were projected to fall as much as 80 percent per year for the next two or three years. Because ABB's sales force focused most of its effort on this market segment, the company had little penetration among the over 3,000 RECs and over 100,000 small municipalities and industrial companies who tended to purchase occasionally or only once. Westinghouse, General Electric, and McGraw-Edison were well-established long-time suppliers to RECs, municipalities, and industrial customers.

---

*This case was developed by Katrin Starke and Arvind Rangaswamy. It describes a real situation using hypothetical data.

New strategy at ABB Electric

ABB Electric's research indicated that the market for electrical equipment would remain flat well into the 1980s. This would cause downward pressure on the prices of all products sold to customers in this market. Daniel Elwing, president and CEO of ABB Electric, concluded that the only way ABB Electric could grow in this environment would be to increase its market share. This meant that ABB Electric had to steal customers away from its competitors.

To support its new marketing strategy, ABB Electric decided to develop a marketing information system (MKIS) to support decision making. To seed the MKIS database, ABB Electric hired a marketing research firm to conduct a survey to provide information about customer needs. This firm thought that it was critical that ABB Electric understand the diverse problems and needs of its potential customers better than its competitors. It also felt that such information would be useful for segmenting the electrical equipment market and would contribute towards making ABB Electric a customer-driven company. ABB Electric hired Professor Dennis H. Gensch to develop segmentation models and to show its employees the value of using formal models to implement its segmentation strategies.

Establishing the MKIS program

ABB Electric hired a marketing research company to design a survey to determine the product attributes most important to current and potential customers. A pretest questionnaire asked electrical equipment purchasers to rate the importance of 21 product and service attributes (e.g., maintenance requirements, invoice price, and warranty) and then to rate the major suppliers in the industry on a poor to good scale on each attribute.

Example Survey Question

Supplier Performance Rating
List the suppliers you are considering or would consider when purchasing your next substation:

_____   _____
_____   _____
_____   _____

For each supplier on your list, indicate your perception of this supplier on the following attributes:

Invoice Price	Poor	Good

Supplier A |————————————————|
Supplier B |————————————————|
Supplier C |————————————————|
Supplier D |————————————————|

The firm used factor analysis techniques (see Chapter 3 of the text) to analyze the responses to determine nine important and fairly independent attributes that influence the purchase of electrical equipment. It mailed its final questionnaire to 7,000 key decision makers at utilities, RECs, municipalities, and industrial firms who purchase electrical equipment. Respondents evaluated each supplier known to them on the nine selected attributes. They also gave an overall rating to each supplier and indicated the supplier from whom they had purchased a particular type of equipment the last time they purchased it. The firm received completed questionnaires from 40 percent of the sample. In a follow-up phone check of nonrespondents, it detected no significant nonresponse bias. This data formed the nucleus of the MKIS database.

Data analyses indicated that the following attributes were the most important to customers when deciding to purchase electrical equipment (not in order of importance):

- Invoice price
- Energy losses
- Overall product quality
- Availability of spare parts
- Problem-solving skills of salespeople
- Maintenance requirements
- Ease of installation
- Warranty

Professor Gensch held the view that different segments of customers would weight these attributes very differently in selecting suppliers, partly because they differed in technical sophistication and partly because they were subject to different sales-force call patterns and different promotional efforts. After reviewing the data, the marketing staff decided on three ways to distinguish between companies: by type, size, and geographic location.

Choice modeling

In addition to determining the important attributes as stated by customers, Professor Gensch suggested that ABB Electric determine the most important factors based on the supplier choices customers actually made. He thought that what customers say is important may not match what actually is important when they decide on suppliers. To get at this, he developed a choice model based on multinomial logit analysis. He then developed a segmentation scheme based on the probability that a customer would choose a particular supplier (the probabilities sum to 1 for each customer):

ABB Electric Loyal Segment (Loyal): Customers in this segment have a probability of purchasing from ABB Electric that is *significantly higher* than the probability that they would buy from the next closest competitor.

Competitive Segment (Competitive): Customers in this segment have a *slightly higher* probability of purchasing from ABB Electric than from the next most preferred supplier. Thus the probability of purchasing from ABB Electric is highest, but not significantly above the probabilities of purchasing from one or more competitors.

Switchable Segment (Switchable): Customers in this segment have a *slightly lower* probability of purchasing from ABB Electric than the most preferred supplier. Thus the probability of purchasing from a competitor is highest, but not significantly higher than the probability of purchasing from ABB Electric.

Competitor Loyal Segment (Lost): Customers in this segment have a *significantly lower* probability of purchasing from ABB Electric than from their most preferred supplier. Thus these customers are highly likely to buy only from a competitor and can be classified as lost customers.

ABB Electric used this segmentation scheme to focus its sales effort primarily at the Competitive and Switchable segments. It redesigned its entire marketing program with this in mind. The sales force spent more time calling on prospects in these segments. ABB customized its brochures to focus on the "hot buttons" specific to each segment. Most important it continuously updated the MKIS database with new data and it institutionalized this approach to targeting across the organization.

Postscript—Situation in 1988

ABB Electric has strengthened its position well beyond expectations. Its market share reached 40 percent in 1988. Along with a larger market share came improvements to its profitability. The overall market remains flat and forecasters predict that it will remain flat into the near future. However ABB Electric was able to establish a competitive edge against much larger competitors.

EXERCISES

Suppose you are the regional sales manager for ABB Electric, and you have been given a budget for a supplementary direct marketing campaign aimed at 20 percent of the companies in your region.

1. At present you have information about the location of customers (districts 1, 2, and 3) and the sales potential of each account or prospect. Based on this information alone, to what companies would you direct the new direct marketing program? Specify the accounts and customer or prospect types.

2. Use the choice modeling approach based on the responses provided by 88 firms from your region. The data consists of the evaluation of ABB Electric and the three main competitors on eight variables: (1) Price, (2) Energy losses, (3) Maintenance requirements, (4) Warranty, (5) Availability of spare parts, (6) Ease of installation, (7) Salesperson problem solving support, and (8) Perceived product quality. Perform a customer-loyalty-based segmentation for your customers and prospects.

   ■ Which variables are the key drivers of choice in this market?
   ■ Based on your analyses, on which firms would you focus your efforts?

3. Assume that marketing efforts targeted at companies in the Loyal and Lost categories result in no incremental gain. On the other hand, suppose that you could retain or win half the companies in the Switchable and Competitive segments with this program. How much improvement in sales productivity can you realize by applying this choice model to allocate your efforts?

4. What other recommendations would you offer to ABB Electric to improve its segmentation marketing program?

5. Comment on the uses and limitations of this modeling approach.

TUTORIAL FOR POSITIONING ANALYSIS

Positioning analysis uses perceptual and preference mapping techniques to visually represent how customers perceive competing products or services and to represent customers' preferences for these products or services. The resulting maps are useful for developing positioning strategies. The perceptual-mapping software we use is based on the MDPREF model, which relies on a factor-analytic approach to derive attribute-based maps. The preference-mapping software produces an external vector model version of PREFMAP3.

The following example illustrates the use of perceptual mapping for developing a positioning strategy for Infiniti G20. We describe the data in detail in the exercise.

From the **Model** menu, select **Positioning Analysis**. You will be prompted for a data file. For this example, select the file called G20.DAT. If you enter your own data sets, make sure that the columns are the products (or alternatives to be evaluated) and the rows contain the attribute evaluations of the products.

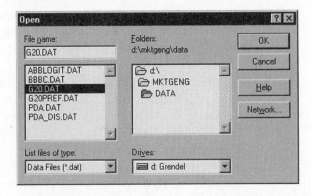

After the file loads, you will see the following split-screen window:

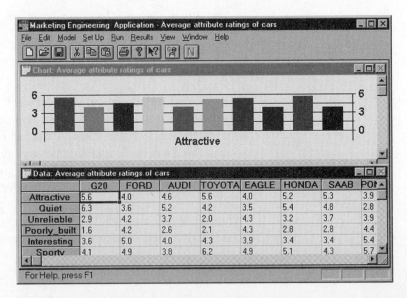

	G20	FORD	AUDI	TOYOTA	EAGLE	HONDA	SAAB	PON
Attractive	5.6	4.0	4.6	5.6	4.0	5.2	5.3	3.9
Quiet	6.3	3.6	5.2	4.2	3.5	5.4	4.8	2.8
Unreliable	2.9	4.2	3.7	2.0	4.3	3.2	3.7	3.9
Poorly_built	1.6	4.2	2.6	2.1	4.3	2.8	2.8	4.4
Interesting	3.6	5.0	4.0	4.3	3.9	3.4	3.4	5.4
Sporty	4.1	4.9	3.8	6.2	4.9	5.1	4.3	5.7

NOTE*: If you make changes to the data to evaluate alternative solutions, the program will not automatically save these changes. To save the changes (under a separate file if necessary) go to the **File** menu and click **Save As***.

On the **Setup** menu, click **Setup** to select the parameters for the run.

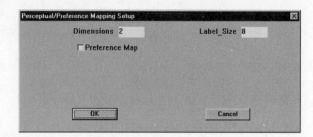

Number of dimensions: Enter either 2 or 3. If you choose a three-dimensional map, the program will produce three two-dimensional maps (Dim 1 with Dim 2; Dim1 with Dim 3, and Dim2 with Dim3).

Label Size: Because long labels might clutter the map(s), you can control the length of labels in the map by specifying between one and 10 characters.

Perceptual Map: This is the default option. For input it relies on the average perceptions of customers on a set of attributes. For this exercise the data is contained in the file G20.DAT. Although this default option generates only perceptual maps and not joint-space maps (containing both perceptions and preferences), you can still obtain simple joint-space maps by including the average preference ratings in your input data matrix.

Preference Map: Select the preference map option if you have a separate file containing information on the preferences of each customer for the selected products. For the G20 exercise, the preference data are contained in the file called G20PREF.DAT. If you choose **Preference Map** you will be prompted to provide this file name.

To run the program, go to the **Run** menu and click **Run Model**.

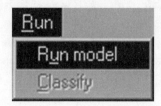

When the program is successfully executed, you will see the following map on the top part of your screen.

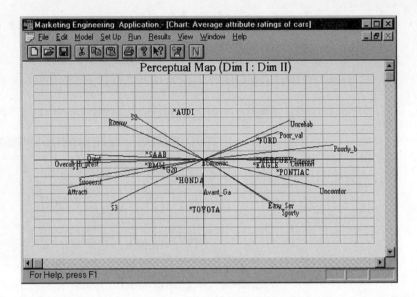

In the map, the length of an attribute vector is proportional to the variance of that attribute explained by the map.

Go to the **View** menu to find commands to customize the display. You have the following choices:

1. ***Zooming in and out***: Use the Zoom command to enlarge any portion of the display. First click **Zoom In**, and then place the cursor anywhere on the map and click. To zoom out again, go back to the **View** menu and click **Zoom Out**.

2. ***Customize the display***: On the **View** menu, click **View Options** to customize the display:

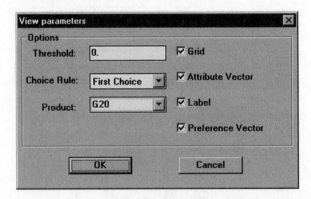

-   Turn the grid on or off.
-   Turn the display of attribute vectors on or off.
-   Display only attributes whose variance recovery is higher than a specified number. Select the threshold values from 0 (default) to 1.0.
-   If you choose to turn off the display of both attribute vectors and labels, the program will display only objects (cars in the example).

The remaining options are used with preference maps, which we describe later.

3. ***Add labels anywhere on the map***: This may be useful for future identification of the map. Click anywhere on the map, and a label dialog box will appear. Anything you enter in this dialog box will be inserted at the selected location on the map. To delete the labels you entered, go to the **Edit** menu and choose **Delete Labels**.

To print a copy of the map on an attached printer, go to the **File** menu and click **Print**. To cut and paste the map into a Windows application (e.g., Word for Windows), bring the map to the foreground, go to the **Edit** menu and select **Cut** or **Copy** and then bring a Windows application to the foreground, go to the **Edit** menu, and select **Paste**.

In the case of 3-D maps, the program displays automatically only a map of dimensions 1 and 2. To view the other dimensions on the **Results** menu, choose **Summary** and then **View Next Chart** as shown below.

Preference maps

If you chose **Preference Map** in the **Setup** menu, the map will include the preference vectors of each individual shown as red lines (vector model). The length of the preference vector is proportional to the variance of that respondent's preferences that are explained by the map. Future versions of the software will include an ideal-point version. The ideal points will be displayed as red dots.

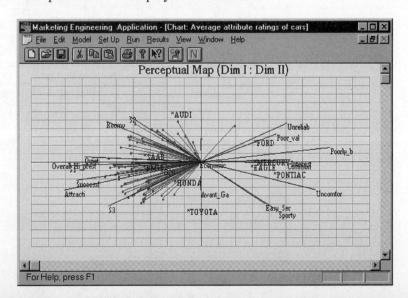

Customize the viewing and analysis options: As with the perceptual map, you can use the options under the **View** menu to customize the display. You will have some new options that were not available with perceptual maps. Go to **View** and choose **View Options.** You can use these options to:

- Turn the display of the preference vectors on or off.
- Select a product whose market share you would like to explore at various locations on the map.
- Select the choice rule to be used for market-share computations. Under the first-choice rule, we assume that each customer will purchase only his or her most preferred product. Under the share-of-preference rule, we assume that the probability that a customer will select a product is proportional to the product's share of preference with respect to all the products included in the model (see Chapter 7 of the text).

NOTE: *The share-of-preference model, as implemented here, arbitrarily sets the preference value of a customer's least preferred product to 0.*

To compute an index of market share at any location on the map for a selected product, place the cursor anywhere on the map and click the **right mouse button**. Cross hairs will appear at that position on the map, along with a market-share figure (at the bottom of the screen) as shown below. It is best to interpret the computed market share as a measure of the *relative attractiveness* of the selected location on the map for the selected product, rather than as an indicator of the absolute magnitude of the market share that will be realized.

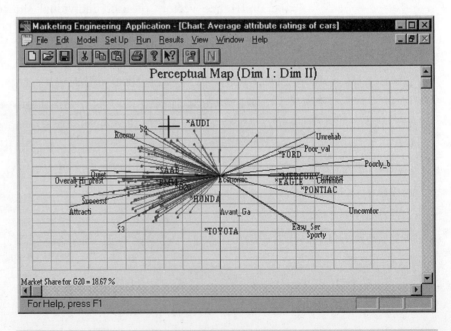

NOTE: *In computing market share, we assume that the selected product is relocated to the new position shown by the cross hairs (the map will*

still show the selected product at its original location for purposes of comparison), while all other products remain at their original positions.

To view additional information of a diagnostic nature, go to the **Results** menu and select **View Diagnostics**. This produces a display of additional information useful in evaluating the statistical adequacy of the generated map. You can print this information to an attached printer by going to the **File** menu and selecting **Print**, or use the Windows cut-and-paste option to copy this information into another Windows application, such as Word for Windows, for further editing.

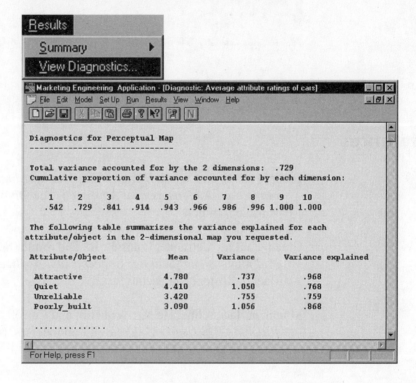

If you had checked **Preference Map** in the **Set Up** menu, you will get additional diagnostics as shown in the screen below:

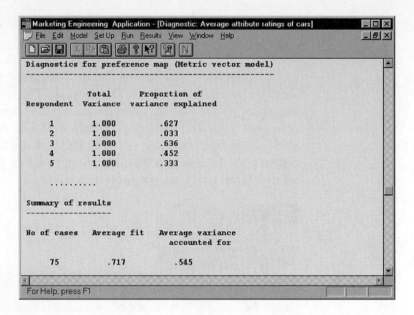

References

Green, Paul E. and Wind, Yoram 1973, *Multiattribute Decisions in Marketing: A Measurement Approach*, The Dryden Press, Hinsdale, Illinois.

Green, Paul E.; Carmone, Frank J., Jr.; and Smith, Scott M. 1989, *Multidimensional Scaling: Concepts and Application*, Allyn and Bacon, Boston, Massachusetts.

Muelman, Jacqueline; Heiser, Wilhelm; and Carroll, J. Douglas 1986, *PREFMAP_3 User's Guide*, Bell Laboratories, Murray Hill, New Jersey 07974.

POSITIONING THE INFINITI G20 CASE*

Introducing the G20

In April 1990, Nissan's Infiniti division planned to introduce the G20, adding a third model to the existing Infiniti line. The G20, equipped with a four-cylinder engine developing 140 horsepower, would be Infiniti's entry-level sports car. Initial market response to the car was disappointing, and management wondered how it might retarget or reposition the car to improve its market performance.

Background

In 1989, three years after Honda first introduced its Acura line, Toyota and Nissan attacked the U.S. luxury car market, a segment previously dominated by American and German manufacturers.

In November 1989, Nissan launched its new luxury Infiniti division with the $40,000 Q45 as its lead car and the $20,000 M30. However Nissan was somewhat late: In August 1989, three months before Nissan shipped its first Infiniti, Toyota had introduced Lexus, its luxury brand with a two-car line comprising the $40,000 LS400 and the entry-level LS250.

As the figures for January to September 1990 showed, Lexus outsold Infiniti by 50,000 to 15,000. The reasons for Infiniti's slow start were threefold.

- First the Infiniti Q45 came to the market after the Lexus LS400 had established a good market position.
- Second Lexus had two very good cars, whereas Infiniti's M30 coupe received poor evaluations from the automobile press and from customers. (Indeed, Infiniti planned to discontinue the M30 in 1992.)
- Finally the eccentric Infiniti advertising campaign that showed scenes of nature, but not the car itself, shared some of the blame. ("Infiniti may not be doing so well, but, hey, at least sales of rocks and trees are skyrocketing," commented comedian Jay Leno.)

Research study

Exhibits 1-3 summarize the results of a study on consumers' perceptions of the G20 in late 1989. The sampling frame for the survey was Infiniti's target audience, which the firm described as people between 25 and 35 with household incomes between $50,000 and $100,000. (When the survey was administered, the Lexus LS250 was not well known enough to

---

* This case was developed by Katrin Starke and Arvind Rangaswamy and describes a real situation using hypothetical data.

the respondents to be included in the study.) Infiniti managers identified three subsegments of the target audience. It used Claritas' databases to obtain demographic and some differentiating psychographic information about these segments.

	G20	Ford T-bird	Audi 90	Toyota Supra	Eagle Talon	Honda Prelude	Saab 900	Pontiac Fire-bird	BMW 318i	Mer-cury Capri
Attractive	5.6	4.0	4.6	5.6	4.0	5.2	5.3	3.9	5.7	3.9
Quiet	6.3	3.6	5.2	4.2	3.5	5.4	4.8	2.8	5.0	3.3
Unreliable	2.9	4.2	3.7	2.0	4.3	3.2	3.7	3.9	2.3	4.0
Poorly Built	1.6	4.2	2.6	2.1	4.3	2.8	2.8	4.4	1.8	4.3
Interesting	3.6	5.0	4.0	4.3	3.9	3.4	3.4	5.4	3.3	3.9
Sporty	4.1	4.9	3.8	6.2	4.9	5.1	4.3	5.7	4.1	5.2
Uncomfort-able	2.4	4.0	2.4	3.7	4.0	3.3	2.8	4.3	3.5	4.4
Roomy	5.6	3.9	5.3	3.5	3.6	3.9	5.1	3.3	4.3	3.6
Easy Serv-ice	4.6	4.9	3.5	4.9	4.6	5.0	3.8	4.7	4.1	4.6
High Pres-tige	5.4	3.5	5.6	5.3	2.8	4.7	5.7	3.8	6.4	3.3
Common	3.5	3.6	3.4	2.9	4.3	3.9	1.9	4.3	2.8	3.9
Economical	3.6	3.7	3.6	3.2	4.9	5.0	4.3	3.1	4.3	4.6
Successful	5.3	4.2	5.0	5.5	3.7	5.6	5.3	4.4	5.9	3.9
Avant-garde	4.3	3.6	3.6	4.9	4.4	3.9	4.7	4.1	3.7	4.5
Poor Value	3.4	4.3	4.3	3.5	3.6	2.6	2.9	4.3	3.3	3.8
Preferences										
Overall	6.3	3.9	6.0	5.5	4.0	6.5	6.8	3.0	6.7	4.0
Segment I	4.3	2.1	6.0	6.1	3.3	6.0	7.5	1.2	8.3	1.7
Segment II	5.9	6.0	7.7	3.5	3.1	5.5	5.4	2.5	5.4	5.8
Segment III	8.6	2.1	3.4	8.1	5.8	8.3	8.4	5.3	7.3	3.4

EXHIBIT 1

Survey results with average perception and preference ratings on a scale from 1 to 9 (G20.DAT)

EXHIBIT 2

Detailed data on customer preferences (G20PREF.DAT)

	G20	Ford	Audi	Toyota	Eagle	Honda	Saab	Pontiac	BMW	Mercury
1	4.0	7.0	8.0	3.0	4.0	5.0	5.0	1.0	4.0	5.0
2	4.0	8.0	6.0	5.0	8.0	7.0	3.0	1.0	5.0	2.0
3	8.0	5.0	9.0	4.0	1.0	7.0	7.0	2.0	4.0	4.0
4	7.0	1.0	8.0	1.0	4.0	6.0	5.0	5.0	7.0	3.0
5	9.0	8.0	8.0	3.0	5.0	4.0	3.0	2.0	8.0	6.0
6	5.0	6.0	5.0	5.0	2.0	4.0	8.0	4.0	4.0	7.0
7	3.0	9.0	7.0	4.0	4.0	3.0	6.0	4.0	3.0	6.0
8	4.0	7.0	9.0	3.0	1.0	7.0	9.0	3.0	6.0	6.0
9	8.0	6.0	6.0	4.0	5.0	5.0	1.0	2.0	8.0	7.0
10	6.0	4.0	6.0	3.0	2.0	8.0	7.0	3.0	1.0	8.0
11	8.0	6.0	8.0	4.0	6.0	8.0	7.0	1.0	2.0	7.0
12	8.0	5.0	6.0	6.0	2.0	3.0	8.0	1.0	6.0	6.0
13	4.0	2.0	9.0	4.0	1.0	5.0	5.0	4.0	8.0	5.0
14	5.0	5.0	8.0	5.0	6.0	4.0	6.0	1.0	3.0	7.0
15	6.0	5.0	9.0	1.0	3.0	6.0	8.0	3.0	6.0	3.0
16	6.0	3.0	9.0	2.0	7.0	8.0	6.0	3.0	7.0	3.0
17	8.0	5.0	8.0	1.0	1.0	8.0	9.0	2.0	5.0	4.0
18	5.0	9.0	7.0	5.0	2.0	4.0	7.0	5.0	6.0	1.0
19	6.0	7.0	9.0	6.0	2.0	6.0	3.0	5.0	4.0	5.0
20	6.0	9.0	8.0	2.0	3.0	8.0	6.0	1.0	7.0	5.0
21	7.0	7.0	9.0	4.0	1.0	3.0	4.0	1.0	4.0	3.0
22	6.0	9.0	6.0	2.0	3.0	4.0	6.0	1.0	6.0	3.0
23	5.0	4.0	8.0	4.0	1.0	4.0	1.0	1.0	8.0	5.0
24	7.0	4.0	8.0	3.0	2.0	3.0	4.0	6.0	9.0	5.0
25	3.0	9.0	7.0	3.0	1.0	7.0	2.0	1.0	5.0	7.0
26	8.0	2.0	1.0	9.0	4.0	8.0	8.0	5.0	8.0	4.0
27	9.0	6.0	5.0	8.0	4.0	8.0	7.0	7.0	5.0	1.0
28	9.0	1.0	2.0	4.0	9.0	9.0	9.0	4.0	8.0	3.0
29	9.0	2.0	4.0	8.0	7.0	8.0	9.0	8.0	5.0	6.0
30	9.0	3.0	4.0	8.0	7.0	6.0	6.0	4.0	5.0	1.0
31	8.0	3.0	2.0	9.0	5.0	8.0	9.0	5.0	7.0	5.0
32	5.0	1.0	2.0	7.0	5.0	9.0	9.0	7.0	8.0	6.0
33	9.0	1.0	4.0	9.0	6.0	9.0	9.0	5.0	9.0	2.0
34	8.0	2.0	6.0	8.0	7.0	9.0	8.0	5.0	9.0	5.0
35	9.0	1.0	7.0	9.0	5.0	7.0	6.0	6.0	4.0	1.0
36	8.0	1.0	4.0	9.0	6.0	8.0	8.0	3.0	7.0	4.0
37	9.0	2.0	3.0	9.0	5.0	8.0	9.0	7.0	9.0	6.0
38	8.0	2.0	3.0	6.0	5.0	9.0	9.0	3.0	9.0	6.0
39	9.0	2.0	4.0	9.0	7.0	8.0	7.0	7.0	9.0	1.0
40	8.0	3.0	2.0	7.0	5.0	8.0	9.0	5.0	6.0	1.0
41	9.0	3.0	4.0	8.0	8.0	9.0	6.0	2.0	9.0	6.0
42	8.0	3.0	2.0	8.0	6.0	8.0	9.0	4.0	7.0	2.0
43	9.0	2.0	1.0	8.0	6.0	7.0	9.0	5.0	9.0	5.0
44	9.0	2.0	3.0	9.0	7.0	8.0	9.0	7.0	5.0	4.0
45	9.0	2.0	3.0	7.0	6.0	9.0	9.0	7.0	5.0	2.0
46	8.0	1.0	2.0	9.0	5.0	8.0	9.0	4.0	9.0	4.0
47	9.0	2.0	3.0	9.0	6.0	9.0	9.0	6.0	8.0	1.0
48	9.0	3.0	6.0	8.0	2.0	8.0	9.0	4.0	8.0	4.0
49	9.0	1.0	2.0	9.0	6.0	8.0	9.0	4.0	7.0	1.0
50	9.0	3.0	6.0	9.0	6.0	9.0	8.0	8.0	7.0	5.0
51	9.0	3.0	5.0	7.0	2.0	8.0	8.0	6.0	8.0	1.0
52	9.0	5.0	4.0	7.0	1.0	2.0	5.0	1.0	9.0	3.0

EXHIBIT 2 cont'd.
Detailed data on customer preferences (G20PREF.DAT)

	G20	Ford	Audi	Toyota	Eagle	Honda	Saab	Pontiac	BMW	Mercury
53	7.0	4.0	4.0	3.0	4.0	9.0	8.0	2.0	5.0	4.0
54	7.0	2.0	6.0	5.0	3.0	7.0	6.0	4.0	8.0	6.0
55	5.0	2.0	3.0	5.0	5.0	8.0	9.0	1.0	9.0	1.0
56	4.0	5.0	6.0	5.0	4.0	9.0	8.0	4.0	6.0	4.0
57	7.0	1.0	7.0	8.0	7.0	7.0	7.0	2.0	6.0	5.0
58	5.0	3.0	3.0	7.0	2.0	8.0	7.0	2.0	9.0	6.0
59	4.0	4.0	5.0	8.0	2.0	6.0	6.0	6.0	6.0	1.0
60	8.0	4.0	9.0	4.0	5.0	5.0	5.0	2.0	7.0	4.0
61	8.0	4.0	5.0	4.0	3.0	6.0	8.0	3.0	7.0	4.0
62	7.0	5.0	7.0	7.0	6.0	6.0	6.0	5.0	7.0	3.0
63	8.0	2.0	2.0	4.0	5.0	8.0	8.0	1.0	9.0	2.0
64	5.0	6.0	4.0	7.0	4.0	4.0	5.0	1.0	8.0	1.0
65	7.0	4.0	4.0	6.0	5.0	3.0	6.0	1.0	6.0	4.0
66	8.0	2.0	9.0	3.0	5.0	7.0	8.0	4.0	6.0	2.0
67	2.0	5.0	8.0	7.0	6.0	3.0	8.0	2.0	9.0	6.0
68	6.0	1.0	3.0	5.0	2.0	9.0	7.0	2.0	6.0	5.0
69	6.0	3.0	8.0	8.0	5.0	8.0	6.0	3.0	3.0	1.0
70	7.0	2.0	8.0	8.0	3.0	9.0	7.0	4.0	4.0	5.0
71	7.0	1.0	7.0	7.0	8.0	8.0	9.0	1.0	9.0	1.0
72	6.0	5.0	5.0	5.0	4.0	6.0	9.0	4.0	8.0	2.0
73	7.0	5.0	4.0	4.0	2.0	6.0	8.0	5.0	9.0	5.0
74	8.0	5.0	6.0	6.0	6.0	7.0	7.0	4.0	7.0	4.0
75	7.0	3.0	6.0	8.0	4.0	7.0	7.0	5.0	5.0	3.0

Segment Type	Segment I (Western Yuppie, Single)	Segment II (Upwardly Mobile Families)	Segment III (American Dreamers)
Segment Size	(25%)	(45%)	(30%)
Education	College Grads	College Grads or Some College	College Grads or Some College
Predominant Employment	Professionals	White-Collar	White-Collar
Age Group	25-35	25-35	25-35
Predominant Ethnic Background	White	White	Mix (Asian, White)
Average Household Income	$81,000	$68,000	$59,000
Persons per Household	1.42	3.8	2.4
Percent Married	32%	95%	65%
Watch Late Night TV	27%	9%	17%
Watch Daytime TV	3%	45%	5%
Read Computer Magazines	39%	6%	10%
Read Business Magazines	58%	23%	27%
Read Entertainment Magazines	3%	14%	30%
Read Infant and Parenting Magazines	1%	17%	2%
Rent Movies	43%	85%	38%
Possess an American Express Card	48%	45%	75%
Own Investment Funds	24%	18%	47%
Go Fishing	2%	30%	3%
Sail, Scuba Dive or Ski	49%	2%	20%

EXHIBIT 3
Data about the segments

EXERCISES

1. Describe the two (or, if applicable, three) dimensions underlying the perceptual maps that you generated. Based on these maps, how do people in the market perceive the Infiniti G20 compared with its competitors?

2. Infiniti promoted the G20 as a Japanese car (basic version $18,000) with a German feel, basically a car that was like the BMW 318i ($22,000), but lower priced. Is this a credible claim, given the perceptions and preferences of the respondents?

3. Which attributes are most important in influencing preference for these cars in the three segments (S1, S2, and S3) shown on these maps? To which segment(s) would you market the Infiniti G20? How would you reposition the Infiniti G20 to best suit the chosen segment(s)? Briefly de-

scribe the marketing program you would use to target the chosen segment(s)?

4. What ongoing research program would you recommend to Infiniti to improve its evaluation of its segmentation of the market and positioning of its cars?

5. Summarize the advantages and limitations of the software provided for this application.

TUTORIAL FOR MULTINOMIAL LOGIT ANALYSIS

Multinomial Logit Analysis is a general-purpose method for identifying the variables that influence customers' choices from among a set of alternatives (e.g., brands). For example, a customer could be choosing among five cars. The variables of interest could be the price of the cars, their features, and the financial packages that dealers offer. This software implements a nonnested multinomial logit model.

The input data should have a particular structure for this program. The first column is the choice variable having a 1 or 0 (purchase or no purchase) for each alternative under consideration. The remaining columns of data correspond to independent variables, one for each column, including dummy variables, if any. The rows correspond to "cases." Each case (e.g., customer) consists of two or more contiguous rows, one for each alternative, where the first column indicates whether that customer chose that alternative (dependent variable) and the remaining columns indicate the data values for each of the independent variables included in the model. Optionally, each case can consist of multiple observations (e.g., purchases made over several purchase occasions). When there is more than one observation per case, the observation sets must be organized sequentially. If there are N alternatives, M cases, and P observations per case, then the total number of rows of data would be N*M*P.

NOTE: *For each case, only one alternative is chosen, i.e., has a choice value equal to 1.*

The following shows how the data are organized for analysis:

1. If you have more than 2 choice alternatives, organize the input data as shown below. The Choice variable column indicates whether a particular choice alternative was chosen by a customer (case) on a particular choice occasion and the remaining columns contain values of the independent variables for each choice alternative for each case. The screen below illustrates this data organization from the file ABBLOGIT.DAT.

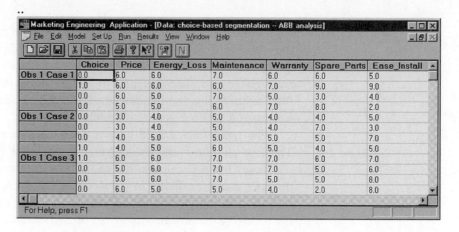

2. If you have two choice alternatives, the data is organized as shown below for the special case of the "binary logit" model. Each customer (case) consists of two alternatives, one of which has a Choice variable value equal to 0 and the other has a value equal to 1 The remaining columns in the data represent independent variables that explain the choices made by customers. In binary logit analysis, one of the choice alternatives serves as a reference—here, for convenience, the reference values of the independent variables are set to zero for the second choice alternative for each customer. The screen below illustrates this data organization from the file BBBC.DAT.

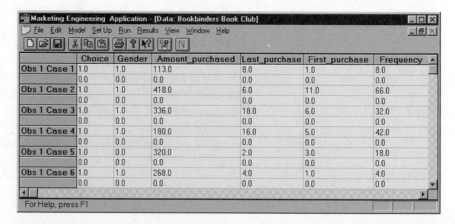

NOTE: *If you make changes to the data to evaluate alternative solutions, the program will not automatically save these changes. You can save the changes (under a separate filename) by going to* **File** *menu and choosing* **Save As**.

The following example illustrates the use of binary logit analysis in Bookbinders Book Club exercise. From the **Model** menu, select **Multinomial Logit Analysis**. You will be prompted for a data file. For this example, use the file called BBBC.DAT. You will then see the following screen (fill in the numbers indicated):

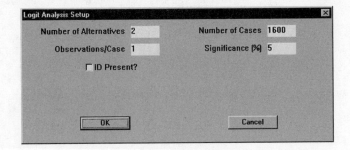

Number of Alternatives: Enter up to nine (choice) alternatives for analysis.

Number of Cases: Enter the number of cases for analysis.

Observations/Case: Indicate the number of observations per case. The default value is 1.

Significance (%): Specify the significance level for the statistical tests. The program uses this to identify statistically significant coefficients from the analysis.

ID Present: This indicates whether a unique name is assigned to each customer. This option is disabled in the educational version.

Click **OK**. To run the program, go to the **Run** menu and choose **Run Model**. After the program runs successfully, you will see a summary of the results in a sequence of screens, similar to the example below. Click **Back** and **Next** buttons to move back and forth among the screens. Click **Print** to get a print out of a screen.

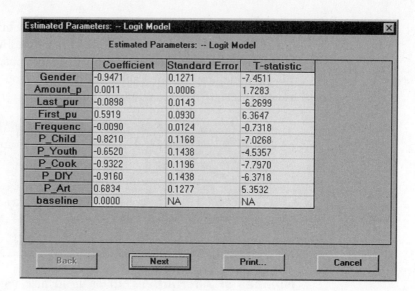

After you look at the summary tables, you will see a graphical summary of the coefficients, elasticities, and predicted shares for each alternative:

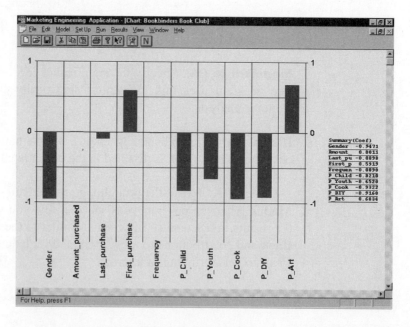

You can see one other chart that gives the market share forecasts for each alternative by going to the **Results** menu, choosing **Summary**, and then **View Next Chart** as shown below:

You can also get additional statistical information about the results by going to the **Results** menu and selecting **View Diagnostics** menu option from the **Results** menu. The extensive set of diagnostics is organized into eight components.

Diagnostics—1

The first set of diagnostics you will see simply indicates the sizes of the data sets. The warning indicates that forecasting is based on the estimation sample, not on a separate holdout prediction sample. This is the only option available in the educational version of the software. The next piece of information indicates the number of rows of data (records) that the model processed.

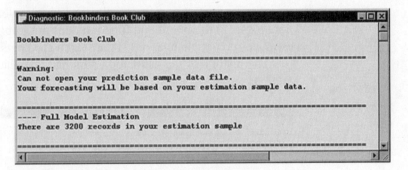

Diagnostics—2

Next, you will see a summary of the mean values of each variable for each alternative. If you use dummy variables, you can use the means of these variables to detect any problems with the data setup. In this example, the first choice alternative (Response) indicates whether someone responded to a direct mail campaign, and the second alternative is a dummy which we can ignore (all means are zero).

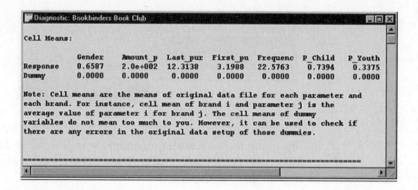

Diagnostics—3

The parameters of the logit model are estimated by a statistical procedure called maximum likelihood. It attempts to find the parameters of the probability distribution for the specified model that will make the observed sample of data to be the most likely sample from the underlying probability distribution. The likelihood of a sample is measured by a likelihood function (or, more conventionally, a log-likelihood function). The iterative maximum likelihood procedure stops if one of the following three criteria is met (within a desired tolerance) for successive iterations: (1) the likelihood function does not improve, (2) the parameter estimates do not change, or (3) the search gradients do not change.

The history of the estimation summarizes what happened at each iteration:

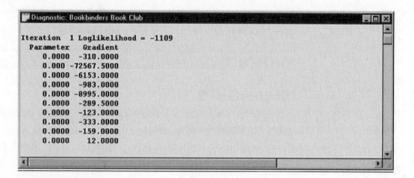

Diagnostics—4

The next set of diagnostics provides information about the parameter estimates and the variance-covariance matrix of the estimates. This information is useful for identifying the parameters that are significantly different from 0 in a statistical sense. A significant variable influences the choice probabilities of each alternative, whereas an insignificant variable does not offer much in the way of explaining the choices customers made.

NOTE: *These are asymptotic results—they are likely to be valid only if the sample is large.*

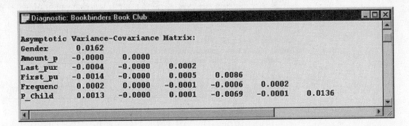

```
Diagnostic: Bookbinders Book Club                                    _ □ X

Asymptotic Variance-Covariance Matrix:
Gender      0.0162
Amount_p   -0.0000    0.0000
Last_pur   -0.0004   -0.0000    0.0002
First_pu   -0.0014   -0.0000    0.0005    0.0086
Frequenc    0.0002    0.0000   -0.0001   -0.0006    0.0002
P_Child     0.0013   -0.0000    0.0001   -0.0069   -0.0001    0.0136
```

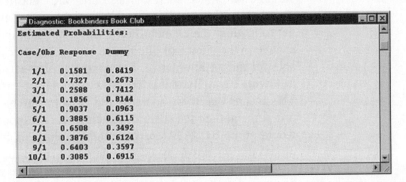

```
Diagnostic: Bookbinders Book Club                                    _ □ X

Estimated Parameters:

Variable    Parameter Estimate      Standard Error      T statistic

Gender             -0.9471              0.1271            -7.4511
Amount_p            0.0011              0.0006             1.7283
Last_pur           -0.0898              0.0143            -6.2699
First_pu            0.5919              0.0930             6.3647
Frequenc           -0.0090              0.0124            -0.7318
P_Child            -0.8210              0.1168            -7.0268
P_Youth            -0.6520              0.1438            -4.5357
P_Cook             -0.9322              0.1196            -7.7970
P_DIY              -0.9160              0.1438            -6.3718
P_Art               0.6834              0.1277             5.3532
baseline            0.0000                 NA                NA
```

Diagnostics—5

The next set of diagnostics indicates the probability of each "case" (e.g., customer) selecting each of the alternatives and the hit rate, which is the percentage of cases for which the predicted choice (each case is assigned the alternative for which it has the highest probability) is equal to the known actual choice.

```
Diagnostic: Bookbinders Book Club                                    _ □ X
Estimated Probabilities:

Case/Obs Response   Dummy

    1/1   0.1581   0.8419
    2/1   0.7327   0.2673
    3/1   0.2588   0.7412
    4/1   0.1856   0.8144
    5/1   0.9037   0.0963
    6/1   0.3885   0.6115
    7/1   0.6508   0.3492
    8/1   0.3876   0.6124
    9/1   0.6403   0.3597
   10/1   0.3085   0.6915
```

Diagnostics—6

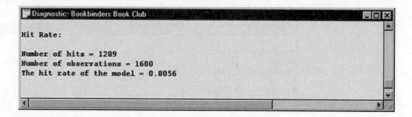

The higher the hit rate, the higher the predictive ability of the model. If the estimation and prediction samples are not distinct (which is the case in the educational version of the software), then the hit rate is a measure of the goodness-of-fit rather than the predictive ability of the model.

In addition, the computed probabilities can be used to derive an estimate of the choice share of each alternative. (If a separate prediction sample is used, the choice shares are computed on that sample, rather than on the estimation sample. This option is not currently available in the educational version of the software.)

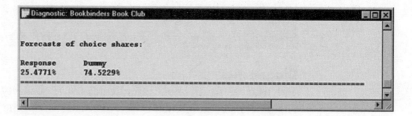

Diagnostics—7

The next set provides information about the elasticity of impact of each variable on choice shares. These are "arc" elasticities (i.e., not "point" elasticities). For each independent variable, the elasticity matrix refers to the following: the element in the (i,j)th position indicates the percentage change in the choice of alternative j for a one percent change of the variable for the ith alternative. For example, elements (1,1) and (1,2) in the following elasticity matrix for amount purchased are 0.1241 and -0.0424. This means that if we increase the amount purchased by a customer by one percent, then the share of the customers responding to the promotion would go up by 0.1241 percent and the share of customers not responding would go down by 0.0424 percent (Here, the magnitudes of these elasticities reflect the fact that only a fourth of the customers in the database responded to the direct mail offer.)

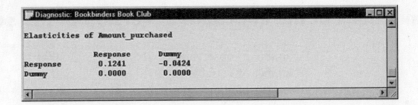

Diagnostics—8

Finally, we provide some statistics that can help you to evaluate how well the proposed model, the "full-parametric model," compares to 1) a "naive" model that assigns equal probabilities to all alternatives (i.e., all parameters are equal to 0) and 2) the constant model (i.e., all parameters except the constant term are zero). The reported Chi-square value is asymptotically distributed as a Chi-square distribution with the indicated degree of freedom (DF).

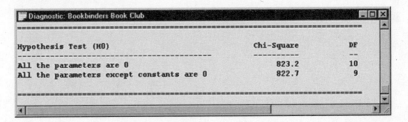

We also compute a Goodness-Of-Fit index that provides additional information about the performance of the model:

Rho-Square is similar to the R^2 measure in regression. It is an index of the extent to which the full parametric model performs better than the constant model. Rho-Bar-Square is another goodness-of-fit measure which is similar to "Adjusted R^2" in regression, which corrects for the number of parameters included in the full-parametric model.

Limitations of the educational version of the software

Number of observations:	3000
Number of variables:	20
Number of choice alternatives:	8
Number of observations per case:	10

TUTORIAL FOR NEURAL NET FORECASTING

A neural network is a general response model that can help firms to understand complex relationships between the dependent and independent variables of a marketing system. The network consists of a number of interconnected nodes (neurons), each of which contributes in a specific way to the overall relationship between the variables. Unlike regression models, neural network models do not require the users to prespecify the nature of the relationship between the dependent and independent variables.

The neural network software is supplied by Cognos Corporation and is called 4Thought. It uses a feedforward network with up to two hidden layers and a sigmoidal activation function. It fits the model using back propagation of errors, and it minimizes the possibility of overfitting by continuously testing the model on a hold-out sample.

NOTE: *4Thought is a comprehensive software program that includes an online help file. Here we describe only the features that you will need for the BookBinders Book Club (BBBC) case.*

For this exercise, you will build a neural net model to explain response to a direct mail offer from Bookbinders Book Club. From the **Model** menu, select **Neural Net Forecasting**. You will then see the following screen.

On the **File** menu, choose **Open** and select **BBBCNN.4TH**. Once this file is loaded, you will see a spreadsheet listing the variables for this exercise. The first 400 observations are from customers who responded to the direct mail offer (Choice = 1), and the remaining 1200 observations are from customers who did not (Choice = 0). The file also contains an additional 2300 observations that you can use for verification or forecasting.

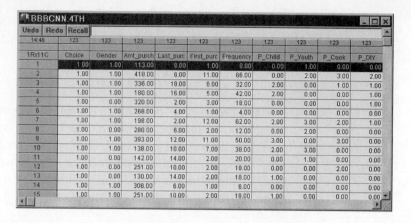

First, go to the **Options** menu and choose **Options...**, and then select the appropriate settings. In particular, check the **Detailed model dialog box**. Until you become familiar with the software, you may also want to choose the **Simple menus** from the **Options** menu.

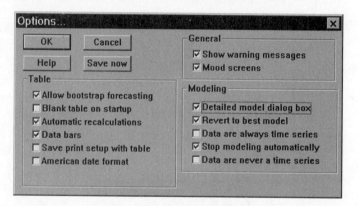

Next, specify a model for analysis. From the **Specify** menu, select **Model**. You will see the following screen:

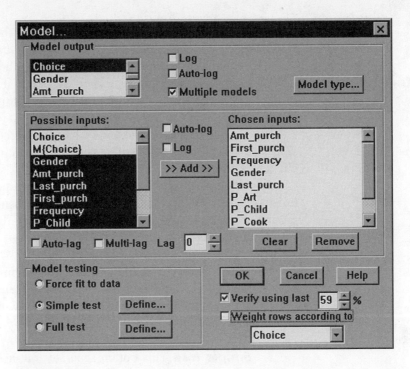

Defining the model

Specifying the dependent variable: First select a dependent variable (here Choice) for **Model output**. The dependent variable can be any table column containing numerical data. If you wish to build models of several columns all at once, all using the same inputs, check the **Multiple models** box and select all the columns you wish to model. If you wish to model the logarithm of the column's contents instead of the raw data, check **Log** before adding the column to the input list. If you want 4Thought to automatically decide whether the distribution of the data in the column merits taking a log of the raw data, then select the **Auto-log** in the check box, before adding the column to the input list.

    Specifying the model type: You can specify the type of neural network model that you wish to explore by clicking on **Model type**. Unless you are very familiar with neural network models, we recommend that you retain the **Chosen by 4Thought** option.

    Specifying the independent variables: Define the independent variables (Possible inputs) in the lower section of the dialog box. You can add items by clicking on the **Add** button. You can remove an item by clicking on the **Remove** button; you can remove all items from the input list by clicking on the **Clear** button. To select multiple columns, keep the Ctrl key pressed as you select each variable.

    If you select a column that is not numeric, and that has not already been categorized, the **Categories** dialog box opens. You can indicate whether data for each input is to be logged or auto-logged as we did with the independent variable. If you are using time-series data, you can also choose to lag an input. This means that instead of using data from the input column's corresponding row number, you can use data from X number of rows forward (down) or backwards (up) in the table. Alternatively, you can select the **Auto-lag** option to tell the system to designate a suitable lag period. In that case, the system will try out different lags, measuring the correlation between the data and the lagged data. It stops when the correlation begins to drop off. Note that if you only one column of data and are building a model of it based upon itself, you have to use lags.

If you wish to add a time and/or seasonality input to the model and you have not previously specified these columns, do so at this point by clicking **Time**.

Specifying model tests: You can choose one of three methods to test the quality of the model you are building using the **Model testing** section of the dialog box. 4Thought uses the test data to decide when to stop the modeling process.

1. *Force fit to data*: In this case, the system does not perform any holdout prediction tests. This option is useful if you wish to compare the results from the neural net with that of a traditional statistical model.

2. *Simple test*: This option separates out a specific region of the data for testing during the model development process. We recommend this option. By clicking on the Define button, you can exercise more control on how specifically the test data is selected. For cross-sectional data, we recommend that you use the **Evenly spread** option. For time-series data, you can select **Contiguous groups** or **At end of data set**. In the case of the contiguous groups, the system selects a number of representative contiguous portions of data for testing. We recommend that you use two contiguous groups.

3. *Full test*: Under this option, the system builds many models with different test points in order to establish an optimum point at which to stop modeling. The system then builds a final model using all the data. We recommend this option if you have a small data set.

If you wish, you can set aside additional data points for verification. This is a wholly independent test, not used in model development or holdout prediction. Data selected for verification should be marked as V under the column titled RU. In that same column, the system marks the data it has selected for model development as M and the data used for holdout prediction as T.

NOTE: *For the BBBCNN.4TH data, you have to mark rows 1,601 to 3,900 with a V before you run the model. This will ensure that these data are not used for model development or testing. However, you will then obtain model predictions for the dependent variable (Choice) for these rows. The simplest way to do this is by checking* **Verify using last** *in the* **Model** *dialog box and setting this value to 59 (=2300/3900) percent.*

After you complete the model specifications, click **OK**. You will see the following screen, which displays the neural net modeling process. (Setting up the screen may take a while, and running the model may take a long time if you have a large data set). If the **Model fit** (shown in blue) and **Test fit** (red) are roughly similar, the model should be reliable. In addition, if you set aside data for verification, the display will include **Verify fit**. If its value is roughly the same as the Model fit, you have further evidence that the is reliable.

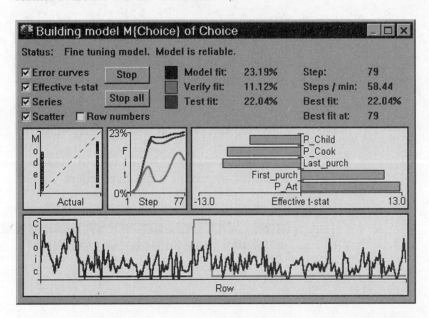

Once the program selects a final model, the spreadsheet will include two new columns. The column titled RU indicates how a particular row of data was used in the modeling process. M indicates use in model development, T in model testing, and V in model verification. The column titled Model (in red) indicates the predicted value of the dependent variable.

	BBBCNN.4TH									
Undo	Redo	Recall	Model of Choice							
15:07	123	123	Model	123	123	123	123	123	123	123
M{Choice}	Actual	Use	Model	0	0	0	0	0	0	0
1Rx1 C	Choice	RU	M{Choice}	Gender	Amt_purch	Last_purc	First_purc	Frequency	P_Child	P
1	1.00	RU	0.19	1.00	113.00	8.00	1.00	8.00	0.00	
2	1.00	T	0.71	1.00	418.00	6.00	11.00	66.00	0.00	
3	1.00	M	0.39	1.00	336.00	18.00	6.00	32.00	2.00	
4	1.00	M	0.28	1.00	180.00	16.00	5.00	42.00	2.00	
5	1.00	M	0.81	0.00	320.00	2.00	3.00	18.00	0.00	
6	1.00	T	0.36	1.00	268.00	4.00	1.00	4.00	0.00	
7	1.00	M	0.60	1.00	198.00	2.00	12.00	62.00	2.00	
8	1.00	M	0.39	0.00	280.00	6.00	2.00	12.00	0.00	
9	1.00	M	0.60	1.00	393.00	12.00	11.00	50.00	3.00	
10	1.00	M	0.39	1.00	138.00	10.00	7.00	38.00	2.00	
11	1.00	T	0.47	0.00	142.00	14.00	2.00	20.00	0.00	
12	1.00	M	0.21	0.00	251.00	10.00	2.00	18.00	0.00	
13	1.00	M	0.30	0.00	130.00	14.00	2.00	18.00	1.00	
14	1.00	M	0.48	1.00	308.00	6.00	1.00	6.00	0.00	
15	1.00	M	0.38	1.00	251.00	10.00	2.00	18.00	1.00	

To interpret the model, use the **Analysis** menu. Select **Statistics…** to see details of model fit. From the **Statistics Summary** dialog box, click **Full Report** to get additional details on the results.

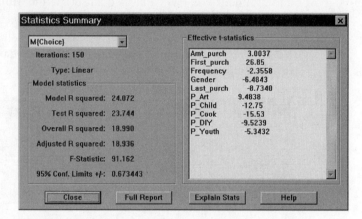

From the **Analysis** menu, select **Cross-section…** to view graphs that depict the impact of each independent variable on the dependent variable.

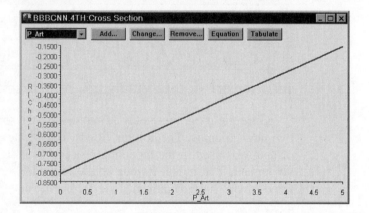

Use **Chart** and **Scenario…** (also under **Analysis** menu) to get further details on model results.

Regression in Excel

As a point of comparison for the Neural Network model, run the BBBC data using ordinary least squares regression. Open BBBC.XLS file.

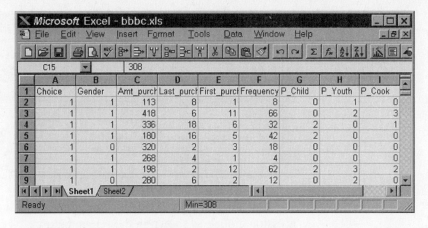

To start the regression-analysis tool, open the **Tools** menu, select **Add-Ins**, and **then Analysis ToolPak**.

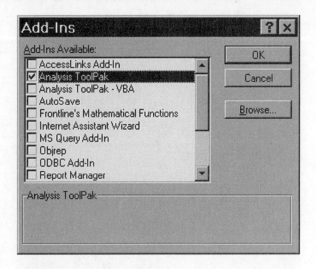

Next, from the **Tools** menu, open **Data Analysis** and select **Regression**.

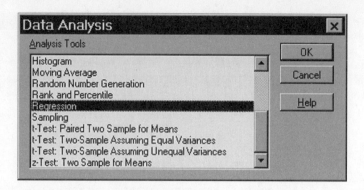

You are now all set to conduct regression analysis. Specify the regression model, as shown in the screen below.

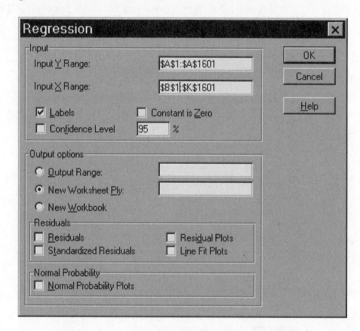

After the model runs, you should get regression results shown in the screen below:

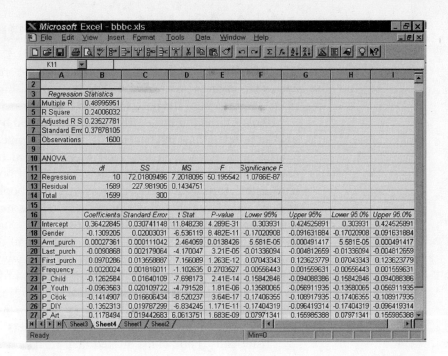

	A	B	C	D	E	F	G	H	I
2									
3	*Regression Statistics*								
4	Multiple R	0.48995951							
5	R Square	0.24006032							
6	Adjusted R S	0.23527781							
7	Standard Erro	0.37878105							
8	Observations	1600							
9									
10	ANOVA								
11		*df*	*SS*	*MS*	*F*	*Significance F*			
12	Regression	10	72.01809496	7.2018095	50.195542	1.0786E-87			
13	Residual	1589	227.981905	0.1434751					
14	Total	1599	300						
15									
16		*Coefficients*	*Standard Error*	*t Stat*	*P-value*	*Lower 95%*	*Upper 95%*	*Lower 95.0%*	*Upper 95.0%*
17	Intercept	0.36422845	0.030741148	11.848238	4.289E-31	0.303931	0.424525891	0.303931	0.424525891
18	Gender	-0.1309205	0.02003031	-6.536119	8.482E-11	-0.17020908	-0.091631884	-0.17020908	-0.091631884
19	Amt_purch	0.00027361	0.000111042	2.464059	0.0138426	5.581E-05	0.000491417	5.581E-05	0.000491417
20	Last_purch	-0.0090868	0.002179064	-4.170047	3.21E-05	-0.01336094	-0.004812659	-0.01336094	-0.004812659
21	First_purch	0.0970286	0.013558887	7.156089	1.263E-12	0.07043343	0.123623779	0.07043343	0.123623779
22	Frequency	-0.0020024	0.001816011	-1.102635	0.2703527	-0.00556443	0.001559631	-0.00556443	0.001559631
23	P_Child	-0.1262584	0.01640109	-7.698173	2.41E-14	-0.15842846	-0.094088386	-0.15842846	-0.094088386
24	P_Youth	-0.0963563	0.020109722	-4.791528	1.81E-06	-0.13580065	-0.056911935	-0.13580065	-0.056911935
25	P_Cook	-0.1414907	0.016606434	-8.520237	3.64E-17	-0.17406355	-0.108917935	-0.17406355	-0.108917935
26	P_DIY	-0.1352313	0.019787299	-6.834245	1.171E-11	-0.17404319	-0.096419314	-0.17404319	-0.096419314
27	P_Art	0.1178494	0.019442683	6.0613751	1.683E-09	0.07971341	0.155985388	0.07971341	0.155985388

BOOKBINDERS BOOK CLUB CASE[*]

About 50,000 new titles, including new editions, are published in the US each year, giving rise to a $20 billion book publishing industry (in 1994). About 10 percent of the books are sold through mail order.

Book retailing in the 1970s was characterized by the growth of chain bookstore operations in concert with the development of shopping malls. Traffic in bookstores in the 1980 was enhanced by the spread of discounting. In the 1990s, the superstore concept of book retailing has been responsible for the double-digit growth of the book industry. Generally situated near large shopping centers, superstores maintain large inventories of anywhere from 30,000 to 80,000 titles. Superstores are putting intense competitive pressure on book clubs, mail-order firms and retail outlets. Recently, on-line superstores, such as www.amazon.com, have emerged, carrying over 1 to 2.5 million titles and further intensifying the pressure on book clubs and mail-order firms. In response to these pressures, book clubs are starting to look at alternative business models that will make them more responsive to their customers' preferences.

Historically, book clubs offered their readers continuity and negative option programs that were based on an extended contractual relationship between the club and its subscribers. In a continuity program, popular in such areas as children's books, a reader signs up for an offer of several books for a few dollars each (plus shipping and handling on each book) and agrees to receive a shipment of one or two books each month thereafter. In a negative option program, subscribers get to choose which and how many additional books they will receive, but the default option is that the club's selection will be delivered to them each month. The club informs them of the monthly selection and they must mark "no" on their order forms if they do not want to receive it. Some firms are now beginning to offer books on a positive-option basis, but only to selected segments of their customer lists that they deem receptive to specific offers.

Book clubs are also beginning to use database marketing techniques to work smarter rather than expand the coverage of their mailings. According to Doubleday president Marcus Willhelm, "the database is the key to what we are doing … We have to understand what our customers want and be more flexible. I doubt book clubs can survive if they offer the same 16 offers, the same fulfillment to everybody."[†] Doubleday uses modeling techniques to look at more than 80 variables, including geography and the types of books customers purchase, and selects three to five variables that are the most influential predictors.

---

[*] The case and the database were developed by Professors Nissan Levin and Jacob Zahavi at Tel Aviv University. We have adapted these materials for use with our software.

[†] DM News, May 23, 1994.

The Bookbinders Book Club

The BBB Club was established in 1986 for the purpose of selling specialty books through direct marketing. BBBC is strictly a distributor and does not publish any of the books it sells. In anticipation of using database marketing, BBBC made a strategic decision right from the start to build and maintain a detailed database about its members containing all the relevant information about them. Readers fill out an insert and return it to BBBC which then enters the data into the database. The company currently has a database of 500,000 readers and sends out a mailing about once a month.

BBBC is exploring whether to use predictive modeling approaches to improve the efficacy of its direct mail program. For a recent mailing, the company selected 20,000 customers in Pennsylvania, New York, and Ohio from its database and included with their regular mailing a specially produced brochure for the book The Art History of Florence. This resulted in a 9.03 percent response rate (1806 orders) for the purchase of the book. BBBC then developed a database to calibrate a response model to identify the factors that influenced these purchases.

Each record in the database consists of two rows of data, one for each of the two choice options: purchase and no purchase. BBBC selected a number of variables that it thought might explain the observed choice behavior. Suppose that a particular customer purchased the book. The first row would then consist of a "1" to indicate choice (dependent variable) followed by the values of independent variables that could influence that choice (see below). The second row then indicates the data values associated with nonpurchase ("0"), followed by the reference data values (set to zero) for all the independent variables. On the other hand, if the customer did not purchase the book, the second row would contain the reference data values (also set to zero) associated with purchase. Data must be structured in this way to properly set up the database for logit analysis.

For purposes of analysis, we will use a subset of the database available to BBBC. It consists of 400 customers who purchased the book and 1200 who did not, thereby over-representing the "response group." Here is a description of the variables used for the analysis:

Choice: Whether the customer purchased the The Art History of Florence. 1 corresponds to a purchase and 0 corresponds to a nonpurchase.

Gender: 0 = Female and 1 = Male

Amount_purchased: Total money spent on BBBC books

Last_purchase (recency of purchase): Months since last purchase

First_purchase: Months since first purchase

Frequency: Total number of purchases in the chosen period (used as a proxy for frequency)

P_Child: Number of children's books purchased

P_Youth: Number of youth books purchased

P_Cook: Number of cookbooks purchased

P_DIY: Number of do-it-yourself books purchased.

P_Art: Number of art books purchased

EXERCISES

BBBC is evaluating three different modeling methods to isolate the factors that most influenced customers to order *The Art History of Florence*: An ordinary linear regression model, a binary logit model, and a neural network model.

1. Summarize the results of your analysis for all three models. Develop your models using the following data files, all of which contain the same data in different formats.

    *   Linear regression: BBBC.XLS—1600 observations for model development.

    *   Binary logit model: BBBC.DAT—1600 observations (3200 rows) for model development.

    *   Neural network model: BBBCNN.4TH—3900 observations with 1,600 observations for model development and 2300 observations for holdout prediction.

    *   In addition, the file BBBCPRED.XLS contains 2300 observations for holdout prediction using the coefficients of the linear regression and binary logit models.

2. Interpret the results of these models. In particular, highlight which factors most influenced customers' decision to buy or not to buy the book.

3. Bookbinders is considering a similar mail campaign in the Midwest where they have data for 50,000 customers. Such mailings typically promote several books. The allocated cost of the mailing is $0.65/addressee (including postage) for the art book, and the book costs Bookbinders $15 to purchase and mail. The company allocates overhead to each book at 45 percent of cost. The selling price of the book is $31.95. Based on the model, which customers should Bookbinders target? How much more profit would you expect the

more data off
clean probability
Logit forces 0/1
Regression
*   intuitive*

company to generate using these models as compared to sending the mail offer to the entire list?

4. Based on the insights you gained from this modeling exercise, summarize the advantages and limitations of each of the modeling approaches. Look at both similar and dissimilar results.

5. As part of your recommendations to the company, indicate whether it should invest in developing expertise in either (or all) of these methods to develop an in-house capability to evaluate its direct mail campaigns.

6. How would you simplify and automate your recommended method(s) for future modeling efforts at the company.

TUTORIAL FOR DECISION TREE ANALYSIS

Introduction

Decision Tree Analysis is useful to managers choosing among various courses of action when the choice (or sequence of choices) will ultimately lead to some uncertain consequences. The TreeÅge software allows you to take into account the potential *payoffs*, *risks*, and *ambiguities* associated with decisions when the decision process can be broken down into a sequence of actions and events. *Payoffs* are the monetary or other consequences of a decision; *risks* are the potential adverse consequences that may result from the decision because the decision maker lacks control over the consequences of the decision (i.e., he or she doesn't know the outcomes with certainty), and *ambiguities* are imprecise information about payoffs and the degree of risk.

A decision tree analysis typically consists of four steps: (1) structuring the problem as a tree in which the end nodes of the branches are the payoffs associated with a particular path (scenario) along the tree, (2) assigning subjective probabilities to events represented on the tree, (3) assigning payoffs for consequences (dollar or utility value associated with a particular scenario), and (4) selecting course(s) of action based on analyses (e.g., rolling back of the tree, sensitivity analyses, Monte Carlo simulations). We describe each step below using the QRS Company example described in Chapter 6 of the text.

TreeÅge is a comprehensive software package that includes a detailed online help file and an electronic manual. Here we describe only the features that you will need for the ICI case.

> **NOTE**: *To view or print a copy of the complete manual, you will need the original CD on which the marketing engineering software was distributed:*
>
> *If you do not have Adobe Acrobat™ installed on your system, run ACROREAD.EXE on the Marketing Engineering CD to install it. Follow the installation instructions that you see on the screen.*
>
> *After Acrobat™ is successfully installed, start the Acrobat program. From the **File** menu, select **Open** and open the file manual.pdf from the x:\treeage\manuals directory, where x is the letter representing your CD-ROM drive. Under the **File** menu, select **Print to** print any part of the manual.*

Step 1—Structuring the problem as a decision tree

When you start the program, you will see an empty root node from which you can construct a tree. To load a pre-existing tree go to the **File** menu and select **Open**. (Choose the QRS.TRE file in the ../mktgeng/data directory to familiarize yourself with the software. If you load QRS.TRE, you can go directly to **Step 2**.)

On the **Options** menu, select **Add Branch** or **Insert Branch** to add branches to any node on the tree. To delete a branch, click **Delete Branch**.

Another method for adding branches to a node is to double-click on the node. When the cursor is over the node's symbol, it will change to a branch cursor to indicate that double-clicking will add branches.

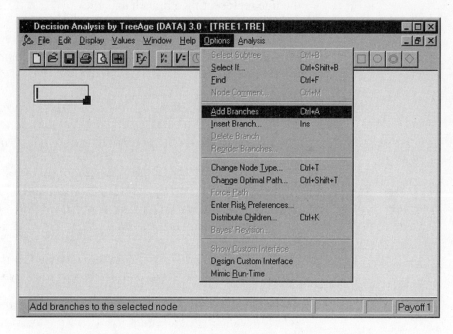

To indicate what a branch stands for, enter descriptive text in the box above it. Place the cursor above the line and click to get the box.

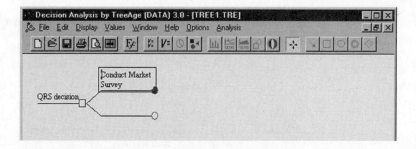

TIP: *Many decision trees have some subtree replication. You can cut and paste a subtree to other locations on the tree. Place the cursor at the root node of the subtree you want to copy and click. Go to the **Options** menu and click **Select Subtree**. Then go to the **Edit** menu and choose **Copy Subtree**. Next place the cursor on the node where you want to insert the subtree and click. Now go to the **Edit** menu and click **Paste**. You can cut and paste subtrees even after you assign names and probabilities to the branches and payoffs to the terminal nodes. (See also the **Clone** command under online **Help**.)*

*The **Edit** menu contains four tree clipboards named Tree clipboard1 to Tree clipboard 4. Thus, you can retain several subtrees at once, each in its own clipboard, to be pasted as needed.*

Step 2—Assigning (conditional) probabilities to branches of the tree

You can insert the probability of an outcome on the branch of the tree in the text box below the line. To get the text box, place the cursor below the line representing a branch and click.

> **NOTE**: *You can enter probabilities only on the branches of a tree that originate from chance node. A decision tree contains several types of nodes:*
>
> *1. A chance node (shown as a green circle) represents an uncertain or risky event. Branches emanating from a chance node represent all possible (non overlapping) outcomes of the event.*
> *2. A decision node (shown as a blue square) represnts a decision the manager faces. Branches emanating from a decision node specify all available (nonoverlapping) decision choices.*
> *3. A terminal node (shown as a red triangle) represents a final outcome: the end of a path, often referred to as a scenario.*
>
> *To change a node type, click the node, go to the **Options** menu and click **Change Node Type** and select the node type from the available choices.. Alternatively, you can click the* 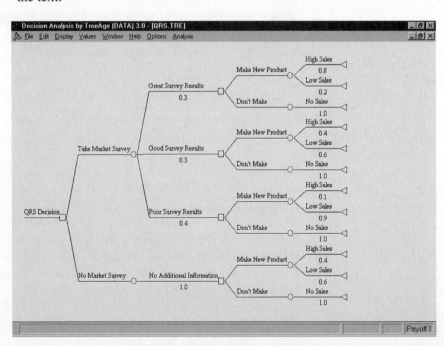 *icon on the toolbar and select the node type you want.*

As an exercise, construct the tree shown below and in Exhibit 6.2 of the text:

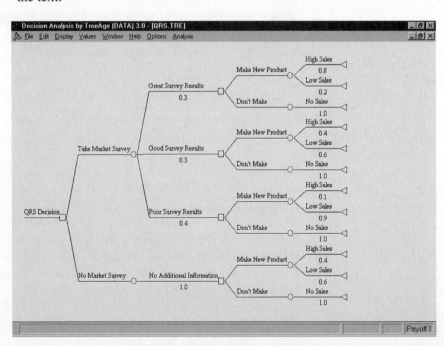

In the rest of the text under **Step 2**, we describe advanced features. You can skip to **Step 3** until you become familiar with the software.

In many cases, you will be uncertain about the accuracy of your probability estimates. Defining the probabilities as variables will enable you to perform sensitivity analyses to help you assess the significance of the uncertainty. To do this, you must define the variable, specify the value(s) it can take, and indicate the location(s) on the decision tree where these values will apply:

1. ***Defining a variable***: Go to the **Values** menu and choose **Define Values**. Click **New** and select **Variable** from the drop-down menu.

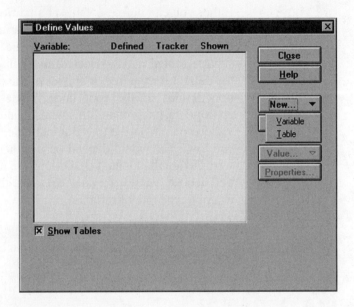

In the **Text Properties** section of the **Properties** dialog box, give your variable a name. If you like, you can also provide a short description or a longer comment, which can be useful for customizing the display,

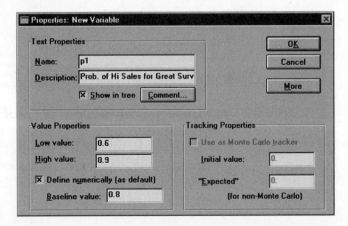

Follow the above procedure to define each variable in your model.

2. ***Specify the default value and, optionally, the range of values a variable takes***. Use the **Value Properties** section to specify a default value (baseline value) for a variable and a range of numeric values to be associated with it. For example, p1 could have the default value of 0.8 and values ranging from 0.6 to 0.9. You can accept or override the suggested range when specifying the parameters of the sensitivity analyses. It is not necessary to provide a range here, although you may find it convenient.

3. ***Indicate the locations on the tree where the values apply***. Click on **Value** and you will be presented with two options. Either you can define a value at a particular node or as a default for the whole tree. If you define a variable at a particular node, the program applies that value of the variable throughout the subtree rooted at the selected node. If you define a variable as the default for the tree, it applies to the entire tree, and its definition resides at the root node. Node-specific definitions are appropriate for probabilities whose values are likely to differ at various points on the tree: for example, the probabilities of high and low sales would depend on whether market research results were favorable. Default definitions are appropriate for probabilities whose values remain constant throughout the tree: for example, the rate of inflation.

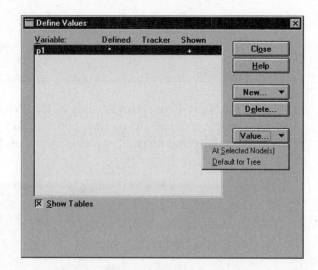

4. ***Associate the variable with probabilities on the tree***: Insert the variable name in the text box below the branches of the tree for which the variable will represent the probability value. In the example below, p1 represents the probability of "High Sales" under the "Make New Product" and "Great Survey Results" scenario.

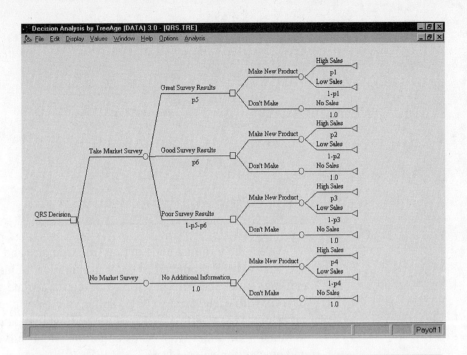

NOTE: *The probabilities along the branches emanating from each chance node must sum to 1.0. Thus, if two branches emanate from a chance node, you can assign one the variable p1 and the other (1 - p1).*

It is very important to make the variable assignments at the correct nodes. For this, you need to understand how the program uses variables in making calculations.

When the program encounters a variable in a probability field during calculations, it searches for the value assignment beginning with the node immediately to the right of the probability field and moves from there leftward to the root node. For a given variable, the program accepts the first definition (value assignment) that it locates as it makes this traversal. Thus, the program will disregard any definitions closer to the terminal node than the node immediately to the right of the probability field in question.

As a general rule, you should avoid using the same variable to define the probability of more than one event. Thus, if you have two subtrees representing the same uncertainty (high versus low sales) but the probability values are different, you should use different variables.

Step 3—Assigning payoffs (preferences) for scenarios

If you are sure about the dollar value (payoff) associated with a scenario, first select the terminal node (place the cursor on the node and click) and then go to the **Options** menu and select **Change Node Type**. You can also click on the icon to change the node type. You will see the following dialog box:

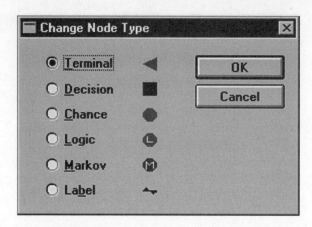

Select the terminal node option (red triangle) and click **OK**.

You will be prompted to enter a numerical value for **Payoff 1**. You can then enter the sure payoffs (You can associate up to four different payoffs with each scenario (e.g., dollar value, costs, utility value, or pay-off realized by a partner firm). In the following example, we selected the terminal node under High Sales under the Great Survey Results scenario, and entered the value 84.

Enter a payoff for each terminal node.

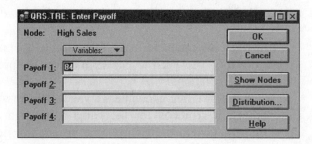

In the rest of the text under **Step 3**, we describe advanced features. You can skip to **Step 4** until you become familiar with the software.

For conducting sensitivity analyses, you can define variables to denote payoffs. The procedure for defining variables for payoffs is the same as the one we described for assigning variables for probabilities. In the following example, we will use the variable v1 to represent payoffs realized under High Sales and with No Market Survey. (You can also use algebraic expressions of defined variables (e.g., *v1 + v2 - v3*) to represent more complex payoffs).

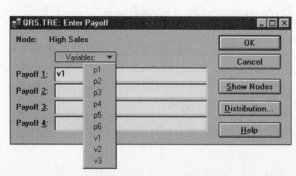

For variables used in calculating payoffs for a scenario, the program will search each node in the scenario, beginning with the terminal node and traversing leftward to the root node, looking for numeric definitions for each relevant variable. For a given variable, the program will accept the first definition (value assignment) that it locates on this traversal. Thus, if the same construct will have different values at two different nodes on the tree, it is best to define two separate variables that apply at those nodes. For example, if unit costs of production are higher at higher volumes, then the cost figures in scenarios with high sales should have larger numbers than cost figures in scenarios that call for lower sales.

Click the **Distribution** button to specify the frequency with which values of the variable would be selected in Monte Carlo analyses. In the example below, we first selected the **Normal** distribution from the palette of distributions and then specified a mean of 80 and a standard deviation of 8 for variable v1.

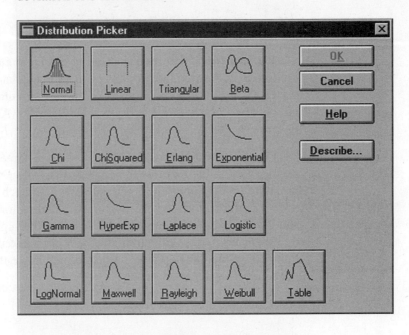

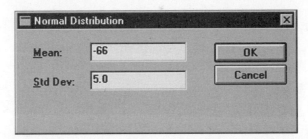

Step 4—Conducting analyses to select decision option(s)

You can conduct many types of analyses with the TreeÅge software. We will describe those you are most likely to use for the ICI exercise. To learn about other types of analyses, play around with the other commands on the **Analysis** menu, which are described in the online help files.

Calculate the expected value of a node: Click on a node, go to the **Analysis** menu, and select **Expected Value**. A dialog box will show the expected value; in this example, the expected value of the Take Market Survey node is $8.

NOTE: *In calculating the expected value, the program uses the baseline values of variables or the mean values of distributions associated with the variables.*

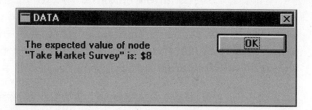

Rolling back the tree: Instead of calculating the expected value of each node in the tree individually, you can calculate and display the expected values and probabilities of all nodes simultaneously. To do this, go to the **Analysis** menu and click **Roll Back.** (Alternatively, you can click on the ⓪ icon on the tool bar.)

Once you roll back the tree, you will see three additional pieces of information on the tree: (1) the expected payoffs (in dollars or other appropriate units) shown in a rectangular box at each chance and decision node, (2) the payoff and the overall probability for each terminal node, and (3) the path along the tree that leads to the highest expected payoff (the branches that are not along this path are marked with the symbol \\). In this example, the "optimal" decision is to make the new product without conducting a market survey.

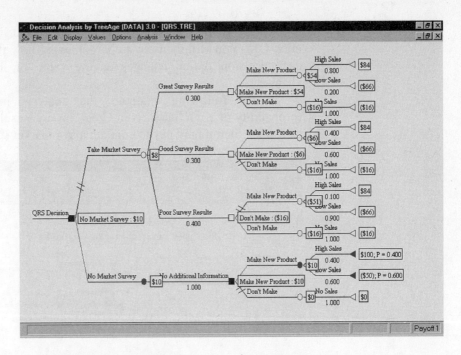

Sensitivity analyses: The TreeÅge software offers several options for conducting sensitivity analyses to determine which factors have great impact on the decisions. The most common way to do this is to select a node and then go to the **Analysis** menu and select **Sensitivity Analysis**. You will then have four choices: (1) analyzing the effects of a change in one variable (One-way); (2) analyzing the effects of changes in any two variables simultaneously (Two-way); (3) analyzing the effects of changes in any three variables simultaneously (Three-way); and (4) Tornado diagram, which is a set of one-way sensitivity analyses on any subgroup of variables in your decision tree. We describe the one-way graphs and Tornado diagrams.

One-Way Sensitivity Analysis: If you choose **One-way**, you will see the following screen.

NOTE: *It is important to first specify the node at which this analysis will apply. Typically you would select the root node to see the impact of the sensitivity analysis on the overall decision.*

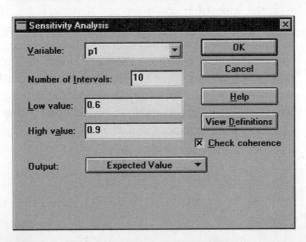

After you specify the variable of interest and its range of variation, click **OK**. You will then see a chart showing how the expected value of each decision option changes as the value of the selected variable changes.

In the following example, the analysis indicates that if p1 (probability of High Sales given Great Survey Results) is equal to a little over 0.84, then it may pay to conduct a test market survey.

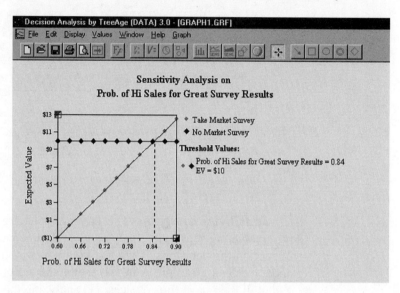

On the **File** menu, click **Close** to get back to the decision tree display.

Tornado Diagram: An alternative way to conduct sensitivity analysis is the Tornado diagram, which is a set of mini-sensitivity analyses set forth in a single graph. It can include all or a subset of the variables defined in your tree. You specify which variables are to be included in the analysis and assign a range of values to each of them. In the resulting graph, each variable analyzed is represented by a horizontal bar. Each bar represents the range of possible outcomes generated by varying the related variable. A wide bar indicates that the associated variable has a large potential effect on the expected value of the decision. (This is called a tornado diagram because the bars are arranged in order with the widest bar at the top and narrowest bar at the bottom, resulting in a funnel-like appearance). A vertical dotted line is drawn on the graph to indicate the expected value at the selected node (often the root node).

To construct a tornado diagram, select the chance node or decision node at which you want to construct the diagram. Next from the **Analysis** menu, select **Tornado Diagram**, and then select **Variables to Analyze**. Click each variable to be included (from **Available Variables**) and then click **Add>>**. You will be prompted to specify the range of variation for each variable.

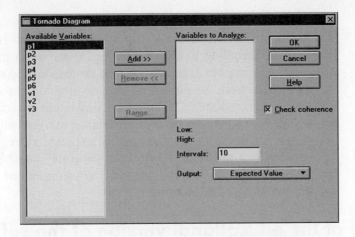

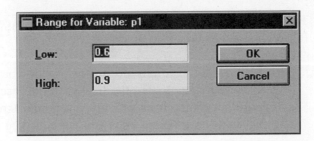

Once you enter the appropriate information, the program will display the results of the sensitivity analysis as bar graphs indicating the expected payoff as the values of the variable(s) change.

NOTE: *The vertical dotted line at the selected node is the "fulcrum" that allows you to view the impact of each variable relative to the original (baseline) expected value. Thus, although the range of p1 is from 0.6 to 0.9, it affects the expected value of the decision only for values from 0.84 to 0.9 - the range in which the expected value of the decision becomes higher than 10, the baseline.*

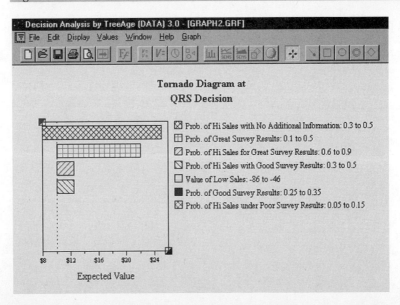

Monte Carlo analysis: In Monte Carlo analysis, the model runs a number of simulated trials. The result of each trial is a single scenario, selected according to the probabilities specified in the model. On most decision trees, no specified outcome corresponds to the expected value. The results from the simulation are a distribution of payoffs, rather than a single expected value. Over many simulation trials, the average result will fall very close to the expected value, but you will also obtain information about the variance around the expected value. You can find more details about the Monte Carlo analysis in the online help and in the detailed manual for the program that you can print out as we described at the beginning of this tutorial.

Limitations of the educational version of the software

The educational (demonstration) version of TreeÅge is identical to the full version in most respects, except:

- You cannot save any documents. Once you complete an exercise, you cannot store the tree for future use (although you can print out a copy from which you can reconstruct the tree). So, do not exit the program until you are sure you have completed all analyses.
- The maximum size tree you can create manually is 50 nodes.
- The maximum size tree you can open is 125 nodes. We have included several example files (with extension *.tre) that you can open to learn more about how decision trees are used in various application areas.

ICI AMERICAS R&D PROJECT SELECTION CASE*

ICI America is a subsidiary of the British-based Imperial Chemical Industries, Ltd (ICI). In 1992, ICI's sales totaled $11.2 billion, making it one of the largest chemical companies in the world. The company reported a net income of $218 million for 1992 before exceptional items and discontinued operations. Its North American subsidiaries included US-based ICI Americas (primarily in polyester film, pharmaceuticals, and specialty chemicals) and Canadian Industries Ltd. (strong in explosives, pulp and paper chemicals, and environmental services). The Canadian subsidiary marketed industrial explosives (e.g., for use in mining operations) throughout North America. ICI Americas focused on the military explosives market. The post-cold-war era has reduced this subsidiary's growth opportunities. To survive within a fast growing company, it needed new products, especially for nonmilitary applications.

ICI Americas' Canadian subsidiary discovered a new but unpatentable application for one of its products (anthraquinine or AQ): use as an agent for reducing pulp mill water pollution. AQ acts by reacting with paper and pulp waste pollutants to form solids that can be filtered out of the paper-mill waste stream.

If Canadian Industries could develop the AQ product and process on a commercial scale, it could create a large global market. Reducing the pollution from pulp and paper processing was a major goal of environmental regulatory authorities worldwide. For example, the state-of-the-art Kraft process produced offensive odors and an effluent that reddened streams. AQ was distilled from coal tar and used principally in manufacturing dyes. Coal tar is a byproduct of coke production, and coke is used exclusively to make steel. Hence ICI's current AQ capacity was directly related to the world demand for steel.

At the time, all the AQ produced in the world would have satisfied only a small portion of the unpatented and unconfirmed market for the product as a pollution reducing agent. One of ICI's competitors, BASF, had an alternative process for synthesizing AQ; if ICI did not move rapidly, BASF might preempt ICI's potential leadership position.

ICI needed to do a quick analysis to decide whether to go ahead with its R&D expenditures or to abandon the project.

The following were the primary issues it considered in making this decision:

- Would market tests confirm that there was a significant market for the product?
- Could the company develop a new process for making this product that was technically feasible?

---

* Adapted from Hess (1993).

- Even if there were a significant market and the process were technically feasible, would the company's board sanction an investment in a new plant necessary to produce the product on a commercial scale?
- Assuming the answers to the above questions were all yes and the plant were built, would the venture turn out to be successful?

Assuming that each of these four issues had a yes or no answer, the management team estimated the probabilities for each event (Exhibit 1).

Event	Probability
Significant market	0.6 ± 0.15
Technically feasible	0.15 ± 0.10
Board sanctions plant expenditures	0.8 ± 0.2
Commercial success	0.8 ± 0.2

EXHIBIT 1
Probabilities for Water Pollution Problem

The following primary economic factors affected the profitability of the venture:

- The research expenses to identify a new production process for the product
- The marketing research cost to determine whether there was a significant market
- The process development costs, including presanction engineering
- The commercial development costs, both before and after the board's sanction
- The venture value (net present value) if successful

Estimates of these values are given in Exhibit 2. The plus-or-minus signs show the degree of uncertainty about the values. (All dollar values are in millions of dollars.)

Expense or Gain	Net Present Value (Million $)
Research expense	$ 1.5 ± 0.40
Marketing Research expense	$ 0.2 ± 0.50
Process development expense (presanction)	$ 3.0 ± 0.75
Commercial development expense (presanction)	$ 0.5 ± 0.25
Commercial development expense (postsanction)	$ 1.0 ± 0.25
Value if successful	$ 25.0 ± 12.50

EXHIBIT 2
Monetary Estimates for Water Pollution Problem

The decisions and actions the firm considered were to decide whether to abandon the product now or:

- To spend on research and marketing development. If marketing research indicates an insignificant market for the product, then abandon the project.
- If process development research indicates that the project is not technically feasible (given positive marketing research), then abandon the project.
- If the process appears technically feasible, then invest in process development. If that research indicates that the process is technically infeasible, cut expenses and quit.
- If the project is technically feasible, spend on process development and begin commercial development. If the company board then declines to sanction the money for the new plant, cut expenses and quit.
- If the board approves, spend on further commercial development. By this time the company has made all of its decisions. If the venture turns out to be a commercial success then it gains the venture value for a success (less expenses so far). Otherwise the company has lost the money spent so far, but that is all.

EXERCISES

ICI managers thought that a decision tree analysis would be appropriate for the problem they faced. Construct a decision tree to represent this problem structure. The managers are interested in the following questions:

1. What is the maximum ICI should invest in presanction process development?

2. What decision would the model recommend under optimistic, pessimistic, and best-guess scenarios?

3. Which probability and payoff estimates have the most impact on the decision?

4. What should ICI do and why?

Reference

Hess, Sidney W. 1993, "Swinging on the branch of a tree: Project selection applications," *Interfaces*, Vol. 23, No. 6 (November-December), pp. 5-12.

TUTORIAL FOR THE PIMS STRATEGY MODEL (PIMS)

The PIMS spreadsheet implements the PIMS return on investment (ROI) models. PIMS (profit impact of marketing strategy) is based on the concept that data drawn from the pooled experience of a diversity of successful businesses and analyzed through regression, will provide insights and guidance for managing businesses profitably. PIMS is based on data from over 3000 businesses from over 200 companies.

We have incorporated data for four strategic business units (SBUs) into the PIMS model here; those SBUs are the ones described in the "Portfolio Analysis" included with the GE: Portfolio Planning exercise.

To start the program, go to the **Model** menu and select **PIMS: Strategy Model** (pims.xls) to see the **Introduction** screen.

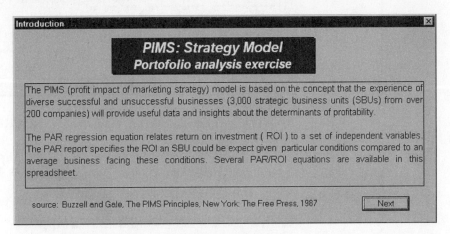

Click **Next** to get to the **Main Menu**. Four SBUs corresponding to the portfolio exercise in the text are built into the program: TRANS, SALT, UBC, and POWER. To select an SBU for analysis, click **Built-In** at the bottom right-hand side of the screen.

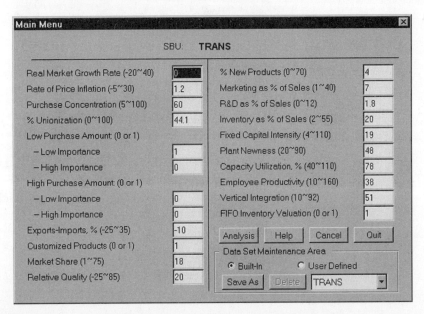

After selecting an SBU and possibly modifying the built-in data, click **Analysis** to activate the par-report models.

Using the next screen, **Model Selection**, you can specify a particular model that best fits your context.

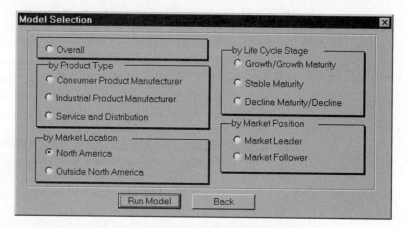

When you have specified your model, click **Run Model** to activate the ROI analysis.

You can now see how sensitive the model output is to changes in a single input. Here we changed Unionization from the original 44.1 percent to 60 percent to produce this report:

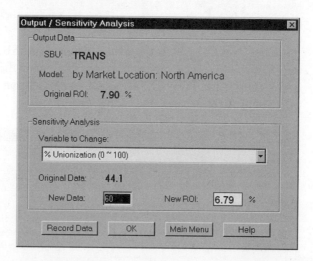

If you want to save this case, click **Record Data** to store your data in the wshRecord sheet. You can access this sheet by going to the **Model** menu in the menu bar, choosing **Main Menu**, clicking **Cancel**, and selecting the wshRecord sheet.

	A	B	C	D	E	F
1	*Sensitivity Analysis Summary Report*					
2						
3	*field* *Case Name*		*TRANS*			
4	Real Market Growth Rate (-20 ~ 40)		0			
5	Rate of Price Inflation (-5 ~ 30)		1.2			
6	Purchase Concentration (5 ~ 100)		60			
7	% Unionization (0 ~ 100)		44.1			
8	Low Purchase Amount -Low Importance (0 or 1)		1			
9	Low Purchase Amount -High Importance (0 or 1)		0			
10	High Purchase Amount -Low Importance (0 or 1)		0			
11	High Purchase Amount -High Importance (0 or 1)		0			
12	Exports-Imports, % (-25 ~ 35)		-10			
13	Customized Products (0 or 1)		1			
14	Market Share (1 ~ 75)		18			
15	Relative Quality (-25 ~ 85)		20			
16	% New Products (0 ~ 70)		4			
17	Marketing as % of Sales (1 ~ 40)		7			
18	R&D as % of Sales (0 ~ 12)		1.8			
19	Inventory as % of Sales (2 ~ 55)		20			
20	Fixed Capital Intensity (4 ~ 110)		19			
21	Plant Newness (20 ~ 90)		48			
22	Capacity Utilization, % (40 ~ 110)		78			
23	Employee Productivity (10 ~ 160)		38			
24	Vertical Integration (10 ~ 92)		51			
25	FIFO Inventory Valuation (0 or 1)		1			
26	Model Selected by Market Location: North America					

wshRecord / wshData /

To save the data as a user-defined case, click **Save As** in the **Main Menu** dialog. You will be prompted to enter a data-set name. The data set will be stored as a user-defined set.

In a similar fashion, you can delete any of the user-defined data sets by going to the **Main Menu** and clicking **Delete**.

Reference

Buzzell, Robert D. and Gale, Bradley T. 1987, *The PIMS Principles*, The Free Press, New York.

GLOSSARY OF VARIABLES USED BY THE PIMS PROGRAM

Capacity utilization: The average rate of capacity utilization during a year. The rate of utilization equals net sales plus or minus change in finished goods inventory divided by standard capacity. The standard capacity is defined as the dollar value of the maximum output possible for the Strategic Business Unit (SBU) under normal operating conditions.

Customized products: Products customized for individual customers (index = 1) or standardized for all customers (index = 0).

Employee productivity (value added per employee): A measure in thousands of dollars obtained by dividing total sales by the number of full-time equivalent employees.

Exports and imports: The percentage of industry sales that is accounted for by exports and imports. Notice that this is defined in terms of the industry in which the Strategic Business Unit competes.

FIFO inventory valuation: Whether the method of valuing inventory is first in, first out (FIFO) (index = 1) or not (index = 0). This factor affects taxes and consequently reported profits.

Fixed capital intensity: The gross book value of plant and equipment expressed as a percentage of sales. This definition excludes depreciation and working capital.

Inventory as a percentage of sales: Average inventories (including raw materials, components, work-in-process, and finished goods) expressed as a percentage of the annual sales of the Strategic Business Unit.

Market share: The market share for the Strategic Business Unit in the market it serves.

Marketing as a percentage of sales: The total annual marketing expenditures (sales force, advertising, media, sales promotion, and other marketing costs) expressed as a percentage of annual sales of the Strategic Business Unit.

Percent new products: The percentage of the Strategic Business Unit's total sales that are derived from products introduced during the three preceding years.

Percent unionization: The percentage of the Strategic Business Unit's total employees (managerial, nonmanagerial; both salaried and hourly) that are unionized.

Plant newness: The ratio of the net book value of plant and equipment to gross book value expressed as a percentage.

Purchase amount: The dollar amount of a typical purchase transaction with an end user or immediate customer. If this is less than $1000, it is generally considered to be low (index = 0). If the purchase amount is high, the index has a value equal to 1.0.

Purchase concentration: The percentage of the Strategic Business Unit's direct customers that accounted for 50 percent of its sales.

Purchase importance: An index based on the proportion of the typical customer's or end users annual purchases that are for the types of products and services the Strategic Business Unit sells. If you think this is high (say >5 percent), you can give the index a value equal to 1.0.

R&D as a percentage of sales: R&D expenses (excluding basic research carried out at the corporate level) expressed as a percentage of the annual sales of the Strategic Business Unit.

Rate of inflation: The rate at which the Strategic Business Unit's selling prices increase.

Real market growth rate: The rate at which the Strategic Business Unit's sales increase in the market it serves, adjusted for inflation. The served market is part of the overall market for which the Strategic Business Unit has a suitable product to offer and uses a marketing program to reach this portion of the total market.

Relative product quality: An index based on the percentage of the Strategic Business Unit's sales volume accounted for by products and services that customers assess as "Superior," "Equivalent," and "Inferior" to those available from the three leading competitors. The index is computed by subtracting the percentage of inferior-quality sales from the percentage of superior-quality sales.

Vertical integration: A measure of value added calculated as the percentage of sales of the Strategic Business Unit, equal to total sales minus all purchases (materials, components, labor, supplies, and energy) by an Strategic Business Unit from other businesses, including businesses within the same parent corporation.

TUTORIAL FOR THE GE PORTFOLIO PLANNING MODEL (GE)

The GE: Portfolio Planning spreadsheet has the GE/McKinsey Portfolio Model at its core. General Electric designed this tool to help it to evaluate a portfolio of strategic business units (SBUs). Based on input on business strength and industry attractiveness, it maps SBUs onto a multifactor matrix. Their position on the multifactor grid provides pragmatic insights for the corporate strategy.

On the **Model** menu, choose **GE: Portfolio Planning** (ge.xls) and then **Generalized Model**) to see the **Introduction** screen.

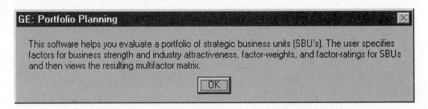

Click **OK** to get to the first of two worksheets, which will prompt you for your input.

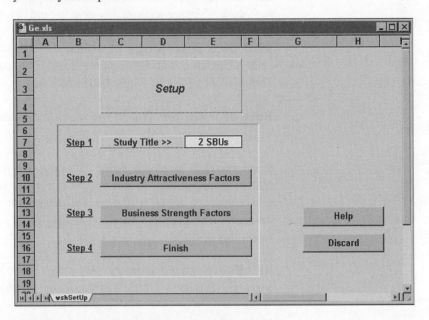

As an example, set up a simple problem consisting of two SBUs. Provide a study title and click **Industry Attractiveness Items** to advance to the next screen and set up the model.

Choose the industry attractiveness dimensions on which the SBUs will be evaluated. Some prospective factors are listed. Click each item in the list that you wish to include and then click **Add,** and the program will include it in your analysis.

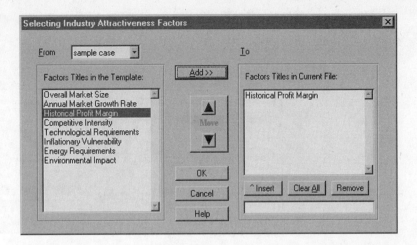

You can also add your own dimensions indicating industry attractiveness. In this example we added the item "Global opportunities" to the list by entering it in the bottom right area and clicking the **Insert** button. If you are dissatisfied with a selection you can highlight an item and click **Remove** or you can **Clear All**.

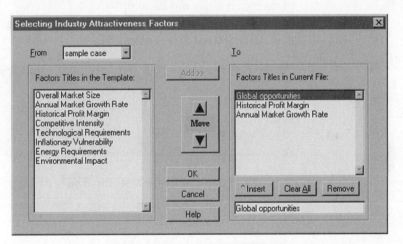

Click **OK** to get back to the initial set-up screen. For step 3, click **Business Strength Factors**.

Now you need to list the factors that serve as indicators of business strength. Choose from Factor Titles in the Template using **Add** or enter your own factors in the lower right area using **Insert** as you did with the Industry Attractiveness factors. Click **OK** when you are finished.

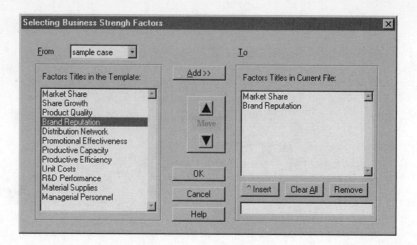

Again click **OK** to get back to the initial set-up screen. Once you have finished the initial set up, click **Finish** (step 4) to continue or select **Discard**.

If you choose **Finish**, the system will customize the worksheet according to your setup and then prompt you for a file name under which to save your basic model setup.

Generally it is a good idea to save your newly configured model now. Give it a name other than GE.

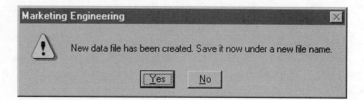

Now you are set to assess the SBUs of interest on the basis of the dimensions you just specified. The following screen shows the **Main Menu** for the evaluation task.

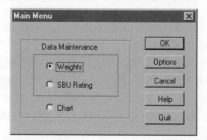

First select **Weights** to indicate the importance weights for each of the factors you chose. The weights are multipliers of the SBU item ratings you will set subsequently.

NOTE: *These are relative weights, so giving every item a '1' is the same as giving every item a '2'.*

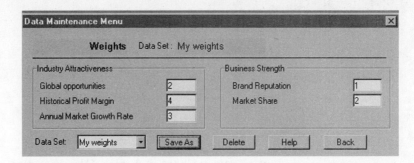

Click **Save As** to save your weights for future use. You can define multiple sets of importance weights, saving each under a different name.

Click **Back** to get back to the **Main Menu**. Next choose **SBU Rating**.

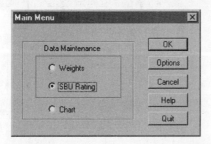

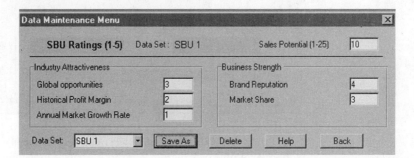

Rate the first SBU on the Industry Attractiveness and Business Strength dimensions and save these by clicking **Save As**.

NOTE: *The rating for Sales Potential does not affect the location of the SBU in the GE matrix, but it will determine the size of the circles in the resulting chart.*

Repeat the procedure to include other SBUs for analysis. Click **Back** to go back to the **Main Menu**.

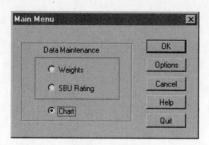

Finally select **Chart** and click **OK**. You will see an empty Multifactor Portfolio Matrix.

To see the result for your input, load the rating information about the SBUs into the chart by clicking **Add from Database**.

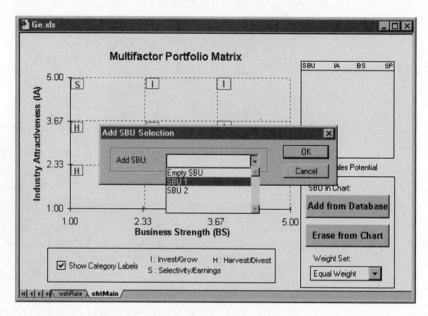

You can test what happens when you apply different weighting schemes, e.g., customized weights versus equal weights (a set of weights that are included as a default option). If different managers weight the factors differently, it can be a very valuable exercise to examine the strategic consequences of those differences.

Strategy implications for individual SBUs can be drawn from their positioning on the matrix, as indicated by the category labels. For example SBU 1 belongs to the category "H" standing for Harvest and Divest.

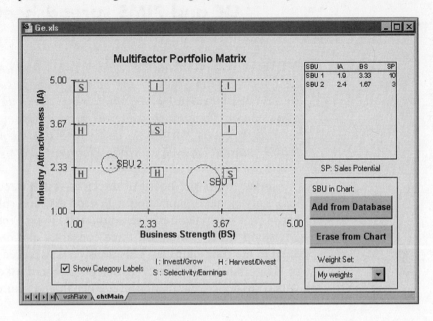

If you need to make changes or additions to the weight sets or the SBU rating sets, go to **Model** in the main menu bar and choose **Main Menu**.

Limitations of the software

Maximum number of industry attractiveness indicators: 15
Maximum number of business strength indicators: 15
Maximum number of cases plotted in chart: 10

Reference

Wind, Yoram; Mahajan, Vijay; and Swire, Donald J. 1983, "An empirical comparison of standardized portfolio models," *Journal of Marketing*, Vol. 47, No. 2 (Spring), pp. 89-99.

PORTFOLIO ANALYSIS EXERCISE
(Exercise to accompany the GE and PIMS spreadsheets)

NOTE: *A version of the GE model, saved as Portfol.xls, contains the data for the four SBUs in the portfolio analysis already entered and saved. Use that version of the spreadsheet to run the exercise, or develop a customized spreadsheet using the general GE model described in the tutorial. To select Portfol.x/s, go to the* **Model** *menu, choose* **GE: Portfolio Planning** *and then* **Portfolio Planning Exercise***.*

In late 1995, the board of directors restructured Conglomerate, Inc. into a divisional organization with each division subdivided into a number of SBUs (strategic business units). Its Food Production and Products Division (FPPD) comprised three consumer and one industrial SBU related to the food industry. This division was placed under the leadership of Henry Antworth, and Conglomerate's board asked Henry to come up with a strategic examination of the health and future for these four businesses.

1. ***The Corn-Transformation Products Group (TRANS)*** is Conglomerate's corn-processing equipment and parts business. TRANS equipment and related supplies are used internally by Conglomerate's other corn-related businesses and are also sold to a range of customers (some of whom compete with Conglomerate in other businesses). In these product markets which have had a negligible growth rate, TRANS is seeing sales of just over $100 million in a global industry that generates about $550 million in sales annually, making TRANS either the second or third largest supplier in this business. Only four percent of those sales come from products TRANS introduced in the last five years. In the last few years, TRANS has been spending about seven percent of sales on marketing activities and about 1.8 percent of sales on R& D. Margins have been tight in this business recently, and investments in new tooling have led to a return on investment of minus two percent in the last year.

2. ***Salted-Corn Snackfoods Group (SALT)*** is one of Conglomerate's consumer products SBUs, producing a range of salted snacks based mainly on corn. Conglomerate has some special plants, expertise, and holdings in corn that have allowed it to maintain a market share of over 22 percent in this $450 million market. This market is growing nearly three percent a year, and SALT earns about seven percent of its sales from products introduced in the last five years. SALT has been spending about nine percent of sales on marketing activities and a bit over two percent on R&D in recent years. Its relatively low plant utilization (75 percent) and stable sales give the firm a healthy (19 percent)

return on the relatively small investment this business has been requiring.

3. ***Unsweetened Breakfast Cereals Group (UBC)*** competes with Post and Kellogg, but with a more narrow range of products based primarily on the firm's expertise in corn. UBC estimates that it has about a five percent market share of the $9.8 billion market, growing at a bit over three percent per year. In recent years it has been spending about eight percent of sales on marketing activities and just under three percent of sales on R&D. New products in this business make up about five percent of sales, and recently the ROI for this SBU has been 17 percent.

4. ***The Powerdrinks Group (POWER)*** is Conglomerate's most recently launched consumer division. The firm considers itself the market leader in this area with about 27 percent of the approximately $470 million market. (Corn and corn products are an important base for all POWER products. It has been spending over 11 percent of sales on marketing activities and over three percent of sales on R&D in this turbulent market. That market is growing at about 5.5 percent annually and POWER sees about 15 percent of its sales from new products. POWER's most recent ROI is 13 percent.

Mr. Antworth scheduled a retreat for the first week of June 1996 with his planning staff and the SBU managers. These are some of the questions that he hoped to answer at the retreat:

1. How well or badly were these businesses performing? (Each SBU manager had to submit a capital and operating budget request by summer's end that justified the level of proposed spending in the business.)

2. Both marketing and R&D budgets were under close scrutiny. How much seemed reasonable (best?) to invest in these activities within the division and how should those expenditures be allocated across SBUs.

3. What type of strategy should Conglomerate pursue with these SBUs? (Invest? Divest? Hold? Harvest?)

Three weeks prior to the retreat Antworth distributed these three questions to the SBU directors. He immediately got four irate phone calls: These questions could be answered only through "business feel" and "experience." Antworth had just participated in a seminar on strategic marketing analysis ("marketing engineering"); he suggested that the group apply some of the analytic structures from that program to answer his three questions. In a half-day session a few days before the retreat, he had each business manager provide the data needed to run two of the models from that seminar, the PIMS model and the GE/McKinsey model. He also led them through an exercise to arrive at best-guess answers to the following questions:

Q1: If your SBU's marketing budget were increased by 1 percent of its present value, what increase in market share would you expect to see (by what percent of the present share)?

Q2: If your SBU's R&D budget were increased by 1 percent of its present value, what increase in relative quality would you expect to see (by what percent of its present level)?

After some discussion, the members of the group agreed on the following answers:

Mkts +1%   R&D + 1% (handwritten)

	Market Share Increase	Quality Increase
TRANS	1.8%	3.1% *too high, wrong* (handwritten)
SALT	2.2%	2.9%
UBC	1.9%	2.7%
POWER	1.5%	2.4%

EXERCISES

1. Using the PIMS model, the GE model, or any other approach you think is appropriate, decide what advice to give Mr. Antworth. (If your approach requires additional information, be specific about what that information is and how you plan to obtain it.)

1. ~~RO~~ try to get PIM ROI close to data. (handwritten margin note)

2. See effect of Δ in mkt share / quality research. (handwritten margin note)

> **TIP**: *When using the PIMS model, look at the impact on ROI of the joint changes (in spending and impact on share and quality, respectively) to see what PIMS has to say about the relative effectiveness of marketing and research spending on profitability—are we under or oversupporting these businesses according to PIMS?*

2. Comment more generally on the uses and limitations of PIMS and the GE model for analyzing these kinds of situations at Conglomerate.

3. How does this approach compare with the Analytic Hierarchy Process, another approach that Antworth's planning staff was considering?

4. Some people claim that these models can be distorted to support any preconceived strategies that managers like those at Conglomerate bring to the table. Comment on this claim.

TUTORIAL FOR ANALYTIC HIERARCHY PROCESS

The Analytic Hierarchy Process (AHP) is a general problem-solving method that is useful in making complex decisions (e.g., multi-criteria decisions) based on variables that do not have exact numerical consequences. We will explain the basics of creating and using AHP models. The software is supplied by Expert Choice, Inc., and this tutorial is based on Expert Choice's online tutorial. We encourage you to work through the online tutorial to get a fuller understanding of all the features of the AHP model.

Decision modeling using Expert Choice (in the Evaluation and Choice mode) typically consists of five steps: (1) Structuring the decision model, (2) Entering alternatives, (3) Establishing priorities among elements of the hierarchy, (4) Synthesizing, and (5) Conducting sensitivity analysis.

Structuring the decision model

You start by breaking down a complex decision problem into a hierarchical structure. You can use the following elements: (1) Overall goal (subgoals) to be attained, (2) Criteria and subcriteria, (3) Scenarios, and (4) Alternatives.

As an example, we will look at how a manager of an ice cream store chain decides where to open a new outlet. The goal is to select the better of two locations. The main criteria in this decision are (1) rental space cost, (2) traffic of potential customers, and (3) the number of competitors. The store locations they are considering are a suburban mall (moderate rent, high population of teenagers and retirees who are known to be purchasers of ice cream) and Main Street downtown (high rent, main traffic is office workers who are not around in the evenings and on weekends).

An Expert Choice model consists of a minimum of three levels: the overall goal of the decision at the top level, (sub)criteria at the second level, and alternatives (the two locations for the store) at the third level. In models with many levels, place the more general factors of the decision in the upper levels of the hierarchy and the more specific criteria in the lower levels.

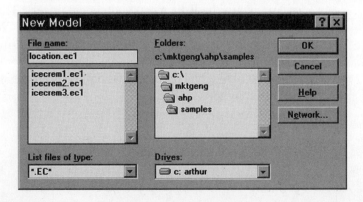

To start a new model, go to the Expert Choice **File** menu, and choose **New**. Enter a name for the file in which to save the model you will build, e.g., location.ec1, and click **OK**.

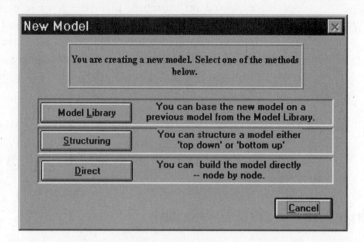

To set up the model node by node, click **Direct**.

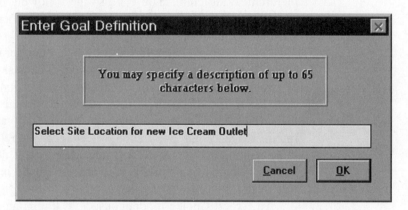

Type in a description of the goal of the decision, e.g., "Select Site Location for new Ice Cream Outlet."

Click **OK**.

For this example, the decision criteria are extent of competition (COMPET'N), customer fit (CUST FIT), and cost (COST). To enter the criteria, go to the **Edit** menu and choose **Insert**. This adds a level to the hierarchy directly below the active GOAL node. When you enter each criterion, e.g., COMPET'N, the program also allows you to give a description of the criterion, e.g., the number of competitors in the area. When you have entered information about all the nodes at this level of the hierarchy, press **<Esc>**.

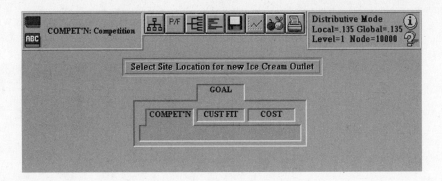

Entering alternatives

To enter the alternatives, first select the COMPET'N node. Next, on the **Edit** menu, choose **Insert**. Type an abbreviation (eight characters or less) for the first alternative, e.g., Mall. You can again enter a more detailed description for the alternative, e.g., "Suburban mall location." Click **OK** to enter the next alternative. When you have entered all alternatives, press **<Esc>**.

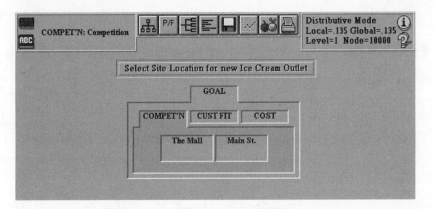

Activate the (sub)criterion node under which you entered the alternatives, go to the **Edit** menu and choose **Replicate children of current node**.

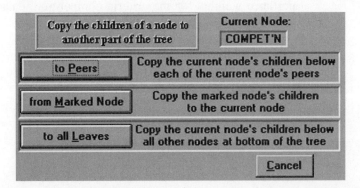

Click **To Peers** or **To All Leaves** to replicate the alternatives to all of the other nodes at the bottom of the model. Once the alternatives have been associated with all subnodes, the alternatives will be displayed at the bottom of the screen.

To save a model, go to the **File** menu and choose **Save**.

Establishing priorities among elements of the hierarchy

Once you specified the decision model fully, you can evaluate the alternatives and criteria at each level to derive "local" priorities (weights) by making pairwise comparisons among elements at the same level in the hierarchy. First select the node for which you want to establish priorities. Go to the **Assessment** menu and choose the assessment method, for example, **Pairwise** or **Data**.

Entering importance weights (Assessment, Data:
You can enter absolute values for the weights of the nodes (instead of relative values such as those derived in the pairwise comparison mode), by clicking **Assessment** and then **Data**. For example, you can assign importance weights for the criteria competition, customer fit, and cost, as shown below.

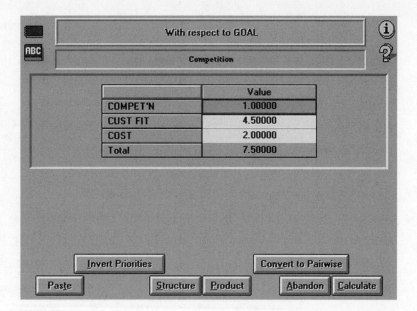

After you enter the importance weights, click **Calculate**. The new values will be reflected in the decision model. (If the decision model does not show the weights, click the **P/F** icon at the top of the screen.)

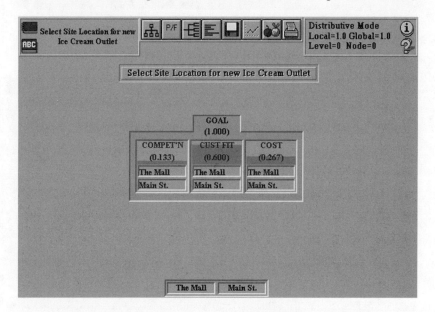

Entering pairwise comparisons (Assessment, Pairwise)

You can make simple pairwise comparison judgments on each pair of items in the comparison set. To begin the pairwise assessment process, move to the first criterion by double-clicking on its node (e.g., COMPT'N). Select **Assessment** and then **Pairwise** (this is only available if there are nine alternatives or less) to compare the alternative sites on this criterion.

Choose the type of comparison (**Importance, Preference, Likelihood**) and the mode of comparison (**Verbal, Graphical, Numerical**). Choose a type and mode that you feel comfortable with. The type you select will not affect any calculations performed by Evaluation and

Choice (the selected type will appear in the comparison statement). Generally, **Importance** is appropriate when comparing criteria, **Preference** is appropriate when comparing alternatives, and **Likelihood** is appropriate when comparing uncertain events.

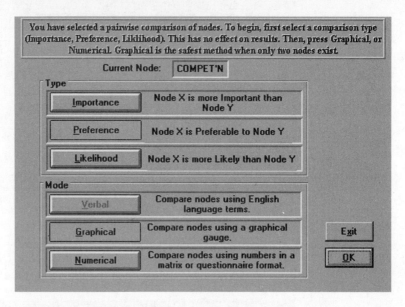

Click **OK**. When only two nodes are to be compared, the **Graphical** comparison mode is the default.

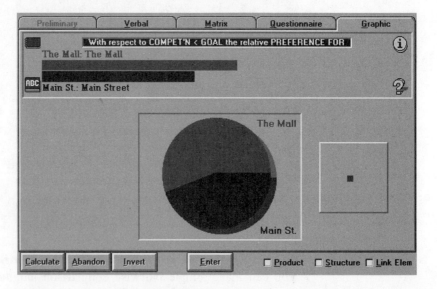

To indicate your preference in the graphical mode, click and drag the upper or lower horizontal, judgment bars. Alternatively, you can enter your assessment in the **Verbal** and **Numerical** mode, in the **Matrix** mode, or **Questionnaire** mode. Choose the appropriate tab.

When you have completed all of the comparisons, the program automatically calculates and graphs the priorities and gives you a measure of the inconsistency of your judgments (Inconsistency Ratio). (In our example, there is only one pairwise comparison, and therefore no redundant information: the inconsistency measure is meaningless.)

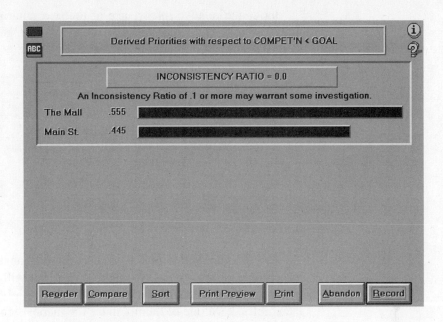

Click **Record** to return to the main screen.

Treat the other criteria in a similar fashion (e.g., double-click on the COST node) to continue the assessment process.

After you finish making the pairwise comparisons and evaluating the alternatives (at the lowest level of the hierarchy), compare the criteria pairwise with respect to the goal. The program uses this information to derive the relative importance of the criteria (cost, customer fit, extent of competition).

To make pairwise comparisons between criteria (instead of directly assigning importance weights earlier in "Entering Importance Weights"), double-click the GOAL node. Select **Assessment** and then **Pairwise** to compare the criteria. Select **Importance for the Type** and **Verbal** for the comparison mode. Clicking **Skip Preliminary Questions** will bring you to the following screen:

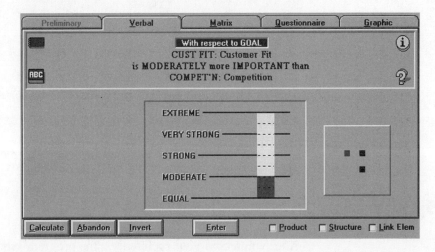

Judge the relative importance of the two criteria and click **Enter** to move to the next comparison. Click **Calculate** to get the measure of the inconsistency of your judgments.

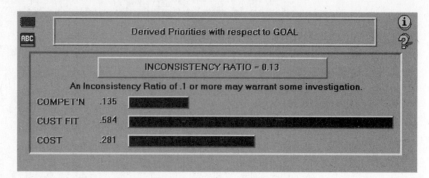

The *Inconsistency Ratio* is purely informational. The program does not enforce consistency. It is unlikely that you will be perfectly consistent in making comparative judgments, particularly when dealing with intangibles. As a rule of thumb, make the inconsistency ratio 0.10 or less. If you wish to improve the inconsistency ratio, go to the **Assessment** menu and choose the **Matrix** mode. Pull down the **Inconsistency** menu and select **1 most** to see which is the *most* inconsistent judgment (highlighted cell). You can enter a new judgment value – perhaps after looking at the "Best Fit" value that the system computes for reference purposes. You can see this value by clicking the words **Best Fit** in the upper left of the matrix or going to the **Inconsistency** menu and selecting **Best Fit**.

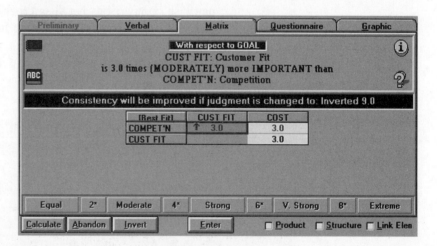

When you have finished entering your judgments, click **Record** to save the values and to return to the main screen.

Synthesizing

After you record your preferences, the program synthesizes the priorities across the hierarchy to calculate the final priorities of the alternatives.

You can choose between two numerical methods of synthesizing the data: the **Distributive** and **Ideal** (default) **Synthesis** Modes.

To synthesize, go to the **Synthesis** menu and select **From Goal**.

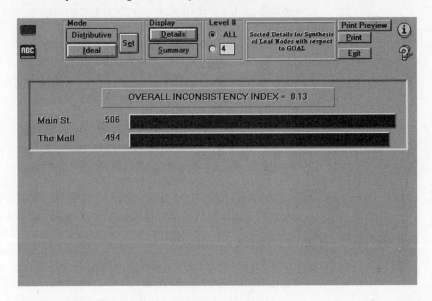

To see the list of the global priorities for all the hierarchy's nodes, click the Details button.

You can select the **Distributive** synthesis button, the **Ideal** synthesis button, or the **Set** button, which will lead you through a series of questions to determine the proper mode. The choice of the appropriate synthesis mode for an application depends on whether you view the decision situation as prioritizing among all the alternatives based on their relative worth (**Distributive**) or picking a single best alternative (**Ideal**). The **ideal** mode preserves the original ranks as alternatives are added. The distributive mode allows ranks to change. Allowing changes in rankings could mean, for example, that alternative A is preferred to alternative B before alternative C is introduced into the mix of alternatives being evaluated, but with the introduction of C, B becomes preferred to A. In the **distributive** mode, criteria weights depend on the degree to which each criterion differentiates between the alternatives being evaluated. This favors (i.e., assigns higher weights) to alternatives that are both better than other alternatives on important criteria and are unusual among the alternatives.

We describe these two modes for synthesizing priorities below. For further information and examples, refer to the Expert Choice online help or tutorial.

Distributive synthesis mode

In the distributive synthesis mode, the program normalizes the weights of the alternatives under each criterion, i.e., it distributes the global weight of a criterion among the alternatives thereby dividing up the full criteria weight into proportions that correspond to the relative priorities of the alternatives. (The normalization is applied at all levels of the hierarchy up to the goal node.)

You should choose the distributive mode if you want your preferences for alternatives to depend on the number and type of other alternatives being evaluated. Use the distributive mode when all the alternatives are relevant, e.g., when the decision task calls for prioritizing alternatives, allocating resources, and planning when the ranking of the alternatives is affected by the other alternatives. In general, if the alternatives are distinct (i.e., not duplicates of each other) and are well separated in their characteristics, you should use the distributive mode.

Ideal synthesis mode

In the ideal synthesis mode, the priorities of the alternatives are divided by the largest value among them and then multiplied by the global weight of the given parent node. Consequently, the most preferred alternative in a group receives the entire group priority of the criterion immediately above it. The other alternatives receive a proportion of the global weight. (Note that if the same alternative is best for all the criteria, that alternative obtains an overall value of one, while the other alternatives obtain proportionately less. The sum for all the alternatives will be more than one.) Unlike the distributive mode, the ideal mode maintains the rank of the best alternative.

The ideal mode is useful when the alternatives are not distinct and you do not want the mere presence of copies or near-copies of alternatives to affect the decision outcome. For example, when comparing three computers, two low-priced computers are very similar to one another and the high-priced computer is better under most other criteria. The two low priced computers are both better alternatives with respect to cost, but they would cut into each others weight if the weight of cost is distributed among the alternatives (as is done in the distributive mode). The ideal mode would give the entire weight for cost to the cheapest computer, thereby making it a stronger competitor to the high-priced computer. The ideal mode divides the numerical ranks of the alternatives for each criterion by the largest value among them, instead of normalizing the entire set. The most-preferred alternative receives the value of one. In this case, the ranks of the alternatives do not depend on each other. Each new alternative added is compared only with the highest ranked alternative for that criterion.

In general, use the ideal mode when your sole concern is for the highest ranked alternative and the others do not matter, or when several alternatives have equal or very similar values along most criteria.

To see distributive or ideal summary weights for alternatives, Click the **Distributive** or the **Ideal** button and then click the **Summary** button.

To see distributive or ideal weights for alternatives and details, click the **Distributive** or the **Ideal** button and then click the **Details** button.

Sensitivity analysis

Use sensitivity analysis to investigate how sensitive the rankings of the alternatives are to changes in the importance of the criteria. Expert Choice offers five modes for graphical sensitivity analysis:

- Performance
- Dynamic
- Gradient
- Two-dimensional
- Difference

Sensitivity analysis from the Goal node will show the sensitivity of the alternatives with respect to the criteria below the goal. You can also perform sensitivity analysis from nodes under the goal—provided the model has more than three levels—to show the sensitivity of the alternatives with respect to lower-level criteria.

To initiate the performance sensitivity analysis, go to the sensitivity-graphs menu and choose **Performance**.

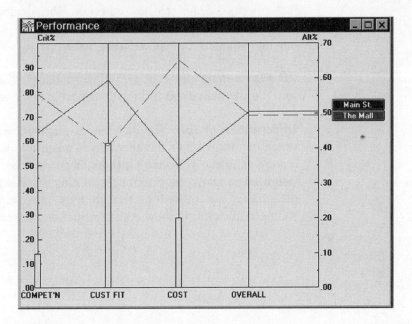

The criteria are represented by vertical bars, and the alternatives are displayed as horizontal line graphs. The intersection of the alternative line graphs with the vertical criterion lines shows the priority of the alternative for the given criterion, as read from the right axis labeled Alt%. The criterion's priority is represented by the height of its bar as read from the left axis labeled Crit%. The overall priority of each alternative is represented on the OVERALL line, as read from the right axis.

To perform what-if analysis, click a rectangular criterion box and drag it up or down to change the priority of that criterion. You can observe the changes this makes in the ranking of the alternatives on the right. In the above example, The Mall has higher overall priority (61 percent) even though it performs poorly on the Cost criterion.

To restore the original priorities, press the **<Home>** key. Returning to the main menu also erases what-if changes and restores the priorities as originally calculated. You can use the Window menu command to change to other sensitivity graphs. (What-if changes will be reflected in the open windows only if you have not pressed the **<Home>** key.)

There are other methods of investigating sensitivity using Expert Choice:

Dynamic sensitivity: The dynamic sensitivity analysis is a horizontal bar graph that you can use to increase or decrease the priority of any criterion and see the change in the priorities of the alternatives. For instance, as you increase the CUST FIT criterion by dragging that bar to the right, the priorities of the remaining criteria decrease in proportion to their original priorities. The program recalculates the priorities of the alternatives based on their new relationship.

Gradient sensitivity: The gradient sensitivity analysis assigns each criterion a separate gradient graph. The vertical line represents the current priority of the selected criterion. The slanted lines represent the alternatives. The current priority of an alternative is where the alternative line intersects the vertical criterion line.

2D Plot sensitivity: The two-dimensional plot sensitivity shows how well the alternatives perform with respect to any two criteria.

Differences graph: The differences graph shows the differences between the priorities of the alternatives taken two at a time for all of the criteria. You can go to the **Options** menu and choose **Weighted** or **Unweighted** to show the differences in either manner. When unweighted, the criteria are treated as though they have equal priorities. When weighted, the criteria show both priorities and differences.

JENNY'S GELATO CASE

Jennifer Edson was putting the finishing touches on the business plan for a new enterprise. Jenny's Gelato, a retail establishment that will serve authentic Italian gelato by the scoop or dish or for carryout. (Gelato is a rich, tasty ice cream sold in Italy.) Wholesale sales to restaurants in the Washington, D.C., Metro area were also included in the plan. The business concept had been in Jennifer's mind since she spent a semester abroad in Florence, Italy, during her undergraduate studies and got "hooked" on gelato.

Jennifer looked over the report and everything seemed in order—it included everything from proforma financial statements to taste test studies that she had conducted. A venture capitalist, in fact, thought the plan was so good that she had obtained a verbal commitment for $50,000 in start-up capital. Restaurant equipment, store fixtures, and gelato-making machines had been comparison priced, and she knew that these fixed costs would eat up the entire $5OK. Everything was "all systems go" for a summer opening save for the selection of a specific retail site. She felt that a downtown location was best because of the preponderance of Yuppies in the area. Negotiations for a specific site had come down to two alternatives, both of which involved leasing space.

She had an option on an off-street site in the fashionable area of Georgetown in Washington, D.C. Twelve-hundred square feet of retailing space was available in a vacant store whose only entrance was via an alley off M Street (a street that was constantly congested with pedestrian and auto traffic). The attractiveness of the Georgetown location was due principally to the heavy entertainment spot and retail shopping traffic. Lots of weekday and evening trade was available, as Georgetown was a haven for tourists arid college and high school students. A long-term lease could be secured for $2500 a month but Jennifer would absorb nearly all the costs of converting the site to a twenty- to twenty-five seat gelateria. The option on the lease had to be exercised in two weeks.

The alternative site was in an attractive, enclosed retailing and office complex on Pennsylvania Avenue only five blocks from the White House. Shops in the minimall included restaurants, men's and women's clothing stores, a jewelry store, a large record and tape store, and a series of international fast-food boutiques. The base for traffic was office workers within a three-block radius, and faculty, staff and students of a large urban university whose buildings were all within three to four blocks of the complex. One thousand square feet was available for $2000 per month on a one-year lease, which would be renegotiated by the developer each year. The developer would also receive 2 percent of the businesses' gross revenues. Since the location was new, the developer would custom build wall partitions and arrange other space configurations to suit the tenant.

Jennifer developed a spreadsheet to summarize market research she had conducted on the two alternative sites (see Exhibit 1). She also prepared a spreadsheet for the proforma income statement for the business (see Exhibit 2). Two of the assumptions underlying this latter spreadsheet were these:

■ The price per serving of gelato was $2.00
■ The cost of goods sold would be approximately 40 percent of the retail price

Exhibit 2 also shows the results of a comparative breakeven analysis on the two alternate sites. As expected, the higher fixed costs associated with the Georgetown site resulted in a higher breakeven point. Jennifer was unsure as to how much importance to attach to this analysis because she felt that breakeven examined only downside risks. The real number she was most unsure about was forecasted sales revenues for the first year of operations.

Based on her review of trade and academic sources, Jennifer developed the following mental model of factors that would influence sales of gelato at a retail site:

Criterion	Pennsylvania Avenue (Foggy Bottom)		'M' Street (Georgetown)	
Traffic *(hourly pedestrian count)*	*afternoon (noon-5 pm)*	*evening (5-11 pm)*	*afternoon (noon-5 pm)*	*evening (5-11 pm)*
Monday	302	142	156	524
Tuesday	286	202	215	426
Wednesday	194	114	187	394
Thursday	371	176	272	404
Friday	226	224	413	735
Saturday	75	110	521	816
Sunday	62	90	795	692
Total	1516	1058	2559	3991
Average	216.6	151.1	365.6	570.1
Average (afternoon & evening)	183.9		467.9	

EXHIBIT 1
Pedestrian Traffic Count Study*

*Each site storefront traffic counts taken during a single week in April. Traffic count is defined as pedestrians passing by.

	Pennsylvania Avenue (Foggy Bottom)	'M' Street (Georgetown)
Revenues	$1,500,000	$1,500,000
Cost of Goods Sold	600,000	600,000
Gross Profit	900,000	900,000
Rent	24,000	30,000
Landlord Percentage	30,000	
Depreciation	5,000	5,000
Utilities	8,500	9,000
General Overhead	50,000	50,000
Advertising	100,000	100,000
Site Preparation	0	20,000
Licenses & Permits	1,500	1,500
Total Operating Expenses	$219,000	$229,000
Net Profit		
Operating Profit	$681,000	$671,000
Interest Expense	9,000	9,000
Taxable Profit	672,000	662,000
Income Tax	248,640	244,940
After Tax Profit	$423,640	$417,060
Breakeven Analysis		
Fixed Costs		
Rent	$24,000	$30,000
Depreciation	5,000	5,000
Utilities	8,500	9,000
General Overhead	50,000	50,000
Interest	9,000	9,000
Advertising	100,000	100,000
Site Preparation Costs	0	20,000
Total Fixed Costs	$196,500	$223,000
Variable Costs per Unit (scoop)		
Cost of Goods Sold	$0.80	$0.80
Landlord Percentage	0.04	0.04
Total Variable Costs	$0.84	$0.80
Contribution (per scoop)	$1.16	$1.20
Breakeven ($)	$338,793	$371,667
Breakeven (scoops)	169,397	185,833

EXHIBIT 2
Proforma Income Statement and Breakeven Analysis

- Sales of gelato would likely exhibit pronounced seasonal trends similar to those of regular ice cream, frozen yogurt, and other frozen desserts.
- Sales of gelato (like those of ice cream and other frozen desserts) represent an unplanned, impulse type of buyer behavior.
- Gelato and other frozen desserts were often bought after consumers had participated in certain activities (after a movie, during a shopping trip, after participating in or watching a sporting event, after dinner at a restaurant).

Criterion	Pennsylvania Avenue (Foggy Bottom)	'M' Street (Georgetown).
Building	Brand new office/retail	Old row house converted to retail space complex
Locale	Enclosed minimall adjacent to PA Ave	Freestanding site in alleyway off M Street
Ambiance	Business offices, university	Upscale shops, restaurants area
Traffic Base	State Dept., World Bank, government employees, faculty, staff of university	Tourists, college students, retail shoppers, patrons of entertainment spots
Avg. hourly traffic	184	468
Size	1000 sq. ft.	1200 sq. ft.
Cost	$2000 per month, developer takes 2 percent of annual gross revenue	$2500 per month
Breakeven volume required		10 percent higher
Site development	Substantial assistance from developer/owner	Lessee assumes all costs of improvement
Competition	Two ice-cream stores within a six-block radius of site	Five ice-cream stores within a six-block radius of site

EXHIBIT 3
Comparison of Site Alternatives

- Gelato demand would be higher among trendy, upscale yuppies who had cosmopolitan interests that often included experimenting with exotic, or so-called gourmet food.
- Like many convenience retail concepts, sales for a gelateria would be heavily influenced by the volume of pedestrian traffic and proximity to complementary retail businesses, restaurants, and places of entertainment.
- Competition from other ice-cream stores was an important factor—some malls, shopping areas and other locations had reached the point of saturation or "overstoring." The uniqueness of the gelato product, however, was expected to offset the heavy competition shown in traditional ice cream sales.

These factors suggest that even though Jennifer Edson had done her homework with lots of conceptualization, financial analyses, and observational studies she still had a complex problem on her hands in making the site-selection decision. Before she actually developed the Expert Choice model she decided to summarize the information that she had collected about the characteristics of the two sites (see Exhibit 2). With this Jennifer Edson began the process of developing her Expert Choice model.

EXERCISES

1. Construct an EC model similar to the one shown in Exhibit 4 to select the best retail site for the gelateria. (Make sure your criteria reflect both the quantitative and qualitative aspects of this problem.)

2. Use EC's sensitivity analysis utility to perform a what-if analysis of the alternative. Document your assumptions.

3. Provide a one-page report (excluding tables and figures) summarizing your recommendations to Ms. Edson.

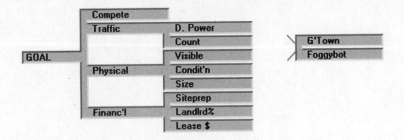

Competition	Competition at site.
Condition	Condition of Store
Count	Count of Traffic During Business Hours
Drawing Power	Drawing Power of Location for this Type of Retail Store
Financial	Financial Considerations
Foggy Bottom	Foggy Bottom Area of Washington, D.C.
Georgetown	Georgetown Area of Washington, D.C.
Landlord $	Percent of Sales Commission to landlord
Lease $	Cost to lease
Physical	Physical Characteristics of Site
Siteprep	Outlay Required to Prepare Site
Size	Size of Store
Traffic	Traffic at Site
Visible	Visibility

EXHIBIT 4
EC Model for Retail-Site Selection: Select the Best Retail Site

TUTORIAL FOR COMPETITIVE ADVERTISING (COMPETE)

The Compete spreadsheet helps you to determine the appropriate level of advertising spending in a two-firm market where both market share and total market size are driven by advertising expenditures.

On the **Model** menu, select **Competitive Advertising** (compete.xls) to see the **Introduction** screen:

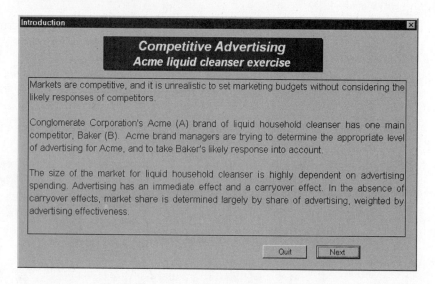

The following screen summarizes the assumptions about the marketplace. Both our firm's brand (Acme) and the competitor's (Baker) are currently spending about $1mm per quarter on advertising, our price is $1.50 per unit, our cost is about $0.75 per unit, and so forth. The "base" figure for the competitor's advertising is the current level if it were fixed as a constant. The "carryover effect" is a number between 0 and 1. Zero means that market share is affected by current advertising only; 0.5 means that market share results equally from the carryover from past advertising share and from current spending on advertising.

	A	B	C	D	E	F	G	H	
1		*Marketing Decisions With Competition (COMPETE)*							
2									
3		$1.00	Initial Brand Advertising ($MM)						
4		$1.00	Initial Competitive Advertising (**Base**: $MM)						
5		15.00	Minimum Market Size (MM units)						
6		30.00	Maximum market Size (MM Units)						
7		$1.50	Unit Price						
8		$0.75	Unit Cost						
9		60.0%	Initial (Base) Brand Market Share						
10			(Fraction 0-1)						
11		5.0%	Market Growth/Decline Rate/period						
12			(Fraction--Could Be Negative)						
13		8	Number of Time Periods (at Least 2)						
14		0.50	Carryover Effect (0=Current Only)					Next Page	
15		1.0	Advertising Effectiveness Relative to Competition						
16			(1=Equal; 2 = Twice as Good, etc)						

Click **Next** to analyze the case.

	A	B	C	D		M	N	O	P
39	Competitive Response?		○ Yes: Set Level						
	Activate Change		○ Yes: Customize						
40			● No, Keep "Base"						
41									
42	**Prev. Page**		**Optimize**						
43							Cumulative		
44	Period	A Adv	B Adv	Tot Adv		A Profit	B Profit	Total Profit	
45	*Base*	*$1.00*	*$1.00*	*$2.00*		*$8.28*	*$6.59*	*$14.88*	
46	1	$1.00	$1.00	$2.00		$16.29	$13.74	$30.03	
47	2	$1.00	$1.00	$2.00		$24.23	$21.25	$45.48	
48	3	$1.00	$1.00	$2.00		$32.22	$29.02	$61.24	
49	4	$1.00	$1.00	$2.00		$40.32	$37.01	$77.33	
50	5	$1.00	$1.00	$2.00		$48.57	$45.19	$93.76	
51	6	$1.00	$1.00	$2.00		$56.98	$53.57	$110.55	
52	7	$1.00	$1.00	$2.00		$65.57	$62.15	$127.71	
53	8	$1.00	$1.00	$2.00		$74.35	$70.92	$145.27	

wshData

In the highlighted area, you should select one of the three options for competitive response.

- *Yes, Set Level*: This assumes that B advertises at a fixed multiple (greater than 0) of A's spending.
- *Yes, Customize*: Here you can use any relationship to link B's advertising spending, in cells C46 and below, to any of the values in the spreadsheet. (For example, you could set up B's advertising to be the square root of A's advertising times a multiplier. You may have to "Unprotect the Sheet" first—see below for instructions.)
- *No, Keep Base*: This sets B's advertising at the base level from the previous page.

After you describe how your competitor will respond, click **Activate Change**.

Click **Optimize** to call Solver, which will allow you to select an objective and specify approximate decision values. For example you might want to maximize A's cumulative profit in period 3 (cell M48) as a result of A's advertising spending in periods 1 through 3.

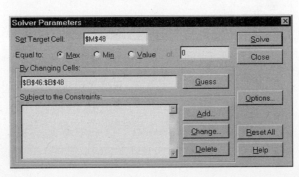

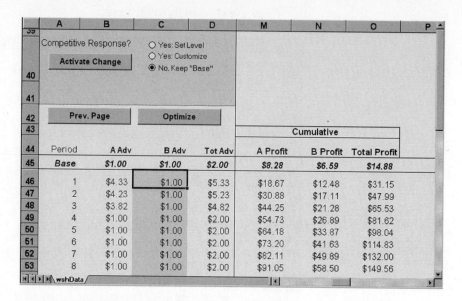

Under **Model**, select **Main Menu** and then choose **Make Charts** to graph the results.

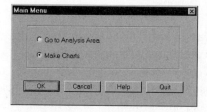

Select the profit chart or the advertising chart. Go back to **Model**, **Main Menu**, and select **Go to Analysis Area** to modify some analyses.

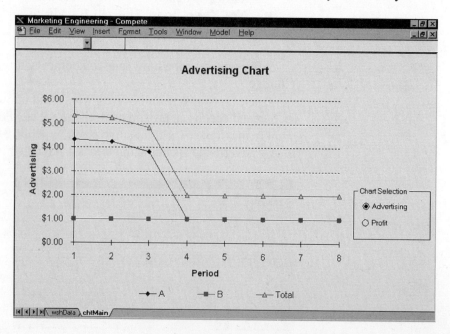

NOTE: *If you want to create your own objective function (e.g., market share target at end of period x), you have to first unprotect the worksheet. To do so, under the **Tools** menu choose **Protection** and then **Unprotect Sheet...***

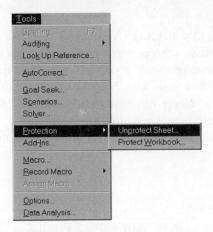

Finally note that columns A through D in the main worksheet are frozen and that you can see other data on sales and market share in columns through 0 by scrolling.

Some hints on using the Compete spreadsheet

1. You must unprotect the spreadsheet—under the **Tools** menu, choose **Protection** *and then* **Unprotect Sheet**—before running Solver.

2. To do analyses like those in the exercise, you will generally be looking at target cells M53, N53, and O53 (Acme profits, Baker profits, and joint profits, respectively) and selecting Changing Cells B46 to B53 (for Acme) and C46 to C53 for Baker.

3. When considering joint profits, work with cells B46:C53; do not try to change cells in column D!

4. For Competitive Response choose **Yes, Set Level** if Baker is matching Acme (or is setting a budget that is a multiple of Acme's spending level). Use the other Competitive Response options to indicate passive response (**No, Keep Base**) or other types of competitive reactions (**Yes, Customize**).

Reference

Lilien, Gary L.; Kotler, Philip; and Moorthy, Sridhar K. 1992, *Marketing Models*. Prentice Hall, Englewood Cliffs, NJ.

ACME LIQUID CLEANSER EXERCISE

Background

Conglomerate Inc.'s Acme (A) liquid household cleanser operates in a highly competitive market segment with its main competitor, Baker (B). Acme brand managers are trying to determine the appropriate level of advertising while considering Baker's likely response.

While this market has many complications, for the purpose of this analysis, Conglomerate is willing to assume that Acme and Baker share the market and that advertising is the main determinant of both total market size and market share.

The Compete model

The company's analytic staff has put together a simple spreadsheet that incorporates its basic assumptions about the market and has called it Compete. In this spreadsheet, a period is a quarter (four periods make up a year) and you want to do a two-year analysis (eight periods or quarters).

The Compete spreadsheet incorporates several of the important effects in the competitive household cleaner market:

- The market is responsive to total advertising spending, and sales vary between a low level (with no advertising) and an upper limit (with unlimited advertising—the most the market can absorb). The market reacts to advertising almost immediately.
- Acme's market share is partly related to its share of advertising spending and partly related to the carryover effect of past spending. (A parameter in the analysis allows you to study the impact of different levels of carryover.) Because of differences in advertising copy and product quality, Acme's spending on advertising has a different level of effectiveness than Baker's.
- To the best of Conglomerate's knowledge, Acme's production costs and Baker's are roughly the same, as are their prices to the trade.

EXERCISES

This market has been in flux recently, and it appears that Baker has been matching Acme's advertising spending pattern closely, but you are not sure that that pattern will continue. By using the spreadsheet, you can analyze different reaction patterns. Acme management has asked you to come up with an advertising budget and projections of market share and profitability for the next eight quarters. Use the spreadsheet and Excel's Solver function to support those proposals.

Scenario 1: Assume that Baker matches Acme's spending over the next eight quarters. What level of advertising spending is best for Acme? ("Best" means maximizes cumulative profit here.)

Scenario 2: Suppose that Baker does not respond (stays with $1mm per period). What is Acme's best level of advertising spending?

Scenario 3: Suppose that Baker does the same analysis that you do in question 2 and based on the solution, optimizes its advertising spending. How much will Baker spend now? And how should Acme respond to this different level of spending?

Repeat this process of Acme → Baker → Acme → Baker until the advertising policies stabilize. Compare the levels of advertising and profit with those in scenarios 1 and 2.

Scenario 4: Suppose Baker becomes more aggressive and spends 50 percent more than Acme does each period (Level of Competitive Response = 1.5). What is Acme's best advertising policy in this case?

Scenario 5: Acme is considering acquiring Baker. If it were to do so [and the Federal Trade Commission (FTC) would permit it to], what should it spend to maximize joint profits? How does that spending level and profitability compare to the other cases.

Scenario 6: Acme has recently replaced its ad agency, and it expects to get ads that perform about 20 percent better from the new agency. Revisiting question 1, what should its level of ad spending be and what is the projected profit in this case?

After running these scenarios (and assuming Acme does not acquire Baker) what ad spending policy do you recommend? (Run any other analyses you feel appropriate here. The policy you recommend can be adjusted annually.)

TUTORIAL FOR CONJOINT ANALYSIS

Conjoint Analysis is widely employed for designing new products. It is a procedure for measuring, analyzing, and predicting customers' responses to new products and to new features of existing products. It enables companies to decompose customers' preferences for products and services (provided as descriptions or visual images) into "part-worth" utilities associated with each option of each attribute or feature of the product. They can then recombine the part-worths to predict customers' preferences for any possible combination of attribute options. They can use this procedure to determine the optimal product concept or to identify market segments that value a particular product concept highly.

On the **Model** menu, select **Conjoint Analysis**. You will see the following window:

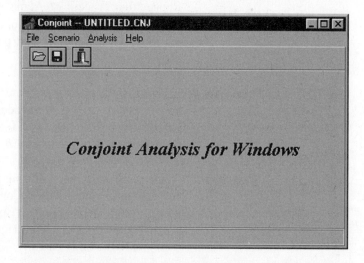

Using the **File** menu you can **Open** an existing conjoint analysis file (if you have one). For the Forte Hotel design exercise, open file hotel.cnj. Otherwise, proceed to the **Scenario** menu. You can also **Save** information from a session to a file and retrieve it later.

The tutorial consists of three sections: (1) Designing a conjoint study, (2) Assessing customer preferences, and (3) Conducting market simulations.

Designing a conjoint study

The first step in designing a conjoint study is to generate a scenario by specifying the product attributes and their possible options. To do this you perform three substeps.

1. Identify the major attributes of the product category of interest. For example, "Leisure activities available to patrons" could be a major attribute in designing a new hotel.

    ■ Identify attributes by asking experts, surveying consumers or conducting focus groups. Attributes can be structural characteristics, product features or options, appearance of product, or even marketing-mix variables, such as price.

    ■ Omit from the analysis attributes on which all products and new product concepts are similar. For example, if all hotels offer express check-out and that service is considered essential in all new hotels, you can omit it from the study. It is also important to use attributes that customers in the target segment care about.

    On the **Scenario** menu, select **Edit Attributes and Levels**:

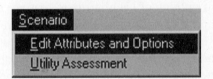

    You will see the following screen:

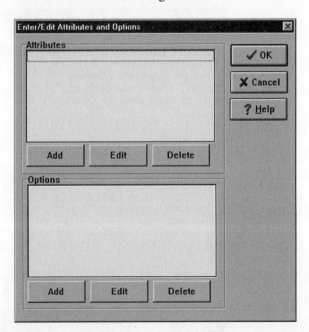

Click the **Add** button under **Attributes** to specify the product or service attributes of interest in the study. You can add up to six attributes. You can edit a previously entered attribute by clicking **Edit**. You can also **Delete** any attribute entered.

NOTE: *The program uses only the first 10 characters of the names you provide.*

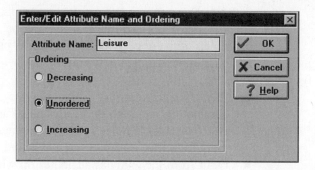

You can use the **Ordering** option to specify whether preferences will be decreasing, unordered, or increasing with respect to levels of this attribute. This educational version permits only the unordered option.

2. Once you have entered your list of attributes, you must enter at least two options of each attribute that are available, as shown in the example below for the attribute Leisure. Use the **Add** button to list levels. You should choose the major options already available in the market, as well as new options being considered for the proposed new product. Use the arrow keys or the mouse to select the attributes for which you want to **Add** the appropriate levels.

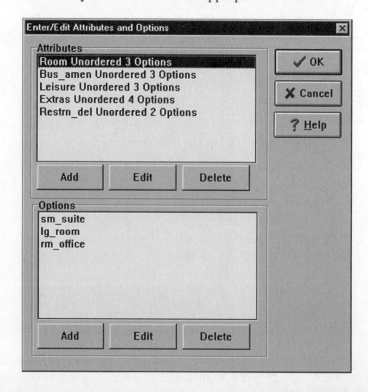

3. To generate a set of products for customer evaluation, describe each product as a combination of attribute options. If you choose, this program will automatically select a subset of products from the total set of all possible combinations of attribute options. After you have entered all the attributes and attribute options, click **OK**. You will see the following screen:

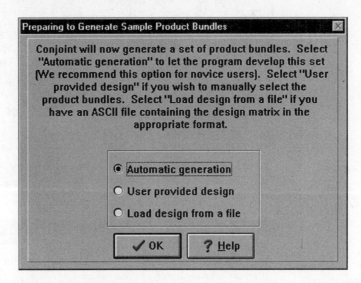

Automatic generation produces a set of orthogonal product profiles. Unless you are experienced in conjoint analysis, select **Automatic Generation** (the default option).

Knowledgeable designers can select their own subsets of products using criteria other than orthogonality. You can specify a set of product profiles for analysis by choosing **User-Provided Design**. The program will then display a list of packages that it selected automatically. You can use this list as a starting point for designing your own set of packages.

NOTE: *Clicking **OK** here brings you back to the initial screen.*

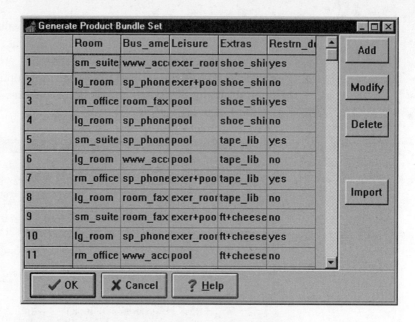

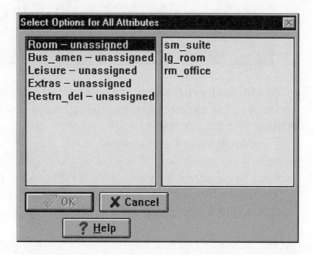

You can also choose **Load Design from File** to load your own design matrix from an external ASCII text file. An example file for a five-attribute design matrix is shown below:

```
0 0 0 0 0
1 1 2 0 1
2 2 1 0 0
1 1 1 0 1
0 1 1 1 0
1 0 1 1 1
2 1 2 1 0
1 2 0 1 1
0 2 2 2 1
1 1 0 2 0
2 0 1 2 1
1 1 1 2 0
0 1 1 3 1
```

```
1 2 1 3 0
2 1 0 3 1
1 0 2 3 0
```

In specifying a design matrix, follow the convention for labeling attribute options shown in the example above: Attribute 1 (the first column) has three options labeled 0, 1, and 2; Attribute 5 has two options labeled 0 and 1.

For this tutorial, we have already specified a design matrix, completing section 1. For the rest of this tutorial, we will use this predefined example. If you have not already done so, go to the **File** menu and click **Open** to load the hotel.cnj file.

Assessing preferences of customers

In this section, we demonstrate how to obtain respondent evaluations for the selected products. For purposes of illustration, you will be the respondent.

Begin the utility assessment procedure by opening the **Scenario** menu and choosing **Utility Assessment**.

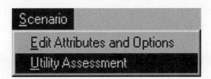

You will see a dialog box requesting an ID under which your preferences will be stored for further analysis. Enter your name or a unique ID and click **OK**.

You will see the following screen:

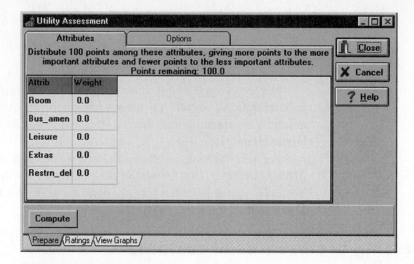

Under **Utility Assessment**, you can select either **Prepare** or **Ratings** procedures or do both in sequence.

1. ***Prepare*** (*also known as self-explicated ratings*): To complete the "Prepare" task, you must provide information regarding (1) relative preferences for the attributes, and (2) relative preferences for the available options of each attribute. You have 100 points to distribute across the attributes.

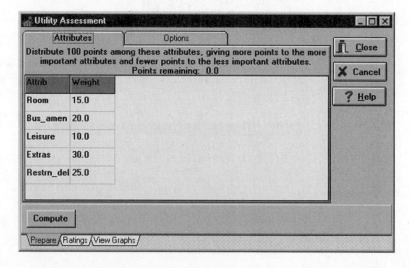

After you assess the importance, or weights, of each attribute, click the **Options** tab and rank the options of the Leisure attribute. Click the **Next Attrib** button to go to the next attribute, which in this case, is "Extras." After you enter your rankings for all the attributes, click **Compute**.

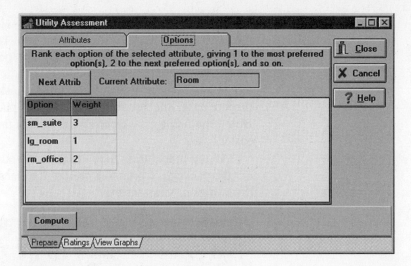

2. ***Ratings option***: Choose the ratings task by clicking the **Ratings** tab at the bottom of the screen. You will see the dialog box below:

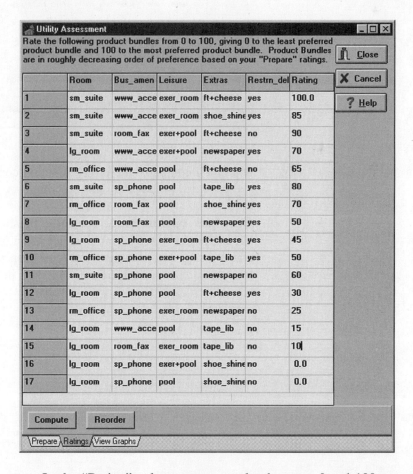

In the "Rating" column, enter a value between 0 and 100 to reflect your preference for each of the hotel packages presented, one per row. If you complete the prepare task before selecting the ratings task, the program will already have sequenced the packages according to your prepared ratings. The most-preferred package appears at the top with a value of 100, and the least-preferred package appears at the bottom with a value of 0. Interspersed between these two packages are a carefully selected set of alternative packages for you to evaluate. If you initiated the ratings task without completing the prepare task, the program will list the packages in random order. Doing the prepare task before the ratings task makes the ratings task easier.

At any time during the ratings task, you can click **Reorder** to order the packages from most preferred to least preferred, which makes the ratings process easier:

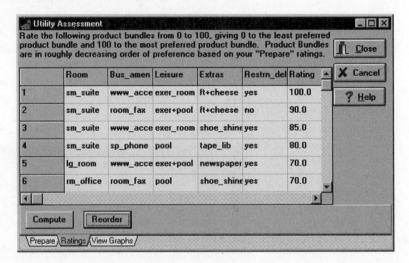

Once you have rated all the packages, click **Compute**. The program then computes the utility function corresponding to the values you provided in the "Ratings" column.

3. **Graphics option**: Once you have finished the ratings task, click **View Graphs** to see a graphical depiction of the utility function generated using your ratings. For consistency the utility function is scaled to lie between 0 and 100 as it does in the prepare task.

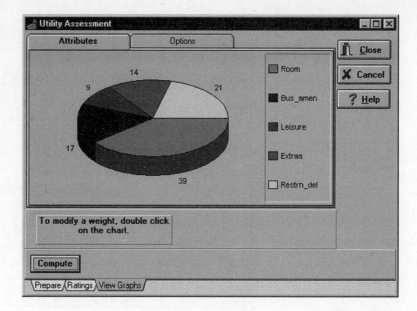

By clicking the **Options** tab, you can see a bar graph of the part-worth utilities corresponding to each option of each attribute, as shown below.

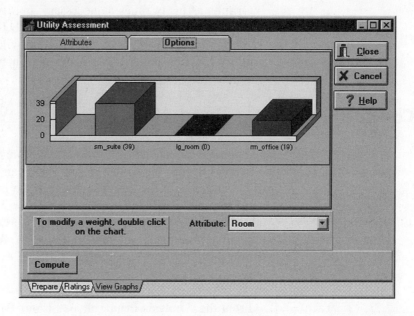

After viewing the graphs, you may think that the relative weights for attributes and attribute options shown in the graphs do not convey your true preferences. In this case, you can alter the weights assigned to any attribute or attribute option. Double-click on either the pie chart (to change part worths of attributes) or the bar graph (to change part worths of attribute options).

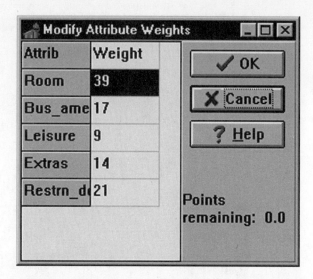

> **NOTE**: *For consistency, attribute weights must sum to 100, and weights for attribute options must range from 0 to a maximum value corresponding to the weight given to that attribute.*

You can go back and forth between **Prepare**, **Ratings**, and **Graphs** as many times as necessary, until you are sure that the utility function shown in the graphs reflects your true preferences. When you finish this task, the program will save a copy of the final utility function under a file name that includes the ID you used to sign on. Click **Close**.

Conducting market simulations

Once you have obtained utility functions from a sample of respondents, the fun part begins. Using the program you can design new products that will be attractive to the target segment in the presence of existing products in the marketplace. The success of new products depends on how well their attribute options match customer preferences compared to the competitive offerings in the market. Go to the **Analysis** menu. You must perform the following tasks before you can evaluate new product concepts:

1. From the **Analysis** menu, choose **Load Part Worth File(s).** Select any subset of respondents for analysis using any suitable criteria. For example, you can select only male respondents for further analysis. You can then repeat the analyses for other subsegments. The program stores utility functions under the ID name of each respondent who provided the data, adding the extension .PRT to the ID name.

> **NOTE**: *Once you have saved part-worth data in a file, you don't have to reload these files each time you run the program. For the Forte Hotel exercise, the hotel.cnj file includes the part-worth files of all 40 respondents. When you do the exercise, you can go directly to*

Create/Edit Existing Product Profiles or to other commands on the Analysis menu.

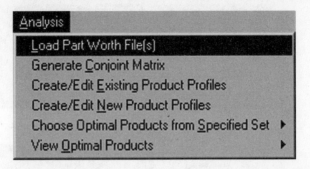

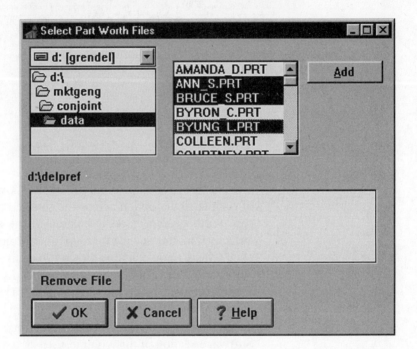

Select all the files you want to include and click **Add**. (To select multiple files at the same time, press the Ctrl key while clicking the file name). For our analysis, we will select all 40 respondents. After selecting the files, click **OK**.

2. Next load these files into the program by selecting **Generate Conjoint Matrix**, as shown below. Use the scroll bar to view sections of the matrix that are hidden from view.

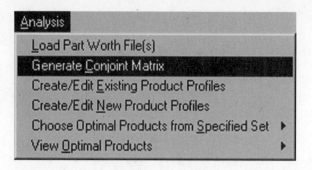

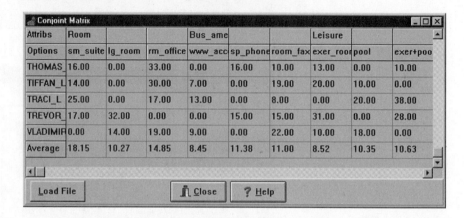

The last row of the conjoint matrix shows the average part worth of each attribute option across the selected respondents. The average part worth gives a good indication of the attribute options that are attractive to the selected group of customers. After viewing this, click **Close**. (You can also directly load an ASCII file containing the part-worth data of a number of respondents by clicking on the **Load File** button and specifying the file name. The file to be loaded should have the format described under "Load an ASCII file containing the data in the appropriate format" described in the **Introduction to Software** section of this volume.)

3. To specify a set of existing products against which proposed new concepts will compete, go to the **Analysis** menu and select the **Create/Edit Existing Product Profiles**.

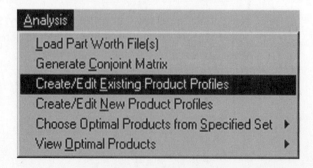

You will see the following screen:

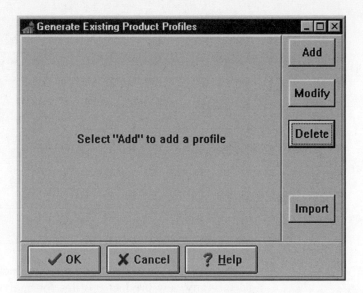

When you click **Add** or **Modify**, you will see the following screen:

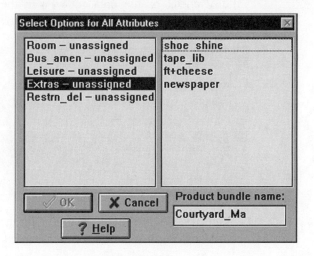

Specify each product by selecting the appropriate attribute options corresponding to that product. It is advisable to include only products that are likely to compete directly with the proposed new product concepts.

If more than one existing product has the same set of attribute options, you should define just one of them. Once you have defined a product, the screen will look as shown. You can also provide a unique name associated with this product. Here, we called this package the "Courtyard by Marriott."

After you define all existing products of interest for this analysis, click **OK**. You will see a screen similar to the following:

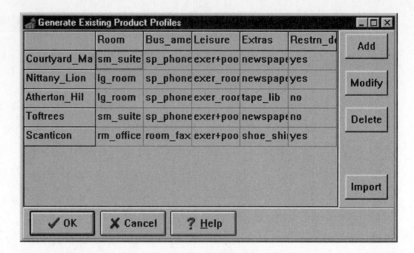

4. Next specify a set of candidate new product-concepts. (If you do not specify any new-product profiles for analysis, you can compute the estimated market shares of the existing products. This serves as a validity check of the data set.) From the **Analysis** menu, choose **Create/Edit New Product Profiles** as shown below.

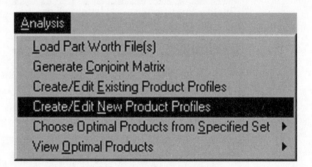

    Specify the attribute options for the new product using the procedure we described earlier for creating existing product profiles.

5. By now, you have specified most of the information that Conjoint Analysis needs to simulate the market performance of the selected products. From the **Analysis** menu, click **Choose Optimal Products from Specified Set**. You will be offered three choice rules for assessing the market performance of the new products:

    Maximum utility rule: Each respondent is assumed to select the product that provides the highest utility among the competing products and a specific new product concept being evaluated. Conjoint Analysis evaluates each new product concept in turn in competition with the existing products. The maximum utility rule is the preferred analysis option if customers buy products in the product category infrequently.

    Share of utility rule: Each respondent's share of purchases of a particular product is considered to be a function of the utility for that product as compared to the total utility for all products in the competitive set. This analysis option is most suitable for products customers buy frequently.

Logit choice rule: The share for each product for each respondent is considered to be a function of the "weighted" utility for that product as compared to the total weighed utility for all products in the competitive set. The weighting is done using an exponential function. This analysis option is an alternative to the share-of-utility model for frequently purchased products.

The market-share predictions made by both the share-of-utility and logit choice rules are sensitive to the scale range on which utility is measured. The market share prediction of the share-of-utility rule will change if you add a constant value to the computed utility of each product, but it is not altered if you multiply all utility values by a constant. On the other hand, market-share predictions of the logit choice rule are not altered if you add a constant to the utilities, but they are altered if you multiply all utilities by a constant.

In computing market shares, we follow Green and Krieger (1985) who first normalized the utility scale for each respondent such that the least preferred option of each attribute has a utility equal to 0, and the utility scale has a range from 0 to K, where K is the number of attributes.

It is best not to interpret the market-share prediction for a new product in an absolute sense. Instead, view the share in a relative sense—those new products that have higher predicted market shares are likely to perform better in the market than those that have lower predicted shares.

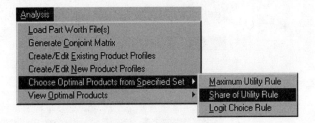

6. After you choose an analysis option, you will see a pie graph showing the market share for the first new-product concept. The following screen shows that the market share for the new-product concept called "Profesnl_1" is 16.44 percent when it is introduced into the market with four existing competitors. Click **Next** to see the graph for the next concept.

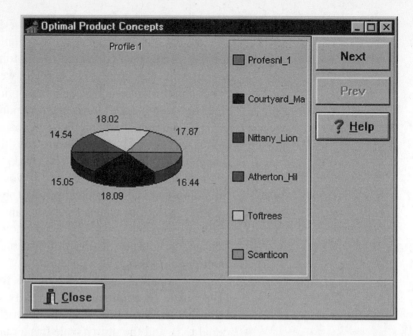

7. You can also do a complete search of all possible product profiles by going to the **Analysis** menu and choosing **View Optimal Products**. If you choose this command the program will select the top four performing product profiles according to the choice rule that you specify.

NOTE: *Products that you have defined in the existing product profiles are excluded from this evaluation.*

Limitations of the educational version of the software:

Maximum number of attributes:	6
Maximum number of levels per attribute:	4
Maximum number of existing product profiles:	8
Maximum number of new product concepts that can be evaluated:	5,000

References

Green, Paul E. and Wind, Yoram 1975, "New way to measure consumers' judgments," *Harvard Business Review*, Vol. 53, No. 4 (July-August), pp. 107-117.

Wind, Jerry; Green, Paul E.; Shifflet, Douglas; and Scarbrough, Marsha 1989, "The Courtyard by Marriott: Designing a hotel facility with consumer-based marketing models," *Interfaces*, Vol. 19, No. 1 (January-February), pp. 25-47.

FORTE HOTEL DESIGN EXERCISE[*]

Forte Executive Innes

Forte Hotels, a large European hotel chain, is developing a new hotel chain in the United States. The chain, named Forte Executive Innes, will combine the ambiance of a European hotel with American functionality and convenience. Forte decided to invest in this hotel chain partly to take advantage of the increasing numbers of business people traveling from Europe to the United States.

Company background

Forte Hotels is the United Kingdom's largest hotel chain. Its hotel brands include Le Meridien, Forte Crest, Forte Posthouse, Forte Agip, and Forte Travelodge. In addition Forte Hotels includes an international group of 80 upscale hotels such as the Watergate Hotel, Washington, D.C., Hyde Park Hotel, London, and King Edward Hotel, Toronto. Recently the company's chairman, Sir Rocco Forte, announced that he plans to sell the Travelodge chain in the United States. In its place Forte Hotels will develop a new chain targeted toward European and American business travelers, Forte Executive Inne.

Forte's strategy in developing the new chain is twofold. European business travelers in the United States will recognize the Forte name and associate it with comfort and service. Forte executives also expect that American business travelers will associate the new chain with "pampering" that is often lacking in the mid-priced hotel chains, while at the same time perceiving the hotel to have all the functionality of American hotel chains. Although the hotels will have a European ambiance, the facilities and services will be comparable to those available in such hotel chains as Hilton, Sheraton, and Courtyard by Marriott.

Preliminary evaluation

A recent survey indicated that the top three reasons business travelers choose a hotel are price, location, and brand name. Forte Executive Innes would be mid-priced, around $100 per night. The company is in the process of securing several prime locations near suburban commercial centers throughout the United States. In addition, the company will leverage the Forte brand name in naming the new chain. Forte now faces the challenge of fine-tuning the specific characteristics of the hotel to insure that it will appeal to both American and European business travelers.

---

[*] This case describes a hypothetical situation. It was developed by Bruce Semisch under the guidance of Professor Arvind Rangaswamy.

A search of business databases provided some preliminary insights on the preferences of business travelers. Among men (60 percent of business travelers in the United States), price, location, and convenience are among the top reasons why a business traveler might try a new hotel. Women travelers place more emphasis on safety and cleanliness than do men. Although these considerations, combined with the overall image of the brand name, are important in generating trial, it is the hotel's unique characteristics (attributes) that encourage repeat visits. Other recent surveys have suggested a range of potential amenities that interest at least 30 percent of business travelers. These include in-room computer facilities; on-site conference facilities; rooms with well-lit work areas with large desks and swivel chairs; and telecommunication facilities, such as speaker phones and data-ports. A survey by a leading credit card company suggests that about half the European business travelers to the United States look for hotels that will look after them and let them relax. The others tended to look for hotels that would let them finish their business assignments quickly and efficiently. Given these preliminary insights, Forte realized that it needed to thoroughly understand the preferences of the hotel's target market to create a successful new hotel chain.

Conjoint Analysis (Matching hotel attributes to customer preferences)

As a first step, the company decided to explore consumer preferences for five key attributes on which Forte Executive Innes could be differentiated: room type, business amenities, leisure facilities, conveniences and extras, and restaurants and dining. Within each attribute, it defined several different options (Exhibit 1). It did not include hotel features that are common to all existing and proposed hotels among the options. Thus for comparison purposes, it considered hotel room types of roughly the same square-foot area, with data-ports and other facilities in the rooms and front-desk faxing services.

Forte's challenge was to decide which combination of the attribute options in Exhibit 1 would most appeal to its target audience. The management team has authorized you to use conjoint analysis to determine this in a "scientific manner." It has recruited 300 business travelers to participate in the conjoint analysis study. For this exercise, you will use the information obtained from 40 of the respondents (Exhibit 2).

EXERCISES

1. **Design**: On the **Scenario** menu of the Conjoint Analysis program, choose **Edit Attributes and Levels** to explore the design of this conjoint study (section 1 of the tutorial). Briefly summarize the advantages and limitations of describing products as bundles of attribute options.

2. ***Utility assessment***. Use the **Utility Assessment** command to explore your own trade-offs for the various attributes and options Forte Inne is considering (section 2 of the tutorial). First complete the prepare task (self-explicated ratings), and then complete the ratings task. Each member of a project group should do a separate utility assessment. When you are finished, note down the final set of weights for each attribute and attribute option.

   Based on your experiences in completing these tasks, summarize the advantages and limitations of conjoint analysis for obtaining preference data from customers.

3. ***Analysis***: Use the **Analysis** menu (section 3 of the tutorial) to assess the viability of the four specific hotel concepts (Profesnl_1, Profesnl_2, Tourist, and Deluxe) that Forte is exploring for the State College area. Base this evaluation on the preferences of a sample of 40 business travelers given in the case and the rough cost estimates summarized in Exhibit 3. The preference data is already included in the hotel.cnj file. The base cost to build each hotel room (without the attributes and options listed in Exhibit 3) is expected to be about $40,000 for a 150 to 200-room hotel, regardless of the mix of room types.

   Identify the optimal product concept from among those Forte is considering. Explain how you arrived at your recommendation.

4. Would you recommend product concepts other than the four Forte is considering for the State College market? Explain how you arrived at your recommendation(s).

5. Summarize the major advantages and limitations of a conjoint study for new-product design. What conditions favor the use of this approach in the hotel industry? (Consider such factors as types of customers and market conditions in responding to this question).

6. After hearing about the study, a manager at Forte claimed that "A conjoint study is a major deterrent to excellence in hotel design. It's a crutch for managers with no vision and conviction. On the surface, it sounds sensible enough: Find out exactly what features customers prefer before you finalize the design. But in practice, this is impossible. Customers cannot tell you what they really prefer without experiencing all the choices available to them. Even if you show them pictures or prototypes, the preferences they express are apt to veer off in the direction of mediocrity. This type of study gives you a Hyundai with a Mercedes grille, Prince tennis rackets endorsed by Ed McMahon, Big Macs with everything, and hotels with no personality! You would not produce a Mazda Miata, a Hermes tie, or the movie "Jurassic Park" with this technique." Do you agree with this statement? Why or why not?

Reference

Green, Paul E. and Krieger, Abba M. 1986, "Choice rules and sensitivity analysis in conjoint simulators," *Working Paper*, The Wharton School, University of Pennsylvania.

Attribute [Abbreviation]	Possible Options [Abbreviation]
Room type (All same size) [Room]	• Small suite [sm_suite] A small suite with a small bedroom area and a separate sitting area with a couch, TV, and coffee table. • Large standard room [lg_room] A room about three feet longer than a standard room with two queen-sized beds. • Room with large desk and swivel chair [rm_office] A room of the same dimensions as the large standard room with only one queen-sized bed and a well-lit work area with a large desk and swivel chair in place of the other bed.
Business Amenities [Bus_amen]	• World Wide Web (WWW) access [www_access] A computer complete with software (e.g. Netscape) with access to Internet and the WWW, at a low hourly connection rate ($2 to $3 per hour). • Speakerphone in room [sp_phone] A speakerphone for group business discussions. • In-room fax machine [room_fax] A fax machine and a private fax number that expires at check-out.
Leisure Facilities [Leisure]	• Exercise room [exerc_room]: A room equipped with Nautilus machines, free weights, stationary bikes, tread mills, stair climbing machines, and a sauna, that is open 24 hours a day. • Pool [pool]: A standard rectangular indoor lap pool with shallow and deep ends. • Small exercise room and small pool [exerc+pool]: An exercise room that lacks some of the features described above (e.g. no sauna, and fewer machines) and a round pool for recreational swimming, not a lap pool.
Conveniences & Extras [Extras]	• Complimentary shoe shine [shoe_shine] Shoes left at the front desk or outside the room at night are shined and returned by a specified time in the morning. • Videotape library [tape_lib] A large selection of tapes will be listed in a catalog in the room and available through room service. • Complimentary fruit and cheese bowl. [ft+cheese] A complimentary fruit and gourmet cheese bowl in the room. • Free newspaper. [newspaper] A complimentary copy of *USA Today* outside the door.
Restaurant Delivery [Restrn_del]	• Yes [yes] From a book of menus from nearby restaurants, patrons can order food through room service, and a hotel employee will pick up and deliver the food. • No [no] No restaurant delivery service available.

EXHIBIT 1
Attributes and Options

	Room	Bus. Amen.	Lei-sure	Ex-tras	Restrn Deli-very	Sm Suite	Lg Room	Rm Of-fice	WWW Ac-cess	Sp phone	Room Fax	Exer-cise Room	Pool	Exer. + Pool	Shoe Shine	Tape Lib.	Ft+ Che-ese	News-paper	Del. Yes	Del. No
1	47	21	16	11	5	47	0	20	21	0	10	12	16	0	10	0	8	11	5	0
2	23	29	7	18	23	23	0	7	0	15	29	7	0	5	9	5	18	0	0	23
3	15	38	9	21	17	15	0	12	0	14	38	4	0	9	5	7	0	21	0	17
4	20	27	10	20	23	20	0	16	10	0	27	8	10	0	0	12	20	16	23	0
5	21	26	21	21	11	21	10	0	12	26	0	0	21	3	21	9	13	0	0	11
6	22	25	12	22	19	8	0	22	13	25	0	0	12	6	22	11	0	15	0	19
7	33	16	13	33	5	16	0	33	0	16	10	13	0	10	0	11	33	18	0	5
8	24	23	14	24	15	13	0	24	10	23	0	14	0	4	8	0	24	12	15	0
9	34	22	6	22	16	0	12	34	9	22	0	0	5	6	15	0	22	8	16	0
10	26	21	16	19	18	26	0	10	21	0	14	9	16	0	0	14	7	19	18	0
11	11	52	10	17	10	0	9	11	52	13	0	0	8	10	17	6	13	0	0	10
12	19	22	18	24	17	0	14	19	9	0	22	10	18	0	24	5	0	7	17	0
13	28	37	19	12	4	12	0	28	5	0	37	0	19	11	8	12	0	6	4	0
14	30	19	20	13	18	14	0	30	7	0	19	20	10	0	4	6	0	13	0	18
15	47	25	9	12	7	0	7	47	0	8	25	9	6	0	4	12	8	0	0	7
16	34	23	12	14	17	34	0	11	23	13	0	4	12	0	5	0	8	14	17	0
17	27	42	7	8	16	27	0	23	0	13	42	0	4	7	8	6	0	3	0	16
18	34	16	16	21	13	34	0	30	0	16	11	0	16	11	21	0	14	8	13	0
19	50	19	11	8	12	50	27	0	0	19	4	11	0	7	0	8	5	4	12	0
20	34	27	14	10	15	34	0	16	6	27	0	8	0	14	4	0	10	8	0	15
21	33	29	3	26	9	28	0	33	11	29	0	0	1	3	6	0	26	4	0	9
22	22	22	12	24	20	0	16	22	5	0	22	12	6	0	24	8	0	12	0	20
23	31	10	10	18	31	8	0	31	8	0	10	10	4	0	0	7	15	18	31	0
24	20	21	9	41	9	20	0	14	0	7	21	9	0	5	41	13	10	0	0	9
25	31	14	25	18	12	14	31	0	14	0	13	7	25	0	13	0	18	8	12	0
26	29	11	31	16	13	10	0	29	7	11	0	0	31	17	2	9	16	0	13	0
27	18	27	27	14	14	0	7	18	0	27	18	12	0	27	4	9	0	14	0	14
28	27	4	56	10	3	0	27	7	4	0	2	56	19	0	4	10	0	6	3	0
29	16	29	29	12	14	0	16	8	16	29	0	0	29	20	0	12	6	9	14	0
30	45	2	32	2	19	45	0	17	0	2	0	0	15	32	2	0	0	1	0	19
31	16	16	33	13	22	6	16	0	0	16	9	7	0	33	5	0	9	13	0	22
32	19	22	32	11	16	0	19	5	10	22	0	32	16	0	9	11	0	3	16	0
33	43	12	25	8	12	13	43	0	11	0	12	10	25	0	0	8	6	4	0	12
34	37	9	39	3	12	10	37	0	0	9	3	0	39	21	3	0	3	0	12	0
35	17	24	32	15	12	17	7	0	7	24	0	5	0	32	2	15	8	0	0	12
36	72	7	10	5	6	72	43	0	7	6	0	7	0	10	0	0	5	5	0	6
37	36	18	24	8	14	36	18	0	18	8	0	0	11	24	0	6	8	8	14	0
38	25	13	38	12	12	25	0	17	13	0	8	0	20	38	0	10	4	12	0	12
39	20	19	32	18	11	11	20	0	9	0	19	14	0	32	4	0	18	12	11	0
40	32	15	31	12	10	17	32	0	0	15	15	31	0	28	12	7	0	5	10	0

EXHIBIT 2
Preference Data

	Incremental fixed costs per room ($) at the time of construction	Average expected incremental contribution per day per room ($)
WWW access	2,500	3.00
Speaker phone in room	200	2.00
In-room fax machine	600	2.50
Exercise room	1500	-2.00
Pool	3000	-4.00
Small exercise room & small pool	3,500	-4.50
Complimentary shoe shine	30	-0.50
Videotape library	300	-0.50
Complimentary fruit & cheese bowl	100	-5.00
Newspaper	-	-1.00
Restaurant delivery	100	-3.00
No restaurant delivery	-	-

EXHIBIT 3
Cost Data

TUTORIAL FOR THE GENERALIZED BASS MODEL (GBASS)

The Excel spreadsheet GBass is a tool for forecasting the adoption of new products. It implements the original Bass model (Bass 1969) as well as an extended version of it, the generalized Bass model (Bass, Krishnan, and Jain 1994). The generalized model extends the original Bass model by including the effects of advertising and price changes.

The software provides two modes for calibrating the model: (1) by analogy and subsequent refinement (i.e., visual tracking), and (2) by fitting the Bass model to past data via nonlinear least squares (Srinivasan and Mason 1986). The forecasting component of GBass is set up for visual tracking: you can watch how changes in model parameters affect forecasts.

On the **Model** menu, select **Bass Model** (gbass.xls) to see the **Introduction** screen.

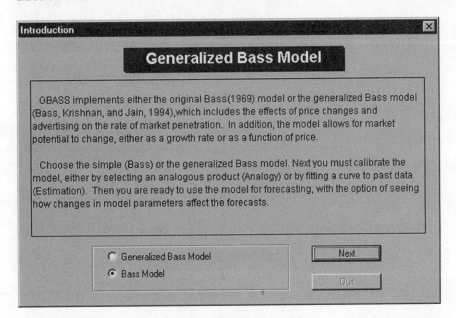

First select either the **Generalized Bass Model** or the **Bass Model** and click **Next**. The generalized Bass model includes two decision variables, pricing and advertising, which are assumed to determine the total number of customers. The Bass model sets up the original model without decision variables and assumes a constant number of customers.

Because the generalized Bass model includes the Bass model, we will describe its use. Both versions have the same setup.

Model calibration by analogy

The model includes a database that contains actual data points, estimated p and q coefficients, and estimates of market potential for various data sets to which the Bass model has been applied. The data come from several product categories. For further information about the database, see

Chapter 7 of the text, which lists the p and q coefficients, the market potential, and the time period of analysis for each case.

You need to identify an analogous product or technology that has market characteristics similar to those of the product you want to analyze. When there are no past data for the product of interest, calibrating the model by analogy can be useful. This can also be useful when you don't have enough data to feel confident about estimating numerical parameters for the model.

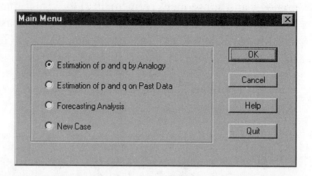

To explore the sales patterns of analogous products, select **Estimation of p and q by Analogy** and click **OK**.

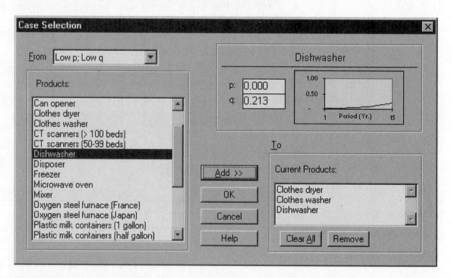

First select a category. All cases have been divided into four categories: (low p, low q), (high p, low q), etc. For example, a high p coefficient indicates a high coefficient of external influence, e.g., advertising was a significant driver for the market penetration of the product. A high q coefficient value indicates a high coefficient of internal influence, e.g., word of mouth was a significant driver for the market penetration of the product. When you click a product in the **Products** list, you will see a preview of its curve and its coefficients.

Now choose a product and click **Add>>** to add a product to the group of potential reference cases in the **Current Products** area. (Add no more than three products, since at most three curves can be graphed at a time.)

After you choose your cases and click **OK**, the program will chart the actual data points and the estimated diffusion curves for them.

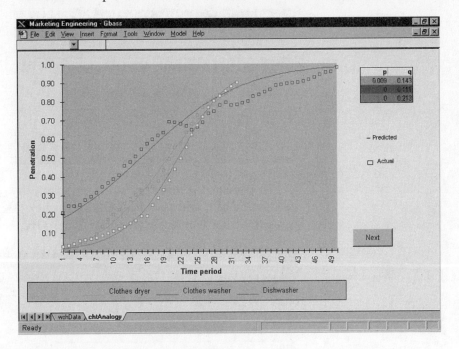

To simplify comparisons we have normalized the available cases to a maximum market penetration equal to 1.

Click **Next** to get to the next box. Indicate the product that you think offers the best analogy and that you want to keep for further reference.

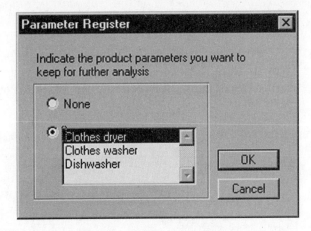

Click **OK** to get to the **Main Menu**.

Model calibration by estimation

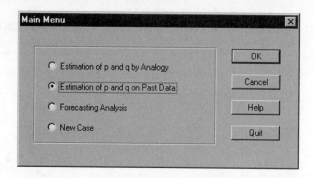

To estimate the model parameters numerically (using Solver), choose **Estimation of q and p on Past Data** and click **OK**. Enter the number of past periods for which you have data. Click **OK**.

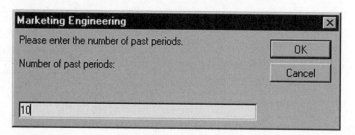

NOTE: *Once you have specified this number you will not be able to change it for subsequent estimations for this product. To make estimates for a different number of periods you must go to the **Main Menu** and select **New Case**.*

Next, enter data for **Cumulative Sales Before Period 1, Market Growth Rate**, **Market Potential at Start** (your estimate of the total market size at the starting period), and **Market Potential Price Elasticity**.

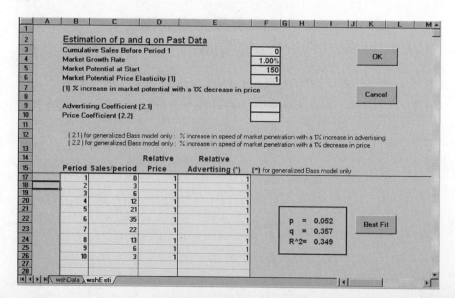

> **NOTE**: *Period 0 serves as an anchor for the display of the curves. Sales in period 0 are always fixed to zero.*

If you chose the **Bass Model,** you don't need to provide values for the advertising or price coefficients. If you chose the **Generalized Bass Model**, you must provide estimates for these coefficients, because historical data rarely have enough variability to permit estimation of these parameters using past data. The advertising and price coefficients can be roughly thought of as "market acceptance speed elasticities," indicating the speed with which the market adopts the new product:

- The advertising coefficient reflects the percent increase in speed of market acceptance with a one percent increase in advertising. (Typical values for the advertising coefficient range between 0.3 and 1.)
- The price coefficient reflects the percent increase in speed of market acceptance with a one percent decrease in price. (Typical values for the price coefficient range between 1 and 2.)

Now enter the data on sales in each period and, optionally, an index for price and advertising in each period.

Click **Best Fit** to start the calibration of the model. The program estimates only the coefficients for p and q. The market potential estimate is fixed at your best guess input.

Click **OK** to go back to the **Main Menu**.

Forecasting analysis

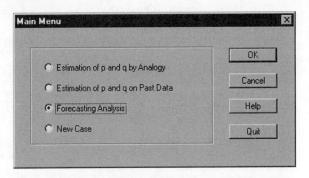

Select **Forecasting analysis** and click **OK**.
You will see the following box:

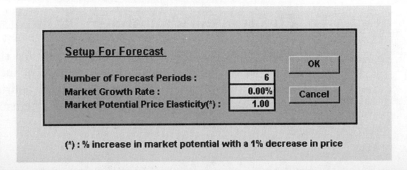

Enter values for the **Number of Forecast Periods**, the **Market Growth Rate**, and the **Market Potential Price Elasticity** (that is, the percent increase in market potential with a one percent decrease in price). Click **OK**.

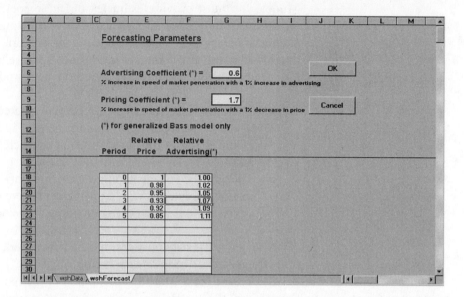

Next specify the expected course of price evolution. For the generalized Bass model you must also specify the evolution of advertising effort. The relative price and relative advertising values are indices with respect to their values in period 0, the last period for which actual data are available.

Click **OK** to get to the next screen.

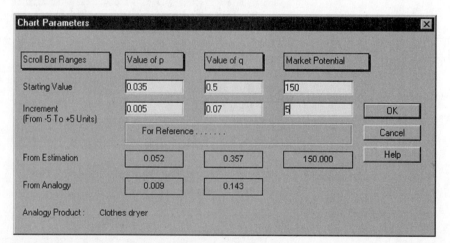

For charting and visual tracking, specify the starting values and increments for the coefficients p and q, and for the market potential. If available, the program displays values from both the best-fit estimates (estimation of p and q on past data) and the reference case (selection of p and q by analogy).

NOTE: *The parameters can be varied by up to five increments on either side of the* **Starting Value**.

Click **OK** to see the estimated sales curves.

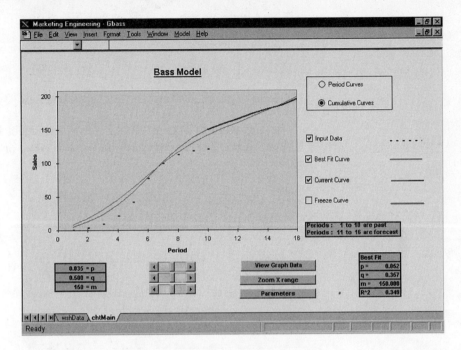

You can view the sales curves either period by period (**Period Curves**) or cumulatively (**Cumulative Curves**). Check the box to the left of **Current Curve** to see the forecasted sales pattern for the values of p, q, and n shown in the left bottom part of the screen. By using the scroll bars under **Period** you can adjust the parameters for the **Current Curve** and observe how changes in the parameter values affect the shape of the graph.

Once you think you have a reasonably good match between your **Input Data** (if available) and the **Current Curve**, you can freeze this curve as a benchmark. All the parameter values for **Freeze Curve** are displayed in the area in the lower right corner. Compare them to the parameter values for the **Best Fit Curve** if you checked that option. You can continue to change the shape of the **Current Curve**, and the **Freeze Curve** will remain fixed.

Clicking the **View Graph Data** button brings up a worksheet listing the raw data. You can only view and not change the data in this data sheet.

Clicking **Zoom X Range** allows you to limit the number of periods for which the data are plotted.

Clicking the **Parameters** button brings back the display **Chart Parameters**. You can enter new values for the starting points of the coefficients and increments.

If you want to try another case or another analogy, modify your data points, or save the current case, you need to bring up the **Main Menu**. To do so, go to the **Model** menu and choose **Main Menu**.

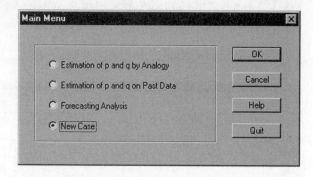

If you want to analyze another product, select **New Case** from the **Model Menu**. Decide whether you want to **Save** or **Discard** the current scenario.

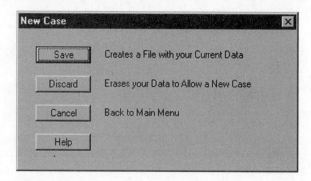

References

Bass, Frank M; Krishnan, Trichy V.; and Jain, Dipak 1994, "Why the Bass model fits without decision variables," *Marketing Science,* Vol. 13, No. 3 (Summer), pp. 203-223.

Bass, Frank M. 1969, "A new product growth model for consumer durables," *Management Science*, Vol. 15, No. 4 (January), pp. 215-227.

Srinivasan, V. and Mason, Charlotte H. 1986, "Nonlinear least squares estimation of new product diffusion models," *Marketing Science*, Vol. 5, No. 2 (Spring), pp. 169-178.

ZENITH HIGH DEFINITION TELEVISION (HDTV)*

On August 1, 1990, Jerry Pearlman, CEO of Zenith Electronics Corporation, met with Bruce Huber, VP of marketing, to discuss the market potential for a new technology called high definition TV (HDTV). At the end of the meeting, Mr. Pearlman asked Mr. Huber to develop, within a month, a preliminary forecast of demand for HDTV sets for a 15-year period starting in 1992. Although they both realized that any forecasts they came up with would just be best guesses they still felt that forecasts would be useful in deciding whether and how the company should respond to this emerging technology. Many strategic decisions would depend on these forecasts, including the level and nature of the R&D and marketing research activities the company would undertake, the strategic alliances it would pursue to get a running start in the marketplace, and the extent of its participation in industrywide lobbying efforts with the FCC (Federal Communications Commission) and the US Congress.

HDTV background

As compared to conventional TV sets, HDTV sets produce better quality pictures with higher resolution and superior sound (CD-like). They also have wider screens. According to the Electronic Industries Association, high definition in TV can be measured by the resolution of the picture, that is, the number of horizontal and vertical lines scanned on the TV screen.

To promote the growth of HDTV several stakeholders would have to adopt a common set of standards:

- Technical specifications for the core functions and manufacture of HDTV sets
- Production standards to enable TV and movie studios to develop content to take advantage of the superior display features of HDTV
- Broadcast and transmission standards regulated by the FCC to ensure high quality transmission within the available frequency spectrum

The Japanese government and industry adopted an HDTV standard in 1984 that had 1125 lines per frame, while the US NTSC (National Television Standards Committee) standard is 525 lines per frame. In addition the US NTSC standard has a 4:3 (or 16:12) aspect ratio (ratio of frame width to height) but the committee is considering a wide-screen aspect ratio of 16:9 for HDTV. Movies made after 1950 typically used wide-screen formats although not always with a 16:9 aspect ratio, while

* This is based on Harvard Business School case 5-591-025 and is used here with the permission of HBS Publishing Division.

TV programs and most movies made before 1950 typically used a 16:12 aspect ratio.

The Japanese standard relied on traditional analog signals for broadcasts, but the transmission was only over satellite channels. Unless consumers had both an HDTV and a way to receive satellite signals, they would not be able to receive these programs.

In 1990, US industry and government were still working together on setting standards. They had to resolve several thorny issues:

Compatibility with existing TVs: The FCC wanted to ensure that whatever transmission standard the industry adopted for HDTV it would not make existing TV sets obsolete. Even with compatibility ensured, an HDTV program would leave the top and bottom of the screen empty when displayed on a standard TV set (Exhibit 1a). On the other hand, when receiving a standard-broadcast TV program, an HDTV would display a squarish picture in the middle of a wide rectangle (Exhibit 1b).

Digital versus analog standard: Several US firms including Zenith were pushing for adoption of digital standards instead of the analog standard the Japanese had adopted. Under a digital standard all images would be converted to the 0/1 language of computers and compressed before being transmitted by cable, satellite, or over the air. The TV receiver would convert the digital streams back into images.

Although a digital standard seemed to be better aligned with the expected convergence of computer and telecommunication technologies, industry members had several concerns. Analog signals typically degenerate gracefully under interference, i.e., a small loss of signal quality results in only a small loss of picture quality. Digital signals however tend to degrade substantially with a small impairment to the signal quality. This may not be a major problem for cable-based transmission. Also people have a lot of experience with analog transmission. A digital transmission standard could require experimentation and testing over several years before adoption.

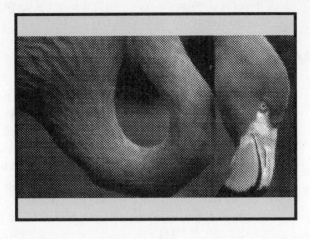

(a)

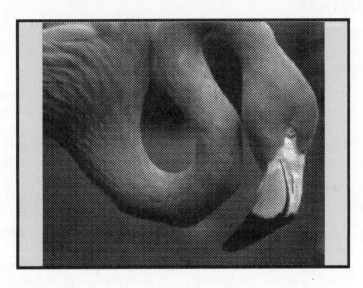

(b)

EXHIBIT 1

(a) HDTV broadcast as it appears on standard TV, and
(b) standard NTSC broadcast as it will appear on HDTV.

Regardless of whether the industry adopts a digital or analog transmission standard, content providers, such as TV and movie studios
would have to invest in costly equipment to produce images with higher
resolution. For example, studios would either need high-definition digital
cameras for shooting or equipment to convert images from a high-
resolution format, such as 35mm film. A studio-quality camera would
cost around $300,000 to $400,000. Production staff at TV studios would
also have to adapt to the new wide-screen-aspect ratio. They would have
to learn new techniques for composing scenes, editing frames, and so
forth. At the same time, broadcasters (e.g., TV stations and cable TV

companies) would have to invest heavily in such equipment as transmitters and towers to broadcast HDTV signals.

Zenith HDTV efforts to date

In 1990, Zenith was working to develop advanced flat-screen picture tubes that could display images in the HDTV format. The development efforts looked promising, so Zenith anticipated marketing 20" and wider screens by 1992. In addition Zenith and its partner, AT&T, had made significant advances in developing a "spectrum compatible" HDTV transmission system that would offer HDTV pictures in the same channel space as existing NTSC standards. (Because of the scarcity of channel bandwidth such a system was considered to be a necessary element in the introduction of HDTV.)

The TV market

Zenith had conducted a number of studies of consumer behavior, which led to the following general conclusions:

- Consumers looked for value for their money and stayed within their budgets. Most consumers were satisfied with their existing TVs.
- Product quality was the most important criterion for evaluating brands. Consumers generally preferred large screens to small screens and considered such product features as stereo, remote control, and style to be important as well.
- Consumers tended to shy away from the lowest priced brands because they were suspicious of poor quality.

Bruce Huber had access to several additional sources of data acquired by Zenith's marketing research department. In particular he thought the data shown in Exhibits 2 to 7 might be useful in forecasting the sales of HDTV sets.

	Size	% units	Average retail price
Small	<19"	42%	$290
Medium	20-25"	40%	$610
Large	27+"	15%	$1,050

EXHIBIT 2
Breakdown of the TV set size distribution in 1989 and the corresponding average prices.

	TV households	Multi-set	Color TV	Cable	VCR	Remote control
1950	10%	–	–	–	–	–
1955	67	4%	–	–	–	–
1960	87	12	–	–	–	–
1965	94	22	7%	–	–	–
1970	96	35	41	7%	–	–
1975	97	43	74	12	–	–
1980	98	50	83	20	–	–
1985	98	57	91	43	14%	29%
1989	98	63	97	53	60	72
1990	98	65	98	56	66	77

Note: Nielsen estimated U.S. TV households = 92.1 million on Jan. 1, 1990.

EXHIBIT 3
Data on the market's time pattern for adoption of past TV-related technologies. *Source: The American Enterprise, 1990, p. 97.*

Year	Total units	Total $	Average $/unit	Total $ in 1989 $*	Avg. $/unit in 1989 $*
1971	11,197	$2,551,997	$228	$7,831,740	$698
1975	11,606	2,684,121	231	6,184,102	533
1980	18,143	4,798,239	264	7,220,650	398
1985	20,829	5,871,854	282	6,766,820	325
1989	24,669	6,899,762	280	6,899,761	280

*Adjusted for the Consumer Price Index

EXHIBIT 4
Summary of factory shipments of TVs in the U.S. since 1971. *Source: EIA Electronic Fact Books 1981-1989.*

Buyer type

Performance or feature	36%
Experience	34%
Price	30%

Note: Performance or feature-oriented buyers consider primarily the performance and the features of the set when making a TV purchase;

Experience-oriented buyers want technology they can trust, i.e., technology that is stable and has been widely used, before they adopt;

Price-oriented buyers base their purchases primarily on the price of the product.

EXHIBIT 5
Summary of the results of a market segmentation study of TV buyers conducted by Zenith.

	1989	1990	1991	1992	1993	1994
Color TV forecast (Econometric model)	22.0	22.2	23.4	24.9	25.7	25.9
—Units—						
First purchase	2.1	1.8	1.6	1.6	1.5	1.5
Replacement	7.7	8.3	8.9	9.6	10.3	11.0
Additional	11.6	11.5	12.3	13.0	13.2	12.7
Institutional	0.6	0.6	0.6	0.7	0.7	0.7

EXHIBIT 6
Zenith's forecast sales of color TVs by purchase occasion (millions of units).

	1992	1993	1994	1995	1996	1997	1998	1999	2000
Industry total (millions of units)	21.4	21.9	22.4	22.9	23.5	24.1	24.7	25.2	25.9
25" and larger (millions of units)	6.0	6.1	6.2	6.4	6.8	7.2	7.5	8.0	8.5
Zenith retail price for HDTV									
26"/31"	$2500	$2000	$1700	$1500	$1400	$1350	$1300	$1300	$1300
22"/27"				1100	1000	900	900	900	
Zenith retail price with conventional tube									
26"/31"	$3000	$2500	$2100	$1900	$1700	$1550	$1550	$1550	$1500
22"/27"				1200	1100	1000	1000	1000	

EXHIBIT 7
Zenith's forecasts of U.S. sales of large screen TVs, which have price points that are likely to be similar to those of the HDTV.

Forecasts of HDTV sales

A few months earlier, the Electronic Industries Association (EIA) had forecast that HDTV would penetrate 25 percent of US households by the year 2000. Jerry Pearlman was not that optimistic but still predicted that HDTV would garner about 10 percent of the TV industry sales by 1999.

Some industry observers believed that both of these forecasts were optimistic because picture quality alone won't sell HDTV sets without significant levels of HDTV programming and broadcasting. They believed that the projected levels of penetration would occur only if (1) the FCC settled on a transmission standard immediately, a highly unlikely prospect, and if (2) broadcasters invested substantial amounts of money in new equipment, which is unlikely before studios produce the content for HDTV broadcasting. There are about 1500 TV stations in the country, each of which would have to incur equipment costs of between $2 and 3 million to upgrade to digital transmission. These observers thought that neither of these scenarios was likely to occur for several years and that by the year 2000, sales would perhaps reach "a few hundred thousand units." Until then, HDTV would be used mostly for viewing closed-circuit TV programs, such as training films (e.g., surgery demonstrations), or for home-viewing of rented or owned movies on high-end entertainment systems.

With this preliminary research behind him, Bruce Huber was ready to tackle "the HDTV forecasting problem." He had recently acquired software called GBass for forecasting new-product sales. He wondered whether this software would be of any help in this forecasting task.

EXERCISES

1. Summarize and justify alternative scenarios (i.e., consistent sets of assumptions) ranging from pessimistic to optimistic with regard to market performance of HDTV.

2. Develop forecasts of HDTV penetration in the US market from 1992 through 2006 for each scenario you develop. Justify and explain your forecasts.

TUTORIAL FOR THE ASSESSOR PRETEST MARKET MODEL (ASSESSOR)

The ASSESSOR system is a set of measurement procedures and models designed to help managers to forecast the market share of new packaged goods before test marketing. Our ASSESSOR Excel spreadsheet incorporates two of its core models: the Trial & Repeat Model and the Preference Model. Both models are essentially self-contained and they complement each other. The ASSESSOR Excel spreadsheet is designed to accompany the Harvard Business School case "Johnson Wax: Enhance (A)."

Part 1—Trial and repeat model

On the **Model** menu, select **Pretest Market Model** (assessor.xls) to get to the introductory screen. Select the **Trial & Repeat Model** and click on the **Next** button.

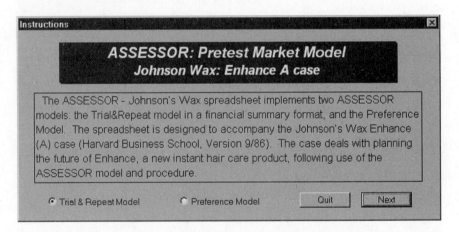

You need to run the Trial & Repeat Model before running the Preference Model. In this implementation, the Trial & Repeat Model generates one of the inputs to the Preference Model (Net Cumulative Trial from Ad).

You will see the input box for the Trial & Repeat Model. Click **Response Mode** to assign parameter values indirectly or click **Manual Mode** to do it directly.

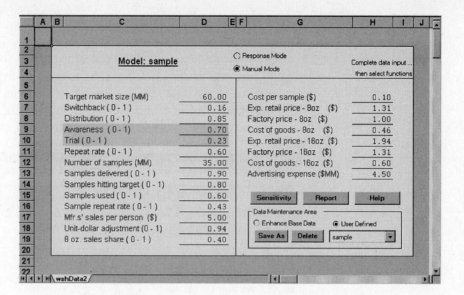

Note that no **Set Up** button is available in the **Manual Mode**.

The response mode allows you to define functional relationships between advertising expenditures and awareness and between advertising expenditures and the trial rate. Variations in the advertising level are reflected in costs and in revenues. In contrast the manual mode represents the simple "dumb spreadsheet" approach, where sales are independent of advertising.

Clicking the **Set Up** button while in the **Response Mode** brings you to the following box.

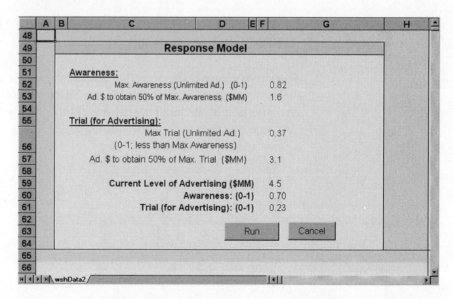

You must provide parameter values to calibrate two simple response curves that represent the effect of advertising expenditure on awareness and trial. The modified exponential function underlies these two response curves. When you are finished, click **Run** to get back to the model input screen.

Once you have provided the necessary inputs for the Trial & Repeat model, save the work. Click **Save As** to save your input data and to assign a name to the data set. Any saved data set can be accessed later by selecting **User Defined** and then selecting the data set from the pull-down menu directly underneath. Click **Delete** to remove data cases.

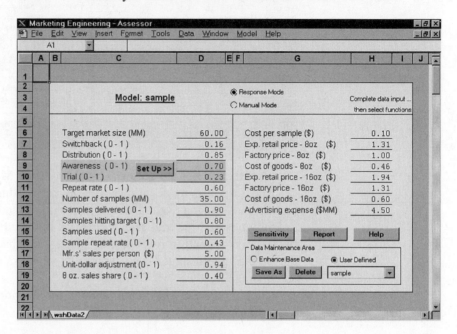

There are two ways to view the results of the Trial & Repeat model: (1) **Sensitivity** and (2) **Report**.

Sensitivity analysis: Selecting **Sensitivity** opens a new dialog sheet that lets you see the effects on Market Share and Return on Sales of changing one of the input parameters. In this box, we have opted to investigate the impact of advertising expense.

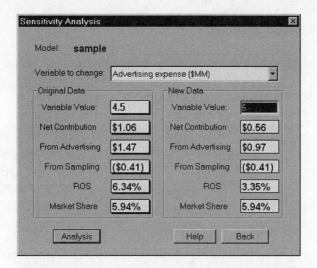

NOTE: *The effects of changing the amount of advertising expense will differ depending on whether the values for Trial and Awareness in the active input data set are based on the Manual Mode or the Response Mode.*

Click **Back** to go back to the model input screen.

Report: Click **Report** to see two pages of output from the Trial & Repeat Model. It shows the effects of advertising and sampling on market share, along with some financial results.

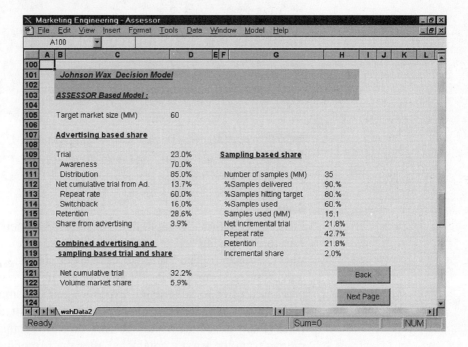

Part 2—Preference model

To switch to the Preference Model, you must go back to the introductory dialog box from the **Model** menu, choose **Introduction**.

Click **Preference Model** and **Next**.

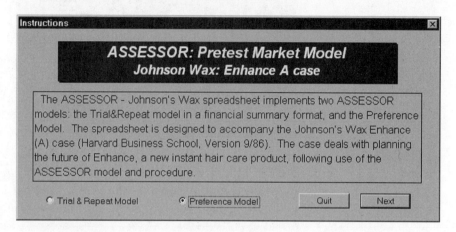

The Preference Model **Main Menu** lists the functions of the model.

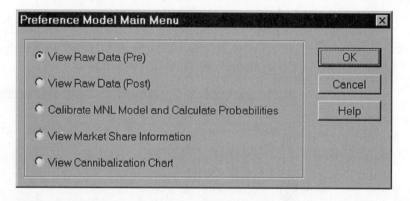

NOTE: *You can access the Preference Model **Main Menu** under the **Model** menu in the menu bar (you cannot access it while working in the Trial & Repeat Model).*

Step 1

First you can view the input data for the respondents prior to their exposure to advertising and to simulated shopping (preusage) and after exposure (postusage). The preusage data sheet shows scaled preference ratings from each respondent for each brand in the test and the brand last purchased prior to advertising exposure and the simulated shopping experience. On the **Model** menu, choose **Main Menu**, and click **View Raw Data (Post)** to see the postusage data sheet. It contains scaled preference ratings from the survey conducted after the respondents have had an opportunity to use the product. The pre- and the post-data sets include information only from respondents who responded to both surveys.

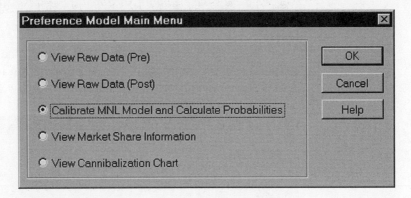

Step 2

Central to the Preference Model is the third option, **Calibrate MNL (Multinomial Logit) Model and Calculate Probabilities**. Click this option to start the estimation of the MNL coefficient (b) and the calculation of the market share estimates based on this estimated coefficient.

First you need to enter the number of brands and the number of respondents. These parameters are dependent on the ASSESSOR test data. For the Johnson Wax: Enhance case, we have already entered this information.

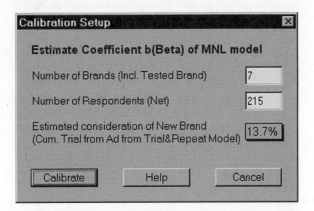

The Trial & Repeat model calculates a value for "cumulative trial from advertising," which serves as a proxy for the likely purchase of Enhance by respondents who are not subjected to the simulated shopping experience. Click **Calibrate** to start the estimation procedure and then **OK**. The program will then display the computed b coefficient. Click **OK** to continue.

The program computes the b coefficient of the MNL model using the Solver tool. It will also compute the choice probabilities of each brand for each respondent, and it will convert these probabilities into market shares using the estimated (b) coefficient. While the macro is running, the status bar will inform you about its progress.

NOTE: *By choosing **View Raw Data (Pre)** and **View Raw Data (Post)** you can access the probability estimates (see also Step 4).*

Step 3

After the program calibrates the MNL model and estimates the probabilities, select **View Market Share Information** to see information on market shares and draw estimates, as shown below:

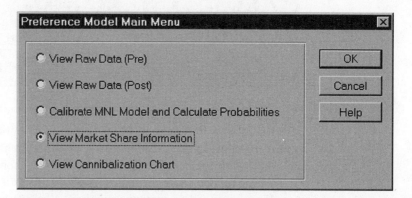

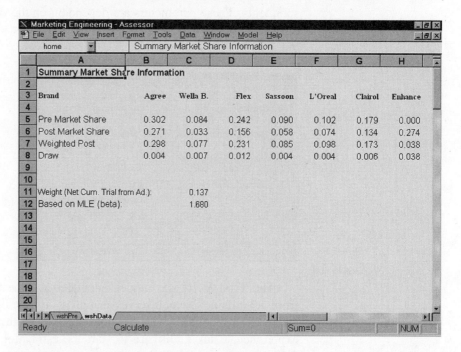

Brand	Agree	Wella B.	Flex	Sassoon	L'Oreal	Clairol	Enhance
Pre Market Share	0.302	0.084	0.242	0.090	0.102	0.179	0.000
Post Market Share	0.271	0.033	0.156	0.058	0.074	0.134	0.274
Weighted Post	0.298	0.077	0.231	0.085	0.098	0.173	0.038
Draw	0.004	0.007	0.012	0.004	0.004	0.006	0.038
Weight (Net Cum. Trial from Ad.):	0.137						
Based on MLE (beta):	1.680						

You can also select **View Cannibalization Chart** to see the chart titled **Market Share Draw** which shows the estimated impact of cannibalization.

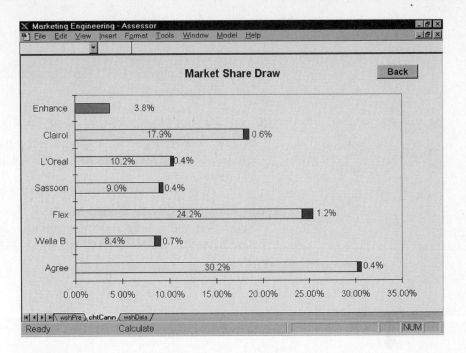

Step 4

If you want to investigate the output of the Preference Model in more detail, you can look at the estimated probabilities (which are based on the b coefficient) for the pre- and post-usage data by going to the **Main Menu** and selecting **View Raw Data (Pre)** or **View Raw Data (Post)**.

Resp. ID	Last Brand Bought	Agree	Wella B.	Flex	Sassoon	L'Oreal	Clairol	Enhance
1	5	1.835	1.416	0.709	1.056	1.916	2.538	0
2	6	0.769	0	0	0	0	1.354	0
3	6	1.236	0	1.825	0	0	3.338	0
4	1	4.67	0	1.774	0	0	0	0
5	2	1.94	4.158	1.152	1.955	4.12	4.961	0
6	1	4.432	3.568	2.757	3.134	0.458	2.314	0
7	4	2.258	3.017	3.509	4.705	0	1.232	0
8	5	1.868	1.636	0.974	0	2.231	0	0
9	4	0	4.472	3.339	1.863	4.605	1.432	0
10	1	3.724	0	0.704	0	0	0	0
11	5	0.99	4.646	0.355	0.166	4.826	3.16	0
12	6	1.355	0	0.65	0	0	3.171	0
13	1	3.784	0.87	2.475	1.445	1.866	2.507	0
14	4	2.347	0	0.252	4.804	0	0	0
15	1	3.411	0	1.316	0.487	3.008	2.074	0
16	2	4.768	4.784	4.71	1.389	1.109	0.418	0

References

"Johnson Wax: Enhance (A)," HBS Case #583046, 1-32, © 1982 Harvard Business School.

Silk, Alvin J. and Urban, Glen L. 1978, "Pre-test market evaluation of new packaged goods: A model and measurement methodology," *Journal of Marketing Research*, Vol. 15, No. 2 (May), pp. 171-191.

Urban, Glen L. and Katz, Gerald M. 1983, "Pre-test market models: Validation and managerial implications," *Journal of Marketing Research*, Vol. 20, No. 3 (August), pp. 221-234.

JOHNSON WAX: ENHANCE (A)[*]

Instant hair conditioner

In April 1979, John Sherman, product development manager for S. C. Johnson & Company, was facing a decision on the future of Enhance, a new instant hair conditioner. Designed as a companion product to Agree, the company's first hair-care product. Development of Enhance had been under way for about a year and a half.

During the development process, Enhance had been tested against the leading existing products through blind comparisons and had undergone a pre-test-market testing procedure called ASSESSOR. The results of these tests would need to play a significant role in Sherman's recommendations, because previous experience had convinced top management that such research was valuable. In fact, the company had performed a number of ASSESSOR or similar analyses in the past, and top management had on occasion seemed anxious to skip the test market and push for introduction when the ASSESSOR results were favorable.

John Sherman's task was to recommend the next steps for Enhance. While his experience and intuitive judgment would be valued, he knew the managerial climate at S. C. Johnson would require marketing research substantiation for his recommendations.

S. C. Johnson & Company

S. C. Johnson & Company, headquartered in Racine, Wisconsin, was founded in 1886 as a manufacturer of parquet flooring. It was incorporated as S. C. Johnson & Son, Inc. and was familiarly known throughout the world as "Johnson Wax." A privately held corporation, Johnson Wax did not publicly report sales or earnings. Still, it was recognized as one of the world's leading manufacturers of products for home, auto and personal care, for commercial maintenance and industrial markets, and for outdoor recreation and leisure-time activities. Johnson Wax and its subsidiaries employed more than 13,000 people worldwide.

The buildings that served as international headquarters had been designed by Frank Lloyd Wright. They had won numerous architectural awards, and were listed in the National Register of Historic Places. U.S.

---

[*] This case was prepared by Associate Professor Darral G. Clarke as the basis for class discussion rather than to illustrate either effective or ineffective handling of an administrative situation. This revision is by Professor Robert J. Dolan. Copyright © 1982 by the President and Fellows of Harvard College. No part of this publication may be reproduced, stored in a retrieval system, or transmitted in any form or by any means—electronic, mechanical, photocopying, recording, or otherwise—without the permission of Harvard Business School. Distributed by HBS Case Services, Harvard Business School, Boston, MA 02163. Printed in U.S.A.

manufacturing operations were conducted at the company's Waxdale, Wisconsin manufacturing plant, about eight miles west of Racine. This plant encompassed more than 1.9 million square feet of floor space and was one of the largest and most modern facilities of its kind in the world.

Johnson Wax maintained sales offices and sales and distribution centers in 20 major U.S. metropolitan areas.

Johnson Wax Associates, Inc. (JWA) was a group of nine associated companies that manufactured and marketed products for leisure-time activities and outdoor recreation. JWA products were distributed nationally and overseas to wholesalers and retailers through a system of manufacturers' representatives and factory salesmen.

The first Johnson Wax overseas subsidiary was established in England, in 1914. In 1979, Johnson Wax had subsidiaries in 45 countries.

The Johnson Wax consumer product line consisted of some of the best-known brands in household, automobile and personal-care products: Brite, Future, Glo-Coat, and Klear floor waxes; Jubilee and Pledge furniture polish, Rain Barrel Fabric Softener, Shout Stain Remover, Glory Carpet Cleaner, Glade Air Freshener, J-Wax auto care products, Raid insecticide, and Off insect repellent.

The Johnson Wax Innochem Division manufactured and distributed a complete line of heavy-duty polishes, cleaners, insecticides and disinfectants for use by commercial and institutional customers and a specialty line of chemicals.

The U.S. consumer products were distributed to supermarkets and drug, discount, and variety outlets through the company's own national sales force. Innochem commercial products distribution was handled through a separate sales force and through a network of more than 400 distributors nationally. Warehouse and distribution facilities were shared by the Innochem and Consumer Products Divisions.

New-product development at Johnson Wax

Development of these numerous product lines over the years had given Johnson Wax considerable experience in new-product evaluation and introduction. New product ideas came from laboratory research, marketing research, and customer contact. The product development process at Johnson Wax was fairly standard: ideas went through various commercial feasibility studies, performance tests against competitive products, and test markets before national introduction or rollout.

In recent years developing a new consumer product had become so expensive that Johnson Wax, like other manufacturers, had sought ways to reduce the cost. One solution was the pre-test-market test. One source[*] estimated the expected benefit from a $50,000 pretest to be in excess of $1 million. Before the Enhance pretest, Johnson Wax had performed many such pretests, most of them ASSESSORS.

The hair conditioning market

During the 1970s, both the variety and the number of hair-care products and brands had increased drastically. Shampoos to combat dandruff were introduced; others were custom-formulated for use on dry, normal, or oily hair. During the same period, new products were introduced that would "condition" hair as well as clean it. According to one manufacturer:

A good creme rinse conditioner can help combat many hair problems. Hair can be easily damaged when it is combed following a shampoo, since hair is weakest when wet. Washing and towel-drying hair tend to tangle it, making it susceptible to breakage during combing. A creme rinse conditioner helps prevent this type of damage because it helps prevent tangles and makes for easy wet-combing. Creme rinse and conditioners also make hair feel softer; add to its bounce, shine, and body; and help prevent the buildup of static electricity that causes hair to be "flyaway."

There were two types of hair conditioners:

- *Instant conditioners*, which were usually left on the hair for one to five minutes before being rinsed off.
- *Therapeutic conditioners*, which generally remained on the hair from five to twenty minutes before rinsing.

The term "creme rinse" was still used occasionally for conditioners that stressed easier combing and manageability. Gradually, the term was being replaced by "instant conditioner." Hair conditioner sales had grown dramatically during the 1970s, spurred by new-product introductions and increased use, especially among young women.

The major instant hair conditioner brands and their market shares in 1978 were Johnson's Agree (15.2 percent), Wella Balsam (4.7 percent), Clairol Condition (9.9 percent), Flex (13.4 percent), Tame (5.4 percent), and Sassoon.

Manufacturers' sales were as follows:

---

[*] Glen L. Urban and John R. Hauser, *Design and Marketing of New Products* (Englewood Cliffs, NJ: Prentice-Hall, Inc., 1980), pp. 52–59. The cost of a 9 month, two-market test market was estimated at about $1MM. The expected savings of ASSESSOR, although also $1MM, are computed from a Bayesian analysis involving: (1) costs of ASSESSOR, test markets, and national introduction; (2) probabilities of success at various stages of the new-product introduction process.

Manufacturers' Sales ($ millions)

Year	Total Conditioner	Instant Conditioner
1975	$132	$116
1976	160	141
1977	200	176
1978	230	202

Instant conditioners were sold in a variety of packages, but generally in either clear or opaque plastic bottles, often with nozzle tops. Popular sizes were 8-, 12-, and 16-ounce bottles. Retail margins generally ranged between 30 and 38 percent.

Agree

In June 1977, Johnson Wax entered the hair-care market with Agree Creme Rinse and Conditioner, soon followed by Agree Shampoo. At that time some creme rinses and conditioners included oil in their formulation. Agree's selling proposition was that the addition of this oil, especially for people with oily hair, caused the hair to look oily, greasy, and limp soon after shampooing. A technological breakthrough by Johnson Wax enabled it to produce a virtually oil-free product (Agree) which helped "stop the greasies." According to Johnson Wax promotional material:

> Agree has exceptional detangling properties making the hair easier to wet-comb. It is pleasantly scented and leaves the hair feeling clean, with healthy shine, bounce, and body. Agree contains no harsh or harmful ingredients and is pH balanced to be compatible with the natural pH of hair and scalp.

Agree had fared well in product comparison tests and an ASSESSOR pre-test-market test. By 1978, Agree had a 4.5 percent share of the shampoo market and 15.2 percent share of the conditioner market.

Enhance product development

Agree's early success created optimism and euphoria at Johnson Wax. Gaining a foothold in the attractive conditioner market offered an opportunity to expand the conditioner product line and subsequently make greater inroads on the even larger shampoo market.

Management felt Agree was successful largely because it solved a specific hair problem for a segment of the market. They also felt that it would be desirable to offer another personal-care product line. Enhance was conceived as an instant hair conditioner targeted toward women 25–45 years old with dry hair, and was formulated to appeal to that audience. Blind paired comparisons were run against Revlon's Flex.

The study, conceived by John Sherman and Neil Ford, of marketing research department, was summarized as follows:

> The purpose of the study was to determine the preference levels for Enhance, both overall and on specific performance attributes, versus those of Flex, the leading instant hair conditioner. A panel of 400 hair conditioner users was preselected by telephone. Each received both Enhance and Flex, blind-labeled and in identical nonidentifiable packages and, following proper rotations, used first one for three weeks, and the other for an identical period. At the end of the six-week usage period, respondents were interviewed regarding their preferences and behavior regarding the test products. A key part of the analysis was to determine preferences of women with specific hair care problems relevant to Enhance strategy and positioning.

A digest of the results appears in Exhibits 1 and 2. The conclusions drawn by Ford in an August 1978 report to Sherman were that:

> Differences between the two products are not great, but where they exist, they tend to be focused on the problems Enhance wishes to address and on the women to whom the brand will be targeted. While work should continue to improve the product, it is suitable for use in ASSESSOR in its current state and, if need be, for use in test-market introduction.

The ASSESSOR pre-test market

Following the blind comparison tests, further work on product formulation, product positioning, packaging, and advertising copy produced an introductory marketing plan. Advertising copy presented Enhance as a solution to the dry and damaged hair problem. Enhance samples were produced in "regular" and "extra conditioning" formulas.

When the marketing plan was agreed upon and samples were available, an ASSESSOR pre-test-market procedure was arranged. The primary objectives were to estimate the ongoing market share of Enhance and determine consumer reaction to the product. Two independent techniques were used to arrive at a market share prediction one year after introduction. The observed trial and repeat levels were used to make one share prediction. Another was made from estimates of brand preference calculated from the respondents' perception of, and preference for, the attributes of Enhance and the existing brands. Additional qualitative and quantitative information gathered during the laboratory phase, and again after use, added support for the primary conclusions of the ASSESSOR study.

ASSESSOR[*], developed in 1973 by Management Decision Systems (MDS), of Waltham, Massachusetts, was one of a number of commercial

---

[*] More detailed descriptions of ASSESSOR may be found in the appendix to this case and in Alvin J. Silk and Glen L. Urban, "Pre-Test-Market Evaluation of New Packaged Goods: A Model and Measurement Methodology," *Journal of Marketing Research*, Vol. XV (May 1978), pp. 171-191.

simulated test-market procedures. The first was the Yankelovich Laboratory Test Market begun in 1968. Elrick and Lavidges' COMP, National Purchase Diary's ESP, and Burke Marketing Research's BASES followed, and by 1979, nearly 1400 applications of these models had been completed.

The Enhance ASSESSOR consisted of a laboratory and a callback phase. During the *laboratory phase*, women were intercepted in shopping malls and asked if they would participate in a test market. Those who were willing and were found to be in the target segment went through a five-step procedure, as follows:

1. *An initial questionnaire* was used to determine the brands about which the respondent could provide meaningful information. This list of brands, called the respondent's "evoked set," included brands used recently or ever, and brands that would, or would not, be considered on the next purchase occasion.

2. *The preference questionnaire* was customized for each respondent to include only those brands in her evoked set. The respondent was asked to allocate 11 imaginary chips between each pair of brands in her evoked set. These allocations were used to calculate the strength of preference for each brand in each respondent's evoked set. If there were N brands, the respondent was asked to give allocations for each of the N(N - 1)2 pairs.

3. *Advertising recall* was measured after the respondent was shown commercials for six creme rinse/conditioning products: Tame, Agree, Flex, Condition, Wella Balsam, and Enhance.

4. *Laboratory purchasing* took place in a simulated store where the respondent was given a $2.25 certificate. If she wanted to buy more than $2.25 in merchandise, she was asked to pay the difference. Respondents who did not purchase Enhance were given a package of Enhance as a gift. Half the nonpurchasers received a 2 oz. container, the other half received an 8 oz. container. A limited number of those who did not purchase the test product were asked a few additional questions probing their impressions of Enhance and reasons for not purchasing it.

5. *Brand ratings*. Respondents were then asked to rate several of their evoked brands on how well they performed on 22 product attributes. Enhance was also rated on these attributes. These ratings, since the respondent had not used Enhance, were based on perceptions created through advertising, price, and packaging. A 7-point rating scale was used.

The *callback phase* was designed to collect information about after-use preferences, repeat purchase rate, and diagnostics concerning product performance. Only those respondents who indicated they had used Enhance were asked to complete the interview. Callback interviews were conducted four weeks after the laboratory interview.

The field research was conducted in three markets—Atlanta, Chicago, and Denver—beginning September 25, 1978, with callback interviews approximately four weeks later. A total of 387 interviews was conducted with users of creme rinse/conditioning products. Respondents included 120 users of Agree creme rinse, a disproportionate number, in order to better determine Enhance's effect on Agree.

ASSESSOR results

ASSESSOR provided results in eight major areas of interest: (1) market structure, (2) advertising recall, (3) trial, (4) repeat purchase, (5) product acceptance, (6) market share prediction, (7) cannibalization, and (8) sampling response.

1. ***Market Structure***: During the laboratory phase of the field-work, respondents were asked to rate several of their evoked brands as well as their "ideal" brand on 22 attributes. These brand ratings were used as inputs to factor analysis[*], a data-reduction technique used for grouping similar attributes into underlying factors or dimensions. From this analysis, four basic perceptual dimensions, or factors, emerged:

---

[*] See Appendix A for description of factor analysis procedure.

Factor	Relative Importance	Attributes Combined to Form the Factor
Conditioning	33%	Nourishes dry hair
		Restores moisture
		Keeps control of split ends
		Makes dry hair healthy looking
		Conditions hair
		Helps keep hair from breaking
		Penetrates hair
Clean	27%	Leaves hair free of residue/flakes
		Leaves hair grease- and oil-free
		Leaves hair clean looking
		Rinses out easily/completely
Manageability/effects	23%	Makes hair more manageable
		Leaves hair shiny/lustrous
		Leaves hair soft and silky
		Gives hair body and fullness
Fragrance	17%	Has pleasant fragrance while using
		Leaves hair with nice fragrance

Besides identifying the possible factors underlying the instant conditioner market, factor analysis provided a graphic representation of the consumer's positioning of the brands in a "perceptual map." This was done by using pairs of factors as axes and assigning each brand a "factor score" that served as a coordinate on each axis. Using these coordinates, a brand was assigned a position on the perceptual map. MDS produced perceptual maps for a number of market segments. The maps for the total market are shown in Exhibit 3. (Maps including the fragrance factor are not presented.)

MDS's report concluded that, in terms of market structure,

The fact that all four dimensions are important to all consumers' segments considered in the study suggests that being strongly positioned on only one dimension may not be sufficient to capture a significant portion of the market.

Agree and Breck Creme Rinse have achieved the "clean" position, while Clairol Condition has succeeded in differentiating itself as the "conditioning" brand. Wella Balsam, based on these maps, appears to have virtually no image, and thus might be vulnerable to a new entry. Sassoon, a relatively new brand, appears to be enjoying a very strong positive image.

2. *Advertising Recall*: Unaided advertising recall provided a measure of how well an ad broke through the clutter of competitive advertising. Total unaided recall for Enhance was 76 percent, about average for ASSESSOR-tested products, but somewhat lower than for other

Johnson Wax products subjected to ASSESSOR tests. Unaided recall did not differ across hair type segments.

Among those who recalled the Enhance ad, almost 50 percent recalled that Enhance was "for dry hair." "Conditions" and "penetrates" received somewhat lower playback. Exhibit 4 summarizes the copy-point recall results.

3. ***Trial Estimation***: Store setups had been designed to reflect local conditions and simulate the anticipated competitive environment. Enhance was available in two sizes for both regular and extra conditioning formulations. Enhance had one facing for each size and formulation, and was featured in the middle of the middle shelf. In all, 24 shampoos and conditioners were represented in 60 facings. Enhance was offered in 8 and 16 ounce sizes at $1.31 and $1.94, respectively. Agree was offered in 8 and 12 ounce sizes at $1.31 and $1.67. Flex was offered only in the 16 ounce size at the same price as Agree. Enhance prices were very similar to those of Breck, Wella Balsam, and Tame.

Trial was measured as a percentage of total laboratory purchasing. Of the 387 respondents, 307 (79 percent) made a purchase in the store. Enhances trial rate was 23 percent. Agree had achieved an overall trial rate of 33 percent in its ASSESSOR test. For purposes of comparison, Exhibit 5 shows trial rates for other ASSESSOR-tested products, both within and outside the health and beauty aids category.

4. ***Repeat Purchase Estimation***: Repeat purchase and product acceptance were determined through telephone callback interviews four weeks after the laboratory interviews. Since all respondents who had not purchased Enhance were given samples, after-use data were potentially available for all respondents. Those who had not used Enhance were not asked to complete the phone interview. Telephone callbacks were completed with 215 respondents (55 percent of all laboratory respondents). This was lower than most ASSESSOR callback completion rates. Of those people with whom callback interviews were *not* completed, 23 percent (42 people) indicated they had not used Enhance because it was specifically formulated for dry hair.

During the callback interviews, respondents were again asked to compare Enhance with other brands in their evoked sets. This information was used to see whether use altered Enhance's position in the market structure (Enh. Post in Exhibit 3).

Respondents were also given the opportunity to purchase another bottle of Enhance at the prices found in the laboratory store. Those who decided to repurchase, plus those who said without prompting that their next conditioner purchase would be Enhance, were classified as repeaters. Repeat rates were as follows:

	Enhance	**Agree**
Repeat among buyers in laboratory	60%	78%
Repeat among nonbuyers (who received sample)	43	63

72 percent of those repeating purchased Enhance's "Extra Conditioning Formula" and 64 percent purchased the 16 ounce size.

The repeat purchase rates of other ASSESSOR-tested products are found in Exhibit 6.

5. **Product Acceptance**: During the callback interview the respondent was asked what she liked best about Enhance. Surprisingly, manageability, not conditioning, was mentioned most frequently, even though it was not considered a main copy point. Those who made a repeat purchase were even more likely than nonrepeaters to mention manageability. Open ended likes and dislikes for Enhance are found in Exhibit 7. Exhibit 8 presents after-use preferences and comparisons with users' favorite brands.

6. **Market Share Prediction**: A major feature that differentiated ASSESSOR from other pretest market procedures was the use of two convergent methods to predict market share. Market share was estimated separately with a "trial and repeat" model and a "preference" model.

Trial and repeat model

The trial and repeat model used the purchase information gathered during laboratory shopping and follow-up interview repeat measurements. The formula used was

$$M = TS$$

where

M = market share,

T = the ultimate cumulative trial rate (penetration or trial),

S = the ultimate repeat purchase rate among those buyers who have ever made a trial purchase of the brand (retention).

Retention (S) was a function of the initial repeat purchase rate and the rate at which previous triers returned to Enhance after buying another product (called switchback). The relationship is explained in Appendix A.

As mentioned above, Enhance obtained a laboratory trial of 23 percent, and a repeat rate of 60 percent. Measured through a series of callback interviews, the switchback rate was 16 percent. Retention was calculated to be 28.6 percent. Since these estimates were achieved in an environment in which every respondent was aware of Enhance advertising, and Enhance was always available, corrections had to be made to adjust these laboratory measurements to actual market conditions. Market trial was estimated by

$$T = FKD + CU - \{(FKD) \times (CU)\}$$

where

F = the trial rate in the ASSESSOR test—the trial rate that would ultimately occur if all consumers were aware of the advertising.

K = the long-run probability that a consumer will become aware of Enhance.

D = the proportion of retail outlets that will ultimately carry Enhance.

C = the proportion of the target market that receives samples.

U = the proportion of those receiving samples that will use them.

Using CU to estimate the trial resulting from sampling, would overstate the extent of sampling trial, since some trial would have resulted from advertising even without sampling. This "overlap" trial $((FKD) \times (CU))$ would be double-counted, and must therefore be subtracted from the sample-induced trial rate.

The market share estimates for Enhance depended not only on data obtained from the ASSESSOR test, but also on John Sherman's estimates of what advertising awareness and distribution levels would be realized for Enhance. Sherman had decided to initially use the advertising awareness and distribution levels realized for Agree:

awareness	70%
distribution	85%

Using these values, and ignoring sampling for the moment, market share was predicted by the trial/repeat model at 3.9 percent. Sherman's computations of Enhance market share, together with those for Agree, are found in Exhibit 9.

Preference model estimates of share

The preference model market share prediction was based on the respondents' answers to the questions about product attributes and the degree to which they perceived these attributes to be present in competing brands. The preference model predicted that Enhance would attain a 27.5 percent share of those consumers in whose evoked sets it appeared. Using the penetration rate found in the laboratory phase of the ASSESSOR study (14 percent), MDS obtained a base market share estimate of 3.8 percent (see Exhibit 9).

7. **Cannibalization**: An estimate of the cannibalization of Agree's share was also computed from the ASSESSOR results by computing Enhance's share separately for Agree users. This analysis demonstrated that Enhance would draw less than proportionately from Agree, with only a share of 2.4 percent among Agree users. This indicated that Agree would lose less than half a share point to Enhance.

More detailed analysis indicated that Enhance would draw more than proportionately to share from Wella Balsam, proportionately to share from Flex and Sassoon, and less than proportionately from Agree, L'Oreal, and Clairol Condition.

8. **Incremental Share from Sampling**: The incremental share that might be expected from sampling could be estimated, since those respondents who had not chosen Enhance had been given a sample of the product at the end of the initial ASSESSOR interview. Their use and acceptance levels were determined during the callback interview.

The effects of sampling were evaluated by first determining the incremental trial rate that would result from sampling. Of those using samples, a certain percentage (equal to net cumulative trial) would have tried the product anyway; the remainder were new triers due to sampling. (See formula above.) These incremental triers would now follow the normal switching process, and their long-run share potential could be estimated like that for the advertising induced triers. These calculations, found in Exhibit 10, estimated or incremental 2 percent share from a 35 million sample drop. Considering the effect of sampling, market share was estimated at 5.8 percent by the preference model and 5.9 percent by the trial/repeat model.

9. **Volume Predictions**: As a final step in the evaluation of Enhance's success potential, it was necessary to convert the share estimates into dollar sales projections. Doing this required a number of additional facts and adjustments. The 1979 volume of instant hair conditioner sales was projected to be $250 million. To find the volume that would result from a given Enhance share, it would be necessary to adjust the share for price and frequency-of-use differences between Enhance and the average for the category.

A use adjustment based on expected source of volume and frequency of use, indicated that Enhance's frequency of use would be about 0.9 times the category average. The tested Enhance prices and share of sales accounted for by the two sizes resulted in a price adjustment of 1.04. Multiplying these two adjustment factors resulted in a factor of 0.94 to be used to convert unit market share to dollar share.

Volume was then predicted, according to the two models, as follows:

	Trial/Repeat Model	Preference Model
Manufacturer's Category Volume	$250MM	$250MM
Enhance Unit Share	3.90%	3.80%
Enhance Dollar Share (Unit Share * .94)	3.66%	3.57%
Enhance Sales	$9.15MM	$8.93MM

Additional Sales From Promotion		
Promotion Unit Share	2.0	
Promotion Dollar Share	1.88	
Enhance Sales	4.7MM	4.7MM
Total Sales	$13.85MM	$13.63MM

Recommendations

MDS, as a result of the ASSESSOR study, was not encouraging about Enhance's prospects. It also thought sampling would not be successful for Enhance. Johnson Wax management had set a market share of 10 percent.[*]

John Sherman knew, however, that the final recommendations were his to make. He could recommend that Enhance be abandoned; reformulated; and/or retested; or that a national rollout begin. The final decision lay somewhere higher up in the organization, but his recommendations would be considered carefully.

---

[*] As a privately held corporation, Johnson Wax did not report financial data publicly. Manufacturers of health and beauty aids in general held cost data close to their chests. Exhibit 11 displays some approximate information on industry cost structure. The data are included for discussion purposes only and should not be considered indicative of Enhance's actual cost structure.

Blind Use Test Results
Incidence of Problems

	All Women	25-29	30-34	35 or Older
Dry/Damage Problems	53%	55%	53%	46%
Split ends	34	42	35	29
Dryness	32	29	35	31
Brittle/breaking	12	13	17	9
Damaged hair	13	10	18	11
Dull/Limp Problems	65%	64%	68%	58%
Hard to manage	38	32	42	39
Dull/no shine	24	16	21	30
Fine/limp hair	44	45	39	46

Each respondent was screened for the presence of any of these seven hair problems. The seven problems, in turn, were subjectively grouped into those to do with "Dry/Damage" and those to do with "Dull/Limp."

Overall Preference

	(BASE)	Prefer Enhance	Prefer Flex	No Difference
ALL USERS	(320)	48%	44%	8%
By Age				
Under 35	(166)	46	47	7
35 or over	(154)	50	40	10
By Hair Type				
Oily	(94)	51	45	4
Normal	(154)	44	47	9
Dry	(72)	53*	35	12
By Hair Quality				
Dry/damaged–net	(168)	50*	40	10
Fine/limp–net	(208)	49*	43	8

*Significant at 90 percent confidence level.

EXHIBIT 1
Johnson Wax: ENHANCE (A)

Blind Use Test Results (continued)

Preference on Specific Attributes

	Prefer Enhance	Prefer Flex	No Difference
Fragrance			
In bottle	27%	32%	41%
While using	34	37	29
After dry	28	28	44
Feels Cleaner			
While using	18	17	65
When dry	26*	19	55
Next day	26	22	52
Conditioning			
Conditioning	28	24	48
Softer	31	26	43
Body	31	32	37
More manageable	32	30	38
Better shine	14	16	70
Relieves dryness	(22)	15	63
Combing			
Easy to comb	22	20	58
Tangle free	16	16	68
Use/Application			
Applies evenly	(30)	14	56
Penetrates better	(28)	18	54
Rinses out easier	22	21	57
Product			
Better color	4	6	90
Better consistency	27	29	44

BASE: 320 Users

( ) Significant at 95 percent C.L
* Significant at 90 percent C.L.

EXHIBIT 2
Johnson Wax: ENHANCE (A)

EXHIBIT 3
Johnson Wax: Enhance (A)

ASSESSOR results
Product map

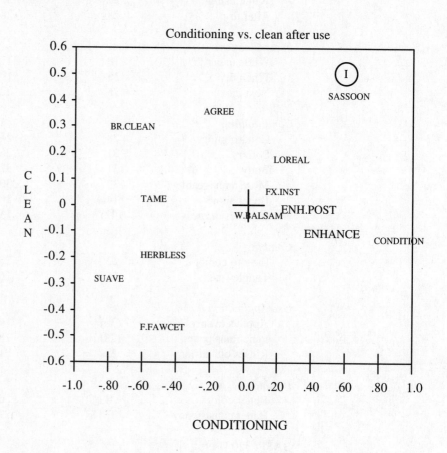

ENHANCE = Before positioning.
ENH.POST = After-use positioning.
I = Ideal brand positioning.

EXHIBIT 3 cont'd.
Johnson Wax: Enhance (A)

ASSESSOR results
Product map

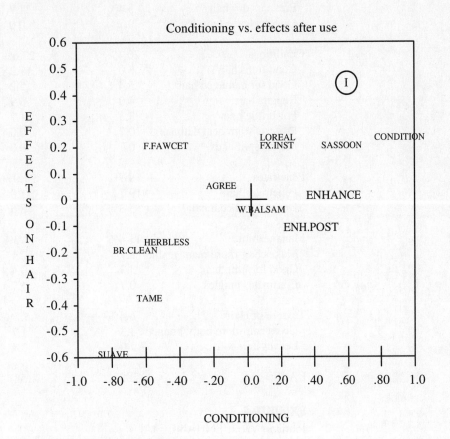

Conditioning vs. effects after use

ENHANCE = Before positioning.
ENH.POST = After-use positioning.
I = Ideal brand positioning.

ASSESSOR Results

Copy Point Recall

	Overall	Buyer	Nonbuyer
For Dry Hair			
Good for dry hair	46.8%	50.0%	46.1%
Nourishes hair	33.1	37.9	32.0
Prevents dry hair	5.4	1.7	6.2
Doesn't leave hair dry	0.7	0.0	0.8
Conditions	20.4%	27.6%	18.7%
Conditions hair	8.0	17.2	5.8
Good for damaged hair	5.4	5.2	5.4
Repairs hair	4.0	6.9	3.3
For brittle hair	3.3	1.7	3.7
Protects from heat damage	0.7	0.0	0.8
Mends split ends	0.7	0.0	0.8
Penetrates	19.7%	31.0%	17.0%
Penetrates hair	19.7	31.0	17.0
Doesn't just coat hair	3.3	8.6	2.1
Manageability	11.4%	17.2%	10.0%
Makes hair more manageable	7.7	12.1	6.6
Good for limp hair	3.3	3.4	3.3
Eliminates tangles	0.7	1.7	0.4
Texture of Hair	6.4%	5.2%	6.6%
Gives hair more body/bounce	4.3	1.7	5.0
Leaves hair soft	2.0	3.4	1.7
BASE:	(299)	(58)	(241)

EXHIBIT 4
Johnson Wax: ENHANCE (A)

Trial Comparison to all ASSESSOR-tested health and beauty aids products

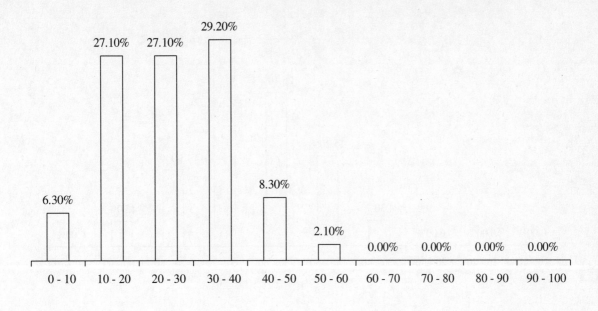

% TRIAL

Trial comparison to all ASSESSOR-tested products

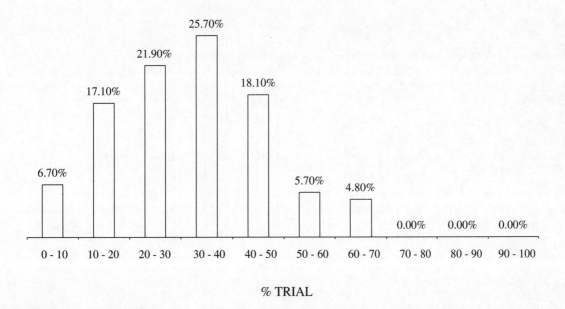

% TRIAL

EXHIBIT 5
Johnson Wax: ENHANCE (A)

Repeat comparison to all ASSESSOR-tested health and beauty aids products

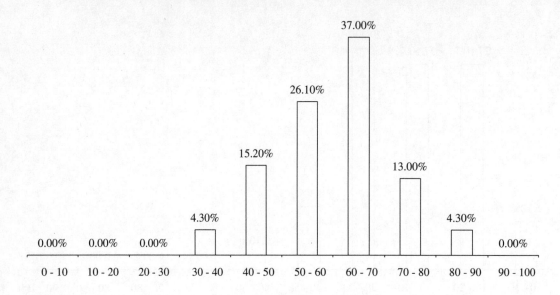

% REPEAT

Repeat comparison to all ASSESSOR-tested products

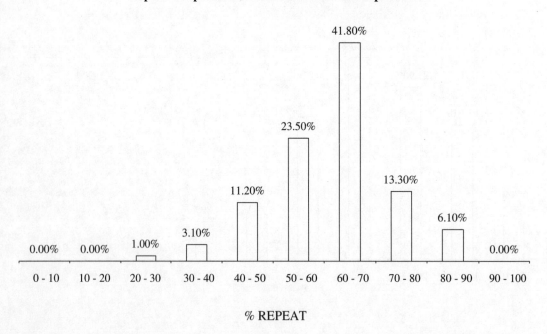

% REPEAT

EXHIBIT 6
Johnson Wax: ENHANCE (A)

ASSESSOR Results

Open-Ended Likes and Dislikes for Enhance (multiple mentions)

Open-Ended Likes	Overall	Repeaters	Nonrepeaters
Manageability	42%	48%	37%
Fragrance	21	14	27
Conditioning	11	12	10
Consistency	7	7	6
Application/ease of use	7	6	7
Penetrates	6	5	7
Clean	5	7	4
Base	(215)	(102)	(113)

Open-Ended Dislikes	Overall	Repeaters	Nonrepeaters
Manageability	24%	9%	38%
Fragrance	16	7	25
Conditioning	11	8	13
Consistency	1	3	0
Application/ease of use	1	1	1
Nothing Disliked	59	74	46
Base	(215)	(102)	(113)

EXHIBIT 7
Johnson Wax: ENHANCE (A)

ASSESSOR Results

After-Use Preferences

	*Percent Prefer Enhance**				
	1st	2nd	3rd	4th	(Base)
Dry Hair	38	32	17	7	(93)
Oily Hair	22	34	20	15	(41)
Normal	23	34	19	12	(69)
Total Sample	28	33	19	11	(215)
Total Sample (Agree)	54	26	12	2	(279)

Comparison to Regular Brand

	Among Triers		*Among Nontriers*	
	Enhance (%)	Agree (%)	Enhance (%)	Agree (%)
Much better	30	44	14	35
A little better	24	25	21	22
About the same	26	13	37	21
A little poorer	14	12	16	13
Much poorer	6	5	12	8
(Base)	(50)	(76)	(165)	(203)

*To be read, of the 93 respondents with dry hair, 38 percent rated Enhance as their favorite brand, for 32 percent it was their second choice, etc.

EXHIBIT 8
Johnson Wax: ENHANCE (A)

ASSESSOR Results
Market Share Prediction Trial Repeat Model

		Enhance	Agree
1.	Trial	23%	33%
2.	Awareness from advertising	.70	.70
3.	Distribution	.85	.85
4.	Net cumulative trial $[(1) \times (2) \times (3)]$	13.7%	19.6%
5.	Repeat	.60	.78
6.	Switchback	.16	.15
7.	Share of triers' choices $\left[\dfrac{6}{1+(6)-5}\right]$ (retention)	28.6%	41%
8.	Base share $[(4) \times (7)]$	3.9%	8.1

Preference Model

		Enhance	Agree
9.	Share for Enhance if everyone evokes it	27.5%	42.0%
10.	Estimated penetration [equal to (4)]	.14	.20
11.	Base share	3.8%	8.4%

EXHIBIT 9
Johnson Wax. ENHANCE (A)

ASSESSOR Results
*Estimated Incremental Share from Sampling
for 35 Million Sample Drop with 90 Percent Delivery*

Enhance vs. Agree

1. Number of samples delivered $[35M \times .9]$	31.5MM
2. Percent hitting target group	80%
3. Percent used*	60%
4. Number of samples used $[(1) \times (2) \times (3)]$	15. 12MM
5. Percent using samples* $[(4) \div 6OMM$ households]	25%
6. Overlap $[(5) \times$ Trial Rate Advertising (line 4, Ex. 9)]	3%
7. Net incremental trial $[(5)—(6)]$	22%
8. First repeat* (repeat among nonbuyers)	43%
9. Share of triers' choices (retention)	22%
10. Incremental share from sampling $[(7) \times (8) \times (9)]$	2.0%

*Measured through ASSESSOR callbacks.

**Calculated from formula $\dfrac{SB}{1 + SB - R}$ where SB is given in line 6 of Exhibit 9
and R is line 8 of this exhibit.

EXHIBIT 10
Johnson Wax: ENHANCE (A)

Approximate Health and Beauty Aid Industry Cost Structures*
(Indexed to Suggested Retail Price)

Suggested retail price	100
Expected shelf price (large 16 oz.)	83
(small 8 oz.)	73
Manufacturer's selling price	56
Cost of goods sold	21%

*These data are not supplied by the Johnson Wax Company, and are not known to be indicative of its actual costs. They are thought to reflect the average market cost structure closely enough to be helpful in the case discussion

EXHIBIT 11
Johnson Wax: ENHANCE (A)

APPENDIX A: JOHNSON WAX: ENHANCE (A)

Market share prediction models

The market share prediction in ASSESSOR was calculated from two independent models.

1. The trial and repeat model was based on:
   trial (measured in the laboratory store), repeat (measured in the callback interview), switchback (measured in multiple call backs).

2. The preference model was based on:
   after-use preferences for the test product (callback), the relationship between preferences and purchasing behavior in the specific market (laboratory).

A convergence between the predictions of these two models serves to increase confidence in the final market share prediction.

Trial and repeat model

The target market for the product is represented by the respondents chosen in the ASSESSOR test. In the test procedure, some respondents buy Enhance in the laboratory store. The proportion of buyers provides an estimate of trial, which must be corrected for probable awareness and availability in the actual marketplace. This corrected trial level is used to estimate the *cumulative* penetration the test product will achieve in the real market. Once cumulative penetration has been estimated, it is necessary to estimate the number of purchases that will be generated on an ongoing basis. This is called "retention," and is a function of the amount of brand switching that will occur.

At any given time, *t*, the purchasers of instant hair conditioners could be segmented into two groups—those who bought Enhance last time and those who didn't. What could happen at time *t+1* is illustrated below. Of those who bought Enhance at time *t*(X), some will also buy it at *t+1*, their next purchase occasion (*R*), whereas others will buy a competitive brand (X-R). At *t+1* some of those who had bought Enhance before *t*, but didn't buy it at *t*, will switch back (SB). Others will continue to purchase a competing brand.

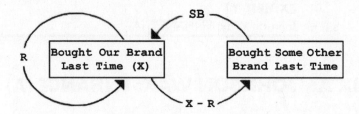

The customers who repeat plus those who don't repeat must equal 100 percent of those who bought the Enhance at their last purchase occasion. Similarly, switchback plus nonswitchback must equal 100 percent of those who bought Enhance at some time in the past, but not on the last purchase occasion. This is illustrated below.

Assume 100 consumers have tried Enhance. If the repeat rate is 81 percent[*] and the switchback rate 20 percent,[*] then on successive purchase occasions we would expect to observe the following:

Purchase Cycle	Eligible to Repeat =	Repeat (R) +	Do Not Repeat	Eligible to Switchback =	Switchback (SB) +	Do Not Switchback
1st	100.0	81.0	19.0	-	-	-
2nd	81.0	65.6	15.4	19.0	3.8	15.2
3rd	69.4	56.2	13.2	30.6	6.1	24.5
4th	62.3	50.5	11.8	37.7	7.5	30.2
5th	58.0	47.0	11.0	42.0	8.4	33.6
6th	55.4	44.9	10.5	44.6	8.9	35.7
7th	53.8	etc.	etc.	46.2	etc.	etc.

Now compute the percentage of triers who have purchased Enhance in any past period that will purchase it in the present period:

Purchase Cycle	Buy Enhance (R + SB)	Buy Other Brands
1st	81.0%	19.0%
2nd	69.4	30.6
3rd	62.3	37.7
4th	58.0	42.0
5th	55.4	44.6
6th	53.8	46.2
7th	52.8	47.2

*These values are used for illustration only.

Notice how the percentage of triers who will repurchase Enhance on a given occasion varies from the previous period value less and less as the number of purchase occasions increases. In fact, if we continued this sequence indefinitely, we would finally arrive at 51.3 percent, and this value would be called the retention rate. The value at which this process finally stabilizes is determined completely by the repeat rate and the switchback rate, so it is not necessary to calculate retention this way. This illustration is an example of what is called a two-stage Markov process. It is not critical to know any more about a two-stage Markov process to understand ASSESSOR than the formula for the final retention rate, or

$$S = \frac{SB}{1 + SB - R}.*$$

*SB and R are expected to be decimal fractions, i.e., .3 instead of 30 percent.

We can compute retention quite simply by using this equation. If, for example, $R = .50$ and $SB = .20$, what would the retention rate be? We might also note that in our example, after only seven purchase occasions, we were getting quite close to .513.

The last step in the calculation is to compute market share as the product of penetration (the percentage who will try the product) and retention (the share of ongoing purchases by those who have tried the product).

Market share = penetration × retention.

To summarize, the procedure used to predict market share with the trial and repeat model is:

1. Measure trial in the laboratory.
2. Multiply this trial rate by expected awareness and availability to compute penetration in a nonlaboratory situation.

3. Measure repeat and switchback in the callback phase.
4. Use Markov formula to compute retention.
5. Multiply penetration by retention to get market share.

Preference model

The preference model for predicting market share is considerably more sophisticated in its derivation than is the trial and repeat model, and much of the detail is beyond the scope of this case. Those interested are directed to the Silk and Urban article referenced earlier.

An overview of the process is as follows:

Analysis of existing brands

1. From a respondent's chip allocations, described in the case, a preference score $V(j)$ is computed for each brand j. These preference scores are computed using a technique borrowed from mathematical psychology.

2. The next step is to use these estimated brand-preference scores to compute the probability of a brand j being purchased by a respondent, $P(j)$. The conversion formula is

$$P(j) = \frac{\hat{V}(j)^{\beta}}{\sum_k \left[\hat{V}(k)\right]^{\beta}}$$

where the summation is over the j brands in the respondent's evoked set.

These steps are taken to estimate the probability of purchase for the brands that existed in the market before Enhance was introduced. In this formulation, β is an estimate of the degree of brand loyalty in the market.

3. The chip allocation procedure is repeated during the callback phase of the ASSESSOR process. β is assumed to remain unchanged with the introduction and trial of Enhance, so the following equation estimates the probability that a consumer would choose Enhance after having tried it.

$$L(i) = \frac{A(i)^{\beta}}{A(i)^{\beta} + \sum_k (A(k))^{\beta}}$$

where

$A(i)$ = estimated preference of the consumer for En-hance after having tried it.

$A(k)$ = estimated preference of the consumer for brand k after having tried Enhance.

$\hat{\beta}$ = a parameter to be estimated.

Summation is over the brands in the consumer's evoked set.

These predicted brand preferences are computed for each consumer separately and are conditional on the evoked set of the consumer. Expected market shares could be computed for the brands by aggregating the individual brand preferences and multiplying by the proportion of consumers who would include Enhance in their evoked sets.

$$M(j) = E(j) \frac{\sum_{k=1}^{N} L_k(j)}{N}$$

where

$M(j)$ = expected market share for brand j.

$E(j)$ = proportion of consumers for whom brand j will be in their evoked set.

$L_k(j)$ = predicted probability of purchase of brand j by consumer k.

N = Number of consumers.

Factor analysis and market maps

Exhibit 3 displayed graphic representations of the relative location of existing and "ideal" brands. They were drawn using a technique called factor analysis. What follows is an intuitive idea of what factor analysis seeks to do and how these "maps" are drawn.

Suppose we had a set of six questions about the attributes of instant hair conditioners like these:

BRAND:_____

Please rate the above brand of creme rinse, hair conditioner, or balsam conditioning product on each of the items below. The *best possible* rating you can give is a 7, the *poorest possible rating* is a 1. Circle *one* number for each item listed. Even if you have never used the product yourself, we would like your impression of what it is like based on what you have seen or heard.

		Best Possible Rating						Poorest Possible Rating
1.	Nourishes dry hair	7	6	5	4	3	2	1
2.	Leaves hair free of residue, film, and flakes	7	6	5	4	3	2	1
3.	Gives hair body and fullness	7	6	5	4	3	2	1
4.	Rinses out easily/completely	7	6	5	4	3	2	1
5.	Restores moisture	7	6	5	4	3	2	1
6.	Keeps control of split ends	7	6	5	4	3	2	1
7.	Leaves hair feeling soft and silky	7	6	5	4	3	2	1

Each respondent would answer these questions about Enhance and the other brands in her evoked set. We would like to see whether there are consistent patterns of response to these questions, e.g., questions 1 and 5 both seem to have something to do with moisture, so we might expect a respondent to give a brand either high or low ratings on both questions. The degree to which questions are answered in similar ways is measured by a number called the "correlation coefficient."

The correlation coefficient simply measures the extent to which two questions are answered above or below their respective averages. If every respondent in this test gave higher than average responses to two questions, the correlation coefficient for those two questions would be 1. If every respondent's answer to one question was higher than the average response while the answer to the other question was always lower than the average, the correlation coefficient for the two questions would be − 1. Correlation coefficients are always between these two extreme values. A correlation coefficient of 0 would mean there was no consistent pattern of response for the two questions.

Exhibit Al is a display of correlation coefficients for the responses to the seven questions presented above.

Hypothetical correlation between responses to selected questions[*]

Question	1	2	3	4	5	6	7
1	1.						
2	.2	1.					
3	.1	-.1	1.				
4	-.3	.9	-.1	1.			
5	.8	-.2	.2	-.2	1.		
6	.7	-.1	.1	-.1	.9	1.	
7	.2	-.1	.8	.2	.1	.3	1.

EXHIBIT Al

Johnson Wax: ENHANCE (A)

*These are not the real correlations, but have been redesigned to illustrate a point.

If we look at the correlations between the responses to the seven questions, we can see that some of them seem to be related, e.g., responses to questions 1, 5 and 6 seem to go together; 2 and 4; and 3 and 7 go together. Let's rewrite Exhibit Al grouping these questions together.

Rearranged correlations between selected questions

	Question	f_1 1	5	6	f_2 2	4	f_3 3	7
f_1	1	1.						
	5	.8	1.					
	6	.7	.9	1.				
f_2	2	.2	-.2	-.1	1.			
	4	-.3	-.2	-.1	.9	1.		
f_3	3	.1	.2	.1	-.1	-.1	1	
	7	.2	.1	.3	-.1	.2	.8	1

EXHIBIT A2

Johnson Wax: ENHANCE (A)

As you examine Exhibit A2, notice how we have three blocks of questions and in each block the correlations between responses to the questions are high, while the correlations between responses to questions in different blocks are low. Suppose we had a set of three uncorrelated variables. Their correlation array would look like this:

$$
\begin{array}{lll}
1. & & \\
0 & 1. & \\
0 & 0 & 1.
\end{array}
$$

That is what Exhibit A2 looks like if you look just at the blocks and not the individual questions. If we considered each block to represent a variable, we would have a new set of variables called factors: factor 1 would consist of questions 1, 5 and 6; factor 2 would consist of questions 2 and 4; and factor 3 would consist of questions 3 and 7.

What are these new variables? We have to name them ourselves, but their properties are given by the questions that define them. In the case, factor 1 was called "conditioning"; factor 2 "cleaning"; and factor 3 "manageability/effects."

This exercise has been quite simplistic; the groupings were clear from the start. This isn't always the case. Frequently many questions are asked to explore consumers' perceptions of products and the underlying dimensions of the market are by no means obvious. Or perhaps a manager would just like to see whether her perception of the market is backed up by objective measurement. In either of these situations factor analysis is very helpful.

What does factor analysis do? It finds the subgrouping of a large set of variables in which the original variables are highly correlated within the subgroup, or factor, and least correlated between factors.

How are graphs like those in Exhibit 3 drawn? That's fairly easy. Each of the original questions (variables) has a coefficient, $a_i.$, that relates it to the factor to which it belongs, much like a regression coefficient. So we can write:

$$ f_1 = a_0 + a_1 v_1 + a_2 v_2 + - - + a_k v_k $$

If we take the mean score attributed to each question for a given brand, we can use this equation to compute what is called the factor score f_1 for that brand. If we have three factors, we can compute three factor scores for each brand. Using these three factor scores, we can locate the brand in a three-dimensional space where each dimension represents a factor.

TUTORIAL FOR ADBUDG ADVERTISING BUDGETING (ADBUDG)

ADBUDG is an advertising sales response model developed by Little (1970) that uses judgmental inputs on market response to determine the best level and timing of advertising expenditures. This implementation of ADBUDG is designed to accompany the Blue Mountain Coffee case.

On the **Model** menu, select **Advertising Budgeting** (adbudg.xls) to see the **Introduction** screen.

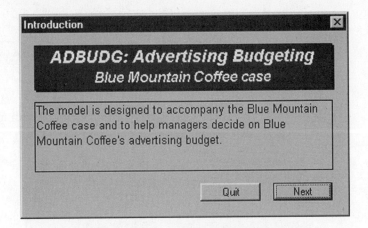

Click **Next** to bring up the **Main Menu**.

First choose **Calibration Based on Managerial Inputs** to calibrate parameter values for the ADBUDG Model.

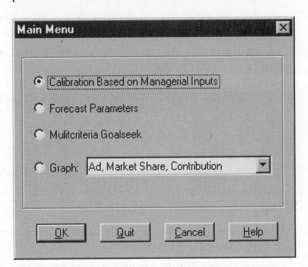

Provide the six input values for calibrating the response model. Then click **Calculate** to see the estimated parameters of the response function (c, d, and "Persistence"). The response curve changes as you change your input values.

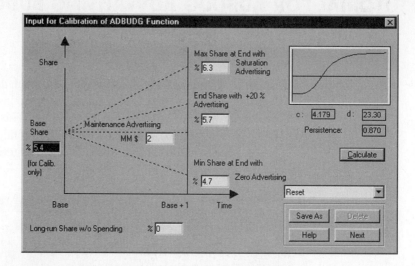

Whenever you have a set of inputs that you want to retrieve later, you can save them by clicking **Save As** and providing a name for the selected inputs.

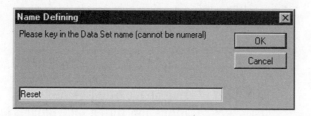

Once you have saved and named a set of inputs and the corresponding coefficient estimates, you can activate it by marking it in the drop-down menu (e.g., "Reset," as shown in the above example). Notice that the name of the data set for the current calibration will then be shown in the left hand corner of the main sheet.

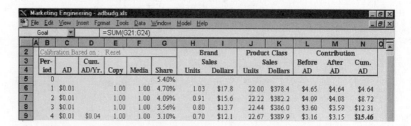

When you have finished the model calibration, click **Next** to get back to the main worksheet.

Next, on the **Model** menu, click **Main Menu** and choose **Forecast Analysis**; click **OK**.

Use the dialog box to set the parameters for the forecasting task. Except for "Initial Share Previous Period," the parameter values will apply to all 12 periods. If your values for "Copy Effectiveness" and "Media Efficiency" vary over time, you have to enter values for each period directly on the spreadsheet.

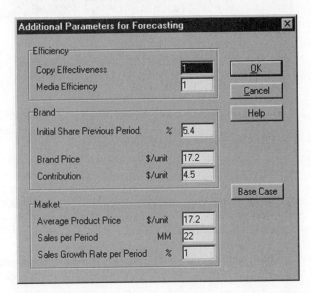

Click **Base Case** to restore the parameter values built into the ADBUDG spreadsheet.

Once you have entered all the data relevant to deciding the advertising budget, you can experiment by entering different values for each period and observing the effects on market share and profit. To try out alternative advertising plans enter these values directly on the sheet in the blue-colored columns. The table will then show how changes in such variables as advertising expense ("AD") and copy efficiency ("Copy") affect market share ("Share") and profit contribution ("Contribution") over time.

For instance in the partial screen shown, advertising expenditure ("AD") increases in the third period whereas "Media" (Media Efficiency) and "Copy" (Copy Effectiveness) drop, mitigating the effect of the increase in market share for this period.

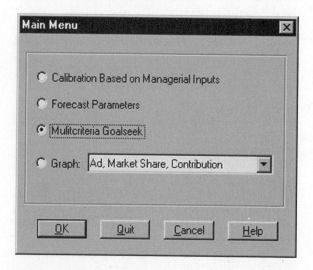

Period	AD	Cum. AD/Yr.	Copy	Media	Share	Brand Sales Units	Brand Sales Dollars
0					5.40%		
1	$2.00		1.00	1.00	5.40%	1.19	$20.4
2	$2.00		1.00	1.00	5.40%	1.20	$20.6
3	$2.50		0.90	0.95	5.51%	1.24	$21.3
4	$2.00	$8.50	1.00	1.00	5.50%	1.25	$21.4

Built into the ADBUDG spreadsheet is a Multicriteria Goalseek feature. On the **Model** menu, choose **Main Menu** and then click **Multicriteria Goalseek**. This feature uses Excel's Solver tool to help you decide the advertising budget.

You can set the goal criterion by providing decision weights for the short-term (four periods) and long-term (12 periods) market share and cumulative profit. Solver will then try to optimize the advertising budget subject to the constraints you impose on the yearly (four periods) budgets.

Weights can be any value. Their relative values are what count. For example in the picture short-term profit ("4") is twice as important as short-term share. You can give weights of 0 to objectives that are irrelevant in a specific decision situation.

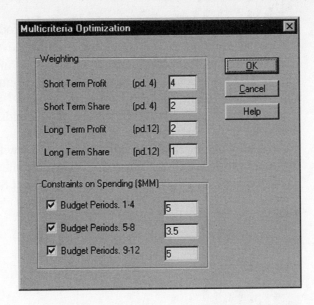

The information you provide is then passed into the worksheet. The objective function for the optimization procedure as implemented in ADBUDG is of a simple additive functional form—it is just one example of how to deal with multiple objectives. In this implementation the criteria (that is, profit and market share) are measured on different scales and have to be normalized before optimization. We do this by computing a scaled value for each criterion. We have chosen the scaling factor arbitrarily such that the scaled values for all of the criteria will be equal to 1.0 if the company freezes the advertising budget at the maintenance level of $2M.

NOTE: *Higher values of goals are more valuable than lower values. Clearly there are other ways to specify the multicriteria objective function.*

X	Marketing Engineering - adbudg.xls													_ 8 X

Goal | =SUM(G21:G24)

	B	C	D	E	F	G	H	I	J	K	L	M	N	Q
2	Calibration Based on :		Reset				**Brand**		**Product Class**			**Contribution**		
3	Per-		Cum.				**Sales**		**Sales**		**Before**	**After**	**Cum.**	
4	iod	AD	AD/Yr.	Copy	Media	Share	Units	Dollars	Units	Dollars	AD	AD	AD	
5	0					5.40%								
6	1	$0.01		1.00	1.00	4.70%	1.03	$17.8	22.00	$378.4	$4.65	$4.64	$4.64	
7	2	$0.01		1.00	1.00	4.09%	0.91	$15.6	22.22	$382.2	$4.09	$4.08	$8.72	
8	3	$0.01		1.00	1.00	3.56%	0.80	$13.7	22.44	$386.0	$3.60	$3.59	$12.31	
9	4	$0.01	$0.04	1.00	1.00	3.10%	0.70	$12.1	22.67	$389.9	$3.16	$3.15	**$15.46**	
10	5	$0.01		1.00	1.00	2.70%	0.62	$10.6	22.89	$393.8	$2.78	$2.77	$18.23	
11	6	$0.01		1.00	1.00	2.35%	0.54	$9.3	23.12	$397.7	$2.44	$2.43	$20.66	
12	7	$0.01		1.00	1.00	2.04%	0.48	$8.2	23.35	$401.7	$2.15	$2.14	$22.80	
13	8	$0.01	$0.04	1.00	1.00	1.78%	0.42	$7.2	23.59	$405.7	$1.89	$1.88	$24.68	
14	9	$0.01		1.00	1.00	1.55%	0.37	$6.3	23.82	$409.8	$1.66	$1.65	$26.33	
15	10	$0.01		1.00	1.00	1.35%	0.32	$5.6	24.06	$413.9	$1.46	$1.45	$27.77	
16	11	$0.01		1.00	1.00	1.17%	0.28	$4.9	24.30	$418.0	$1.28	$1.27	$29.05	
17	12	$0.01	$0.04	1.00	1.00	1.02%	0.25	$4.3	24.54	$422.2	$1.13	$1.12	**$30.16**	
18											Note: All $ are in millions.			
19	**MULTICRITERIA**			**Scaled**	**Weighted**			**Subject to**						
20	**GOALSEEK**		Weights	Values	Values	**GOAL**		Constraints						
21	Short Term Profit		4	1.12789	4.51157	7.22563								
22	Short Term Share		2	0.57387	1.14775			AD Budget 1st Year		5				
23	Longterm Profit		2	0.68866	1.37732			AD Budget 2nd Year		3.5				
24	Longterm Share		1	0.18899	0.18899			AD Budget 3rd Year		5				
25														
26														

| wshData / |

Ready   Sum=7.22563

Sometimes the optimization procedure produces an apparently suboptimal solution for allocating the ad budget over time—Solver may have settled on a local maximum. In other cases, running Solver may not lead to convergence at all. You may sometimes obtain a (better) new result by providing different starting values for the advertising expenditures in each period. Please see the appendix to Chapter 2 in the text.

If you want to conduct additional analyses with Solver directly on the main worksheet, you must first unprotect the spreadsheet: on the **Tools** menu select **Protection** and then **Unprotect Sheet**.

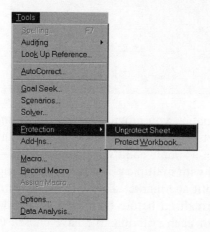

Go to the **Model** menu, choose **Main Menu**, select **Graph,** and click **OK** to view a chart showing your advertising plan and its impact on market share and contribution.

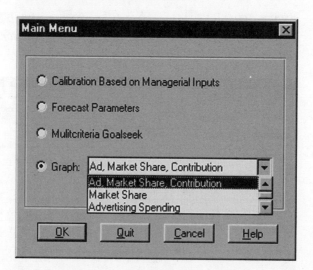

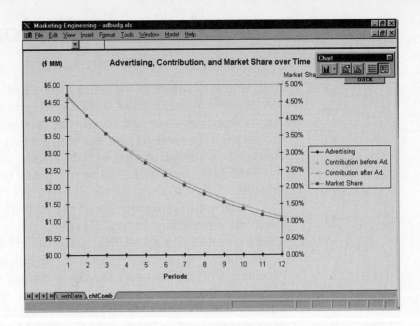

Reference

Little, John D. C. 1970, "Models and managers: The concept of a decision calculus," *Management Science*, Vol. 16, No. 8, pp. B466-B485.

BLUE MOUNTAIN COFFEE COMPANY CASE[*]

Blue Mountain's share of the coffee market had slipped badly during the past decades, although brand share has recently stabilized. The advertising manager was concerned because the increased advertising budget he had obtained the previous year had been cut back in midyear because top management was dissatisfied with the results. In addition, he thought it was vital to increase Blue Mountain's share so it would not lose distributors.

The advertising manager faced the problem of preparing and justifying an advertising budget for the coming fiscal year. He was considering using the ADBUDG model to help him.

In May 1994, Reginald Van Tassle, advertising manager for the Blue Mountain Coffee Company, tugged at his red mustache and contemplated the latest market share report. This was a dismal moment. "Blimey," he muttered, "I've got to do something to turn this darned market around before it's too late for Blue Mountain and for me. But I can't afford another mistake like last year's..."

Reginald Van Tassle had been hired by James Anthoney, vice president of marketing for Blue Mountain, in the summer of 1992. Prior to that time he had worked for companies in the Netherlands and in Singapore and had gained a reputation as a sharp and effective advertising executive. Now, in the spring of 1994, he was fighting to reverse a long-term downward trend in Blue Mountain's market position.

Indeed, Lucinda Pogue (the president and a major stockholder of the Blue Mountain Company) had been dismayed to hear that Blue Mountain Coffee's share of the market was dropping back toward 5.4 percent where it had been a year before. She had remarked rather pointedly to Reggie that if market share and profitability did not improve during the next fiscal year she might have to take "some rather drastic actions" and had murmured something about "a ticket back to Singapore."

Blue Mountain's market position

Blue Mountain Coffee was an old, established company in the coffee business, with headquarters in Squirrel Hill, Pennsylvania. Its market area included the East Coast and Southern regions of the United States and a fairly large portion of the Midwest. During its "good old days" in the 1950s, the company had enjoyed as much as 15 percent of the market in these regions. The brand had been strong and growing, and the company sponsored such popular radio and TV programs as "The Blue Mountain Comedy Hour" and "Blue Mountain Capers."

[*] This is a revised version of a case written by Professors William F. Massy, David B. Montgomery, and Charles B. Weinberg which appeared in G.S. Day, G.J. Eskin, D.B. Montgomery, and C.B. Weinberg, *Planning: Cases in Computer and Model Assisted Marketing* (Scientific Press, Redwood City, California, 1973). The case was revised by Gary L. Lilien and Katrin Starke. The new revised software was designed by Katrin Starke and John Lin under the supervision of Professor Gary L. Lilien.

Blue Mountain began to experience some difficulties in the 1960s: TV production and time costs rose and competition stiffened as many other regional old-line companies were absorbed by giant marketers, such as General Foods and Proctor & Gamble. Furthermore, the advent of freeze-dried products and the increasing promotion and popularity of instant coffee put additional pressure on Blue Mountain which stuck with its traditional ground vacuum-packed coffee as its only line.

Nonetheless, Blue Mountain's troubles had only started. U.S. coffee consumption dropped steadily in the 1970s and 1980s after peaking in 1962 when 74 percent of Americans drank about three cups per day. By the end of the '80s only about half of all Americans drank coffee and they were drinking an average of 1.7 cups per day. At the same time, the coffee market became more oligopolistic, and the "Big Three," i.e., Procter & Gamble (Folgers), Kraft General Foods (Maxwell House), and Nestle (Nescafe) together controlled over three quarters of the national market. Coffee was considered a commodity and competition was mainly on price. Under these circumstances, Blue Mountain's share slipped from 12 percent at the beginning of the 1980s to about five and half percent at the end of the decade.

Since then, however, its share has been fairly stable. Management attributed this to a hard-core group of loyal buyers combined with an active (and expensive) program of consumer promotions and price-off deals to the trade. Jim Anthoney, the vice president of marketing, believed that they had halted the erosion of share just in time. A little more slippage, he said, and Blue Mountain would begin to lose distributors. This would have been the beginning of the end for this venerable company.

Operation breakout

When Lucinda Pogue became president in 1990, her main objective was to halt the decline in market position and, if possible, to bring about a turnaround. She had succeeded in the first objective. However, she and Anthoney agreed the strategy they were using—intensive consumer and trade promotion—would not win back much of the lost market share.

They both thought that they needed to increase consumer awareness of the Blue Mountain brand and develop more favorable attitudes about it to improve its market position. This could be done only through advertising. Since the company produced a quality product (it was noticeably richer and more aromatic than many competing coffees), they thought that a strategy of increasing advertising weight might succeed. They initiated a search for a new advertising manager, eventually hiring Reginald Van Tassle.

After a period of familiarizing himself with the Blue Mountain Company, the American coffee market, and the advertising scene, Van Tassle began developing a plan to revitalize Blue Mountain's advertising program. First, he released the company's current advertising agency and requested proposals from a number of others interested in obtaining the account. While he told them that the amount of advertising might increase somewhat, he emphasized that he was most concerned with the kind of appeal and copy execution. The company and the various agencies agreed that nearly all the advertising budget should go into spot television. Network sponsorship was difficult because of the regional character of Blue Mountain's markets, and no other medium could match the impact of TV for a product like coffee.

The team from Aardvark Associates, Inc., won the competition with an advertising program built around the theme "Blue Mountain Pure." Aardvark recommended a 30 percent increase in the quarterly advertising budget to give the new program a fair trial. After considerable negotiation with Lucinda Pogue and Jim Anthoney and further discussion with the agency, Van Tassle compromised on a 20 percent increase. The new campaign was to start in the autumn of 1993, which was the second quarter of the company's 1994 fiscal year (the fiscal year started July 1,1993 and would end June 30, 1994). It was dubbed "operation breakout."

Blue Mountain had been advertising at an average rate of $2.0 million per quarter for the last several years. This seemed to be enough to maintain market share at about its current level of 5.4 percent. Neither Reggie Van Tassle nor Jim Anthoney anticipated that competitors' expenditures would change much during the next few years regardless of any increase in Blue Mountain's advertising.

One basis for the 1994 plans was the expectation that the quarterly spending level of $2 million (ignoring several variations) would be enough to maintain market share at its current 5.4 percent level. Reggie felt that increasing advertising by 20 percent would increase market share to six percent.

This projected result sounded pretty good to Lucinda Pogue, especially after she had consulted the company's controller. The controller wrote her a memorandum about the advertising budget increase and its results (Exhibit 1).

August 1, 1993   CONFIDENTIAL MEMO

To: Lucinda Pogue, President
From: I. Figure, Controller
Subject: Proposed 20 percent increase in advertising

I think that Reggie's proposal to increase advertising by 20 percent (from a quarterly rate of $2.0 million to one of $2.4 million) is a good idea. He predicts that we will achieve a market share of six percent, compared to our current 5.4 percent. I can't comment about the feasibility of this assumption: that's Reggie's business, and I assume he knows what he's doing. I can tell you, however, that such a result would be highly profitable.

As you know, the wholesale price of coffee has been running about $17.20 per 12-pound case. Deducting our average retail advertising and promotional allowance of $1.60 per case and our variable costs of production and distribution of $11.10 per case leaves an average gross contribution to fixed costs and profit of $4.50 per case. Figuring a total market of about 22 million cases per quarter and a share change from 0.054 to 0.060 (a 0.006 increase), we would have the following increase in gross contribution:

change in gross contribution   = $\$4.50 \times 22$ million $\times .006$
= $\$0.60$ million

By subtracting the amount of the increase in advertising expense due to the new program and then dividing by this same quantity, we get the advertising payout rate:

Advertising Payout Rate $= \dfrac{\text{change in gross contribution - change in ad expense}}{\text{change in ad expense}}$

$= \dfrac{\$0.10 \text{ million}}{\$0.20 \text{ million}} = 0.50$

That is, we can expect to make $\$.50$ in net contribution for each extra dollar spent on advertising. You can see that as long as this quantity is greater than zero (at which point the extra gross contribution just pays for the extra advertising), increasing our advertising is a good deal.

I think Reggie has a good thing going here, and my recommendation is to go ahead. Incidentally, the extra funds we should generate in net contribution (after advertising expense is deducted) should help to relieve the cash flow bind which I mentioned last week. Perhaps we will be able to maintain the quarterly dividend after all.

EXHIBIT 1

Reggie had, of course, warned that the hoped-for six percent share was not a sure thing and, in any case, that it might take more than one quarter before the company saw the full effects of the new advertising program.

The new advertising campaign broke as scheduled on October 1, 1993, the first day of the second quarter of the fiscal year. Reggie was a bit disappointed with Aardvark's commercials and a little worried by the early reports from the field. The store audit report of market share for July, August, and September showed only a fractional increase in share over the 5.4 percent of the previous period. Nevertheless, Van Tassle thought that, given a little time, things would work out and the campaign would eventually reach its objective.

The October, November, and December market share report came through in mid-January. It showed Blue Mountain's share of the market to be 5.6 percent. On January 21, 1994, Reggie received a carbon copy of a memorandum to Lucinda from I. Figure (Exhibit 2).

January 20, 1994   MEMO
To: Lucinda Pogue, President
From: I. Figure, Controller
Subject: Failure of Advertising Program

       I am most alarmed at our failure to achieve the market-share target projected by Reginald Van Tassle. The 0.2 point increase in market share we achieved in October-December is not sufficient to return the cost of the increased advertising. Ignoring the month of October, which obviously represents a start-up period, a 0.2 point increase in share generates only $200,000 in extra gross contribution per quarter. This must be compared to the $400,000 we have expended in extra advertising. The advertising payout rate is thus only -0.50: much less than the break-even point.

       I know Mr. Van Tassle expects shares to increase again next quarter, but he has not been able to say by how much. The new program projects an advertising expenditure increase per quarter of $400,000 over last year's winter-quarter level. I don't see how we can continue to make these expenditures without a better prospect of return on our investment.

cc: R. J. Anthoney
        R. Van Tassle

EXHIBIT 2

       On Monday, January 24, Jim Anthoney telephoned Reggie to say that Lucy wanted to review the new advertising program immediately. Later that week, after several rounds of discussion during which Reggie failed to convince Lucy and Jim that the program would eventually be successful, they decided to return to fiscal 1993 advertising levels. Reggie renegotiated the TV spot contracts and by the middle of February had cut advertising back toward the $2 million per quarter rate. Aardvark Associates complained that the efficiency of their media buy suffered during February and March, because of Blue Mountain's abrupt reduction in advertising expenditure. However, they were unable to say by how much. Blue Mountain also set the spring 1994 rate at the normal level of $2.0 million. Market share for the quarter beginning in January turned out to be slightly over 5.6 percent, while that for the one starting in April was about 5.5 percent.

Planning for fiscal year 1995

In mid-May of 1994, Reginald Van Tassle faced the problem of recommending an advertising budget for the four quarters of fiscal 1995. He was already very late in dealing with this assignment, since the company would have to up its media buys soon if it was to effect any substantial increase in weight during the summer quarter of 1994. Alternatively, it would have to act fast to reduce advertising expenditures below its tentatively budgeted "normal" level of $2.0 million.

During the past month, Van Tassle had spent a lot of time reviewing the difficulties of fiscal 1994. He remained convinced that a 20 percent increase in advertising should produce somewhere around a six percent market-share level. He based this partly on hunch and partly on studies performed by academic and business market researchers.

One lesson he had learned from his unfortunate experience the previous year was that presenting too optimistic a picture to top management was unwise. On the other hand, if he had made a conservative estimate he might not have obtained approval for the program. Besides, he still believed that the effect of advertising on share was greater than implied by the company's performance in the autumn of 1993. This judgment should be a part of top managers' information set when they evaluated his proposal. Alternatively, if they doubted his judgment and had good reasons to do so, he wanted to know about them. After all, Lucinda Pogue and Jim Anthoney had been in the coffee business a lot longer than he had, and they were pretty savvy.

Perhaps the problem lay in his assessment of the speed with which the new program would take hold. He had felt it would take a little time but had not tried to pin it down further. That's pretty hard, after all. He had said nothing very precise about this to management. Could he blame Mr. Figure for adopting the time horizon he did?

As a final complicating factor, Van Tassle had just received a report from Aardvark Associates about the quality of the advertising copy and the appeals used the previous autumn and winter. Contrary to expectations, these ads rated only about 0.95 on a scale that rated an "average ad" at 1.0. These tests were based on the so-called theater technique, in which the agency inserted various spots into a filmed "entertainment" program and determined their effects on the subjects' choices in a lottery designed to simulate purchasing behavior. Fortunately, the ads currently being shown rated about 1.0 on the same scale. A new series of ads scheduled for showing during the autumn, winter, and spring of 1995 appeared to be much better. The agency could not undertake theater testing until it completed production during the summer, but experts in the agency were convinced that the new ads would rate at least 1.15. Reggie was impressed with these ads, but he knew that such predictions were often optimistic. In the meantime, he had to submit a budget request for all four quarters of fiscal 1995 to management within the next week.

To help him with this problem, Reggie decided to use a marketing planning model, an adaptation of Little's (1970) ADBUDG model.

The marketing planning model

After describing his problem to Jill Stillman, director of research for Blue Mountain, Van Tassle asked Stillman to give him a list of the basic inputs the model required. After much tugging at his red mustache and several conferences with Stillman, Van Tassle arrived at a preliminary set of estimates for the basic inputs (Exhibit 3). Only the estimates relating to market share and the advertising plan itself required a lot of head scratching.

Market share at start of period	5.4%
Maintenance advertising per period ($MM)	2.0
Market share at period end with	
Saturation advertising	6.3%
20 percent increase in advertising	5.7%
No advertising	4.7%
Market share in long run with no advertising	0.0%
Copy effectiveness	1.0
Media efficiency	1.0
Previous period market share	5.4%
Brand price ($/unit)	$17.20
Contribution ($/unit)	$4.50
Average product price ($/Unit)	$17.20
Product sales per period (MM cases)	22.0
Product sales growth rate per period	1.0%

EXHIBIT 3
ADBUDG basic input values

After some thought Van Tassle concluded that, if his advertising budget were reduced to zero, he would lose perhaps half his market share in the next year or about an eighth of it in the next quarter. He settled on the figure 4.7 percent as the market share at the end of the first quarter with no advertising. Similarly, he arrived at the figures of 6.3 percent for a saturation advertising program and 5.7 percent for a 20 percent increase in advertising (figuring it would take him about three quarters of this 20 percent increase to reach a six percent share).

He then began experimenting with different values for his market share estimate and media—and copy-effectiveness estimates. He was hoping he could use the results of his analysis to explain past results and to help prepare his 1995 plan. He constructed Exhibit 4—a table of events—to help him recall the history of the program.

ADBUDG Period	Month	Yr	Fiscal Year 94/95	AD Budget	Copy and Media	Market Share	Events
0						5.4 %	
1	July	93	1st qtr	$2.00	1.00	5.4 %	
1	Aug.	93	(FY 94)				
1	Sept.	93					
2	Oct.	93	2nd qtr	$2.40	0.95	5.6 %	Operation "Breakout"
2	Nov.	93					
2	Dec.	93					
3	Jan.	94	3rd qtr	$2.10	0.95	5.6 %	Budget cut
3	Feb.	94					
3	Mar.	94					
4	Apr.	94	4th qtr	$2.00	1.00	5.5 %	Copy effectiveness up
4	May	94				→ **5.4 %**	**Now!**
4	June	94					
1	July	94			1.00		
2	Oct.	94			>1.00		

EXHIBIT 4
Blue Mountain table of events

Recent developments: The U.S. coffee market in transition

Even though advertising budgeting was preoccupying her, Pogue kept thinking that in the light of recent trends more could be done to help Blue Mountain's long-term position in the coffee market. What for a long time seemed to be a rather static market was now undergoing profound structural changes. In recent years, the coffee bean had had a renaissance as consumption in the U.S. slowly climbed after more than two decades of decrease—but Blue Mountain, along with such other traditional roasters as Procter & Gamble, Philip Morris, and Nestle, had been unable to capitalize on this trend. The growth was primarily due to specialty brews and the expansion of coffee and coffee accessory chains, such as Starbucks Coffee Company of Seattle. Pogue was wary that specialty coffees, growing at about 20 percent annually, continued to grab market share at the expense of supermarket ground coffee sales. In fact, according to the latest figures, Starbucks, other regional cafes, and the gourmet, whole-bean roasters had obtained nearly a quarter of the multibillion coffee market.

Pogue was wondering how best to respond to these changes and worried that Blue Mountain might already have missed the tide. It did not seem to her that the price-cutting and couponing approach of her major competitors in the ground coffee market was the answer. Pogue had been carefully following the development of Starbucks, which was holding on to its premier position in the specialty coffee business despite the increasing level of competition and imitation it encountered. Its business design differed significantly from Blue Mountain's, as Starbucks also operated a national mail order program to complement its hundreds of corporate-owned stores and its collaboration with Barnes & Noble bookstores, Nordstroms, and fine restaurants. According to a study Pogue came across, consumers of gourmet coffees were college-educated 25- to 45-year-olds who earned over $35,000 a year. They drank gourmet coffee for its prestige as well as for its taste. Gourmet coffee with price tags 80 to 100 percent higher than canned coffee was viewed as an affordable luxury. What could be a successful business model for Blue Mountain? Pogue still heard the warning of an industry analyst in her ear: "It's just like cars. Generation Xers wouldn't be caught in their fathers' Oldsmobiles, and they're not going to drink their parents' coffee brands. The traditional marketers have to come up with new appeals; the same old grind isn't going to make it."

EXERCISES

1. State precisely what you think the objectives of Blue Mountain's 1994 advertising plan should have been. Were these Van Tassle's objectives? Lucinda Pogue's? I. Figure's?

2. Evaluate the results obtained from the 1994 (FY) advertising funds. What do you think the results would have been if the 20 percent increase had been continued for the entire year?

3. What should Van Tassle propose as an advertising budget for 1995? How should he justify this budget to top management?

4. How should Van Tassle deal with the issues of seasonality and copy quality?

5. Comment on the uses and limitations of the ADBUDG model as a decision aid for this case and more generally as an advertising-budgeting decision aid.

TUTORIAL FOR COMMUNICATIONS PLANNING (ADVISOR)

The Advisor models offer descriptive information on the product and marketing characteristics that are most important in determining the level of marketing spending for industrial products. While the Advisor Excel spreadsheet is designed to accompany the Convection Company Case, it is more general and can provide budgeting guidelines for marketing other products as well.

On the **Model** menu, select **Communications Planning** (advisor.xls) to see the **Introduction** screen.

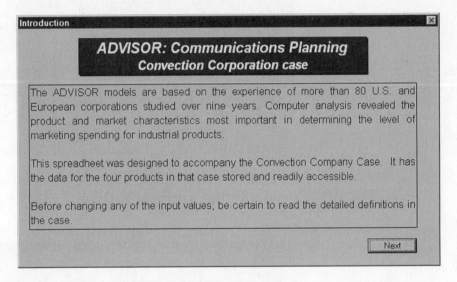

Click **Next** to get to the **Main Menu.** This is the **Main Menu** with no data (Empty Product).

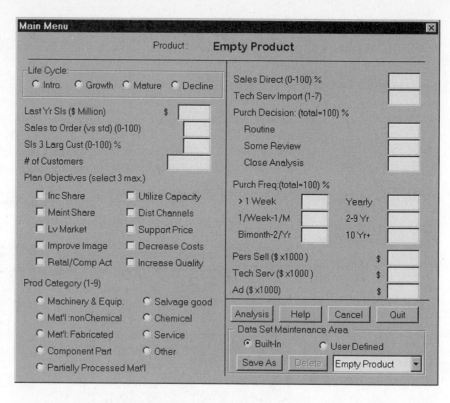

Select the **Built In** option in the Data Set Maintenance Area to view the data for the Convection Company case. Click the arrow to the right to select the different products pertaining to this case.

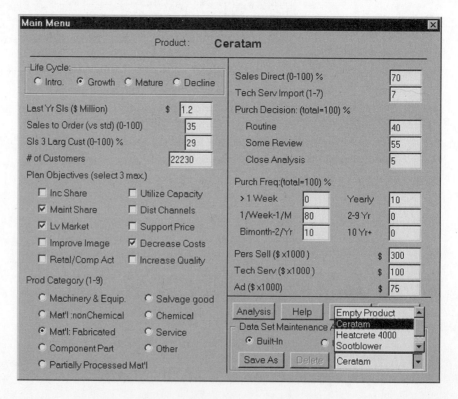

Once you have selected a case, click **Analysis** to get the following par report. A par report compares your budgeting practices with the norm, that is, the practices of other companies with similar products.

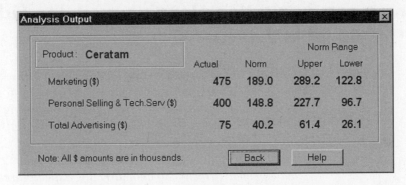

Click **Back** to go to the **Main Menu** dialog that contains the product data. You can then change input data and redo the analysis. Click **Save As** in the **Main Menu** to save your new data set as a **User Defined** product.

References

Lilien, Gary L. 1993, "Convection Corporation case," *Marketing Management: Analytic Exercises for Spreadsheets,* second edition, Boyd and Fraser, Danvers, Massachusetts.

Lilien, Gary L. 1979, "Advisor 2: Modeling the marketing mix for industrial products," *Management Science*, Vol. 25, No. 2 (February), pp. 191-204.

Lilien, Gary L. and Weinstein, David 1984, "An international comparison of the determinants of industrial marketing expenditures," *Journal of Marketing*, Vol. 48, No. 1, pp. 46-53.

CONVECTION CORPORATION CASE[*]

Using a communication planning model to aid industrial marketing budget decisions

One of Paul Warren's major tasks following his appointment as group marketing coordinator at Convection Corporation, was to develop a systematic approach to communications budgeting. The assignment was not an abstract exercise, however, since he was also to present and support his budget and media recommendations for Convection products in the annual budget review. The task was further complicated by a top management directive to cut marketing expenditures by one-third.

Background

Convection Corporation (CC) is a midwestern corporation founded in 1880 to produce steam boilers for use in the nearby northern Indiana steel mills. This initial product provided the experience base and opportunity to develop a more general expertise in high-temperature production process machinery and high pressure hydraulic systems. Over the years, CC developed a diverse product line that served a wide range of industrial customers.

CC's sales reached the $2 billion level in 1997[†] despite increased competition and economic uncertainty in the utility industry, one of its major markets. During this same time period, CC sought to establish a more systematic approach to marketing. Part of this process included a reorganization that created Mr. Warren's position.

In the new organization, CC marketing was directed by a senior vice president for marketing. Reporting to him were three vice presidents, each of whom supervised a number of group marketing coordinators. A number of brand managers reported to the group marketing managers. This new organization replaced the production line-oriented structure that had evolved over the years. Roles and responsibilities of the various managers were still somewhat fluid.

Mr. Warren had been given the task of recommending and justifying the marketing and communications programs for four related products managed by three product managers, Vera Stapleton, Stan Bloch, and Wayne Collins.

Vera Stapleton was the product manager for Heatcrete 4000 and Ceratam. Her background included both field sales experience and a period of time in the controller's office. Stan Bloch had been with the company for 22 years. He had done some of the development work for the Flowclean Sootblower in conjunction with several large boiler

---

[*] This is an updated and abridged version of a case by the same name by Gary L. Lilien and Darral G. Clark. Copyright © 1982 by the President and Fellows of Harvard College.

[†] At the time of this case, it is the end of the third quarter (both calendar and fiscal) 1997. The 1997 "actual" figures are projections from three quarters of actual data and one quarter of forecast data.

manufacturers. For the past four years he had been selling Flowclean and based on this considerable knowledge of its application, had been appointed product manager. Wayne Collins had joined the company three years earlier after completing an advanced degree in materials science. His first assignment had been research on improving the corrosion resistance of conventional steel alloys, and the first application of his work was the Corlin valve.

Mr. Warren and his three product managers directed the marketing efforts for four industrial equipment products. The products varied in the technical nature of the selling task, size of the sale, and age of the products.

Heatcrete 4000

Heatcrete 4000 is a castable concrete refractory material used in the construction of high-temperature furnaces, chemical reactors, and other process applications. It can be used both as a mortar for fired brick refractories and for casting special shapes and had been available from CC for a number of years. Similar products were offered by full-line refractory product manufacturers. Three new competitors had entered the refractory supply business during the past year, bringing the total number of competitors with over 1 percent market share to 28. Heatcrete 4000 sales usually occurred in conjunction with the sale of other refractory products. Ms. Stapleton estimated that there were approximately 600 Heatcrete customers that were reached through a direct sales effort (50 percent of sales) or through about 100 distributors. Heatcrete salespeople reported that they usually dealt with about three different people in a customer company involved in a given purchase decision. Industry refractory product demand in 1988 was forecast at $230 million and a growth rate of about 8 percent was anticipated. Industry sales of Heatcrete-type products were forecast to be $63 million in 1988.

Ms. Stapleton was concerned about scattered sales reports of customer dissatisfaction with Heatcrete 4000 as well as its low market share. She felt that some research into possible product problems should be undertaken, and if no problems existed or if existing problems could be solved, advertising and promotion for Heatcrete 4000 could probably reach 5 percent of sales before it would start to cut into margins.

Ms. Stapleton submitted a tentative budget for Heatcrete 4000 as follows:

	1998 (plan)	1997 (actual)
Heatcrete sales	$632,000	$601,000
Market share	1%	1%

Marketing Expenses	Amount	Percent of Sales	Dollar Amount	Percent of Sales
Personal selling	$28,000	4.4%	$20,000	3.3%
Technical service	5,300	0.8%	3,900	0.6%
Advertising	25,000	4.0%	20,000	3.3%

Ceratam

Ceratam is a ceramic material used for coating machine tool cutting inserts. Beginning in the mid-seventies, ceramics found increasing use in cutting inserts for lathes because they provided reduced friction and temperature at the tool-work interface. However, recent trends in the machine tool industry and heavy manufacturing had not been favorable and Ceratam was not yet profitable.

Making a case for coated cutting inserts required new esoteric arguments, and most end users were concerned that the coating would substantially affect their machining operations. Vera Stapleton felt that "the substantial marketing effort required to gain acceptance for the product has seriously cut into our margin. We are not sure where the market is going. We would like to hold our position and try to reduce selling costs on the one hand, but if this technology catches on we want to have a reasonable market position. We cut marketing expenses from 46.7 percent of sales in 1996 to 39.5 percent in 1997. I think we should hold marketing under 40 percent of sales to prevent further erosion of our margin."

Ceratam had about 2,000 potential customers and 40 to 50 independent distributors. About 35 percent of Ceratam orders were produced to order, which somewhat limited the role of distributors. Ms. Stapleton felt that the decision process required for an initial Ceratam purchase was complex and estimated it to require sales contact with about 11 people at each buying location. Industry sales growth was 11 percent in 1997 and industry sales for the same year were $5 million. Ceratam had 3 competitors with over 1 percent market share.

Ms. Stapleton's tentative Ceratam budget was as follows:

	1998 (plan)	1997 (actual)
Sales	$1,200,000	$800,000
Market share	24%	18%

Marketing Expenses	Amount	Percent of Sales	Dollar Amount	Percent of Sales
Personal selling	$300,000	25.0%	$250,000	31.0%
Technical service	100,000	8.3%	50,000	6.3%
Advertising	75,000	6.3%	75,000	7.5%

Flowclean Sootblowers

Due to environmental pressures and increased fuel costs during the 1970's and thereafter, sootblowers were either designed into or planned to be retrofitted to virtually every large-scale fossil fuel steam boiler because they increase efficiency, reduce the need for cleaning, and reduce boiler downtime. Since sootblowers extract airborne heavy particulates from the combustion chamber, they had been adapted recently for pollution control and combustion efficiency purposes. Convection's current line of sootblowers was developed about 25 years ago and had only been slightly modified since. There were about 1,000 customers in the marketplace. Salespeople visit about five decision-makers at each location. Selling a sootblower requires working the system manufacturer as well as the buyer to understand the design parameters of the complete boiler system.

Convection was the largest of only three companies in the market. The applications are so technical that only a company with a complete understanding of boiler systems can manufacture sootblowers. Mr. Bloch explained the selling situation as follows: "When I was selling sootblowers, everybody knew me and knew that I understood the product. Sometimes I would talk to final users because the sootblowers would have to work with their existing equipment or special environmental protection procedures. In such cases it was nice to be able to show these people our ads in the key industry publications, to let them know that we were the biggest. It was always good to have some brochures that let people know that Convection was a major firm with an excellent reputation for engineering. Beyond that, it was the product specs and applications engineering that sold the product."

In 1997, Flowclean sales were $23.5 million, which represented a 50 percent market share. Forecasts for 1998 presented a muddled picture. The utilities, a major market segment, appeared to have a declining rate of expansion in generating capacity. At the same time, many facilities were converting from gas to coal. Exactly how these two oppositely directed forces would balance out for sootblower demand was uncertain.

Mr. Bloch's tentative budget for Flowclean was as follows:

	1998 (plan)	1997 (actual)
Sales	$24,160,000	$23,500,000
Market share	50%	50%

Marketing Expenses	Amount	Percent of Sales	Dollar Amount	Percent of Sales
Personal selling	$2,338,000	9.7%	$2,166,000	9.2%
Technical service	314,000	1.3%	304,000	1.3%
Advertising	248,000	1.0%	388,000	1.7%

Corlin Valve

The Corlin valve is made from a special alloy that provides higher resistance to corrosion than was previously possible with stainless steel. The Corlin valve was felt to have a substantial potential market since it could replace existing corrosion-resistant valves that were much more expensive. Some applications involving highly corrosive substances still required existing corrosion-resistant valves. But for a wide variety of uses, the Corlin valve offered much better performance per dollar.

It hadn't been easy to convince chemical companies to switch to the Corlin valve. Mr. Collins said: "I think we need to convince customers that our product can meet their technical performance requirements. A lot of engineers just expect that any valve for corrosives must be titanium-lined. I think we should get some articles in the technical press with some specific test results for Corlin in comparison with other materials."

The market for corrosive-resistant valves was estimated at $23 million in 1996, and was growing at 15 percent. There were nearly 4,000 potential customers. Selling the Corlin valve usually required dealing with about five different people at each potential customer firm. Corlin had seven competitors with over 1 percent market share.

Mr. Collins' tentative budget was as follows:

	1998 (plan)	1997 (actual)
Sales	$500,000	$100,000
Market share	1.9%	0.43%

Marketing Expenses	Amount	Percent of Sales	Dollar Amount	Percent of Sales
Personal selling	$225,000	45%	$130,000	130%
Technical service	30,000	6%	20,000	20%
Advertising	80,000	16%	55,000	55%

ADVISOR: An approach to marketing budget planning

Mr. Warren felt that whatever method of budgeting he developed, he would need to have at least a consensus of approval from his product managers. To achieve this consensus, he felt a meeting would be necessary to discuss various budgeting methods. During the evenings since be had been appointed to his new position, he had done considerable reading on the budgeting of industrial advertising.

He was dubious about finding a method that was better than "gut feel," but he found a description of a major cross-sectional study of industrial marketing spending behavior known as the ADVISOR Project, and thought it interesting enough to attend an ADVISOR seminar. There he learned that the ADVISOR study was based on the idea that successful industrial managers have learned how to make good communication decisions, and the project was designed to understand and generalize managers' decision experience.

ADVISOR tried to identify product and market characteristics that would affect the marketing and advertising levels for a given product. The data upon which the ADVISOR project was based were drawn from over 300 industrial products supplied by over 100 companies. Data were collected on 11 different factors found to impact budget levels, and models were constructed that computed norms called par reports for marketing and advertising spending.

When the seminar was over, Mr. Warren had no illusions that ADVISOR would solve all his budgeting problems, but he felt that the approach was sufficiently interesting to do an ADVISOR analysis on each of the four products for which he was responsible.

Summaries of the results he got are found in Exhibits 1a to 1d. (A discussion of the terms used in these exhibits is found in Exhibit 2 and an associated data form in Exhibit 3 at the end of this discussion.) When he examined the ADVISOR par reports, he felt that they made sense to him, but he wasn't sure if the product managers would feel the same way.

ADVISOR RESULTS

Product Name/ID → Ceratam

	Actual	Norm	Range
Marketing ($000)	475.0	189.0	122.8 — 289.2
Personal Selling/Tech Serv ($000)	400.0	148.8	96.7 — 227.7
Total Adv ($000)	75.0	40.2	26.1 — 61.4

EXHIBIT 1a

ADVISOR RESULTS

Product Name/ID → Heatcrete 4000

	Actual	Norm	Range
Marketing ($000)	58.3	139.3	90.6 — 213.2
Personal Selling/Tech Serv ($000)	33.3	99.4	64.6 — 152.1
Total Adv ($000)	25.0	39.9	25.9 — 61.1

EXHIBIT 1b

ADVISOR RESULTS

Product Name/ID → Soothblower

	Actual	Norm	Range
Marketing ($000)	2900.0	1335.5	868.1 — 2043.3
Personal Selling/Tech Serv ($000)	2652.0	1262.0	820.3 — 1930.9
Total Adv ($000)	248.0	73.5	47.8 — 112.4

EXHIBIT 1c

ADVISOR RESULTS

Product Name/ID → Corlin

	Actual	**Norm**	**Range**
Marketing ($000)	335.0	505.3	328.4 — 773.1
Personal Selling/Tech Serv ($000)	255.0	346.8	225.4 — 530.6
Total Adv ($000)	80.0	158.5	103.0 — 242.4

EXHIBIT 1d

Budget task force meeting

On his return to the office, Mr. Warren called his product managers together to review their budgets. He reviewed the results of his initial runs with the ADVISOR model and gave each of them a Marketing Engineering/Excel version of the program, so they could re-analyze their products, if they wished.

At this point, he asked: "Do you all feel confident of your proposed budgets? Are you sure they're right? There is one final problem I hate to bring up, but I just received a memo from John Smiley, the Comptroller, telling me to cut last year's budget by a third because of the difficult economic conditions facing the firm. His current 1998 profit projections for our products are these:

Heatcrete	$ 12,640
Ceratam	(57,200)
Flowclean	4,212,000
Corlin Valve	(197,000)

"Where do we make cuts? 1 don't think we'll settle this now. Will you all please meet with me again Monday morning? For that meeting I would like a justification for your present budget. Second, I need a new budget in which the total of your 1998 budgets is two-thirds of your 1997 budgets, along with a justification."

ADVISOR: A set of mathematical models that provides comparison of common industry budgeting practices among products exhibiting similar marketing characteristics.

Advertising: As used in par reports, advertising covers the following kinds of activities associated with the product:

All sales promotion	Direct mail
Trade shows	Brochures and catalogs
Space advertising	TV and radio

Customer: A purchase influencer, user or reseller. If the industry has 10 customer locations, each with 5 people involved in the purchasing decision process, it has 10 x 5 or 50 "customers." The number of customers includes distributors and any other outsiders (consultants, e.g.) who might influence the decision process.

Life Cycle: We break up the product life cycle into four phases: Introduction refers to the period when the initial growth of the product is rather slow. This is followed by the growth stage in the life cycle. The growth stage can last many years; generally if the industry volume is growing by 8-10 percent or more, we consider the product to be still in the growth stage. As growth settles down and sales remain stable from year to year, the product reaches maturity. As the product begins being replaced by competitive technologies, it enters the decline stage of its life cycle.

Marketing: As used in par reports, marketing includes these activities:

All advertising
All personal selling
Technical service

Direct costs and overhead are included; sales management expenditures are not included.

Par: Par refers to the level of advertising spending that most companies agree upon. A par report compares your budgeting practices with those of other companies with products like yours.

Product or Product Market: A product market, defined by customer need, is the basis for completion of this questionnaire. Thus, if you make a unique plastic product to satisfy a need currently satisfied by steel, your competitors might include manufacturers of the competitive steel product and industry sales must be defined accordingly.

A product can be a line of products sold together or a product-market combination. Flexibility in the definition should be one that has operational meaning in your organization. The definition should rarely be so narrow that the product is considered to have no competitors, nor so broad that the questions of unit price or market share become ambiguous.

Range: Budgeting levels vary, even of similar product and marketing situations. The range gives a measure of the variability in budgeting levels in the sample. About three-fourths of the products find themselves within range. Being outside the range means you are significantly different from the norm.

Sales: Dollar value transaction of the product (by the company or industry) to external organizations. Thus internal company product transfers are not included.

EXHIBIT 2
ADVISOR Dictionary

EXHIBIT 3

Convection Product Data

Product Name/Identification	Ceratam	Heatcrete	Sootblower	Corlin
1. In what stage of its life cycle would you say the total market for this type of product is?				
Introduction = 1				
Growth = 2				
Mature = 3				
Decline = 4	2	3	3	2
2. What were your company's product sales ($ millions) to your end users plus independent resellers	1.2	0.632	24.1	0.5
3. What percent of your product's sales volume is...				
a. Produced to order?	35	100	100	10
b. Standard: carried inventory	65	95	0	90
4. What percent of the industry's total dollar sales is purchased by its 3 largest customers?	29	40	63	15
5. How many customers (individuals influencing the purchase process in any way) were there for the industry last year?	22,230	1,650	5,224	22,480
6. If plans and objectives were developed for this product this year, indicate the main emphasis of those plans by a '1' (no more than three items should be indicated as '1').				
a. Increase share	0	1	0	1
b. Maintain share	1	0	1	0
c. Leave unprofitable market	1	0	0	0
d. Improve image	0	1	1	0
e. Retaliate against competitive action	0	0	1	0
f. More fully utilize capacity	0	0	0	1
g. Stimulate distribution channels	0	1	0	1
h. Support price	0	0	0	0
i. Decrease selling costs	1	0	0	0
j. Increase product quality	0	0	0	0

EXHIBIT 3 cont'd.
Convection Product Data

Product Name/Identification	Ceratam	Heatcrete	Sootblower	Corlin
7. Which one of the following categories best describes this product?				
Machinery and equipment = 1				
Raw material (not chemical) = 2				
Fabricated material (e.g., glass) = 3				
Component part = 4				
Salvage good = 5				
Chemical = 6				
Service = 7				
Partially processed material = 8				
Other = 9	3	3	1	1
8. Approximately what percent of your product's dollar sales volume is sold directly to users (versus through resellers/distributors)	70	51	25	80
9. How would you rate the importance of technical service in this product category? (from 1 = not very critical, to 7 = a key element in the marketing mix)	7	4	7	3
10. What percent of industry customers consider that the decision to purchase this product				
a. Is routine?	40	60	15	0
b. Needs some review?	55	35	60	10
c. Requires close analysis?	5	5	25	90
11. What is the distribution of how frequently industry customers make a decision to buy this product (as opposed to merely ordering after a purchase decision has been made)? Enter percent of customers in each category.				
a. Weekly or more frequently	0	0	0	0
b. Once/week—once/month	80	5	15	40
c. Bimonthly—twice/year	10	22.5	17.5	30
d. Yearly	10	22.5	17.5	30
e. Once/2—9 years	0	40	50	0
f. Once/10 years or less frequently	0	10	0	0
*12. What was the total amount of money ($thousands) your company spent on personal selling (including applicable overhead) for this product this year?	300	28	2338	225

EXHIBIT 3 cont'd.

Convection Product Data

Product Name/Identification	Ceratam	Heatcrete	Sootblower	Corlin
*13. What was the total amount of money ($thousands) your company spent on technical service (including applicable overhead) for this product this year?	100	5.3	315	30
*14. What was the total amount of money ($thousands) spent on advertising for this product this year?	75	25	248	80

*This information is provided for reference and comparison only; it is *not* used in developing the ADVISOR norms.

EXERCISES

Using the ADVISOR system, prepare an analysis that

1. (a) Identifies the products/markets, their problems and their marketing needs.
    (b) Recommends a total level of marketing spending and its breakdown into advertising and personal selling/ technical service for each product.
    (c) Justifies the recommendation.
    (Check your assumptions carefully—i.e., product plans in particular: re-run ADVISOR for assumptions that appear more appropriate.)

2. Viewing this set of products as a portfolio, review your analysis using the BCG Growth/Share matrix framework (Chapter 6 of the text) Is that framework useful?

3. Is it appropriate to cut 1/3 from the budget? Where should that cut come from? Why?

TUTORIAL FOR AD COPY DESIGN (ADCAD)

Introduction

ADCAD is an expert system designed to help firms to develop TV commercials for frequently purchased products. The system combines inputs describing the user's view of the market situation with its internal knowledge base of research findings about what types of advertising are effective in various situations. The system then develops a customized list of recommendations for those elements of the advertising strategy that the user can put into effect. The system includes explanations with its recommendations. You should treat these recommendations as you would any other expert advice—with caution and skepticism.

The interaction or dialogue the user has with the system about a particular decision is called a *consultation*. ADCAD asks for any information it needs as the dialogue proceeds.

Operation

NOTE: *If you are running ADCAD under Windows 3.1 you may need additional system files to make it work properly. Check your windows and windows\system directories to see if you have a file called win32s.ini. If you don't have this file, you need to download and install a free patch file called pw1118.exe from Microsoft's ftp site:*

ftp://ftp.microsoft.com/Softlib/MSLFILES/

Place the self-extracting file pw1118.exe in a directory of its own, because it expands into many files. (Alternatively you can copy the file into a temporary directory that gets cleaned out regularly.) First execute pw1118, which will generate a set of installation files including Setup.exe file. Next execute setup.exe.

If you are running ADCAD under Windows 95 or Windows NT, you may have system files that are incompatible with ADCAD. If you encounter errors such as "Failed to open empty document" then you need to replace some files. (This change may adversely affect the running of other programs on your computer. Please follow these instructions carefully.) First, copy the file threed.vbx located in c:\windows\system or c:\winnt\system directory under a different name (e.g., threed.kp). Next, copy the file threed.vbx from the directory in which ADCAD is installed to the Windows system directory. If you later encounter any problems related to threed.vbx, restore the saved version (e.g., threed.kp) into the Windows system directory.

On the **Model** menu, select **Ad Copy Design**. You will see a window with three boxes and a menu bar. On the **Run** menu, click **Start**. You will then see the following screen:

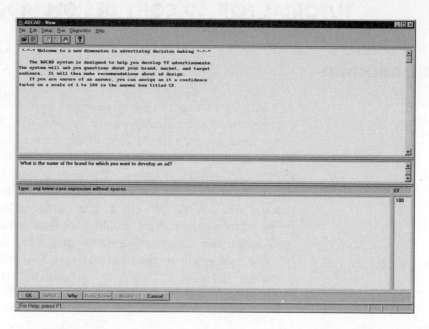

The consultation window contains three dialog boxes. In the top box ADCAD displays the information it generates during the consultation. In the middle box ADCAD displays questions. In the bottom box you answer questions and assign each answer a confidence factor (the default value of the confidence factor is 100).

You can respond to the questions ADCAD asks in one of the following ways:

- Click an answer the system provides (if any) and type in a confidence factor under the CF column (if any). After you choose your answer, click **OK** to register the answer.
- For some questions, you type your answer in the answer box.

> **NOTE**: *Do not type blank spaces or capital letters.*

- For more information on a question, click **What**, **Why**, **Modify**, or **Don't Know**. **What** provides further details about the question. **Why** summarizes the reason why or context under which ADCAD is asking this question, **Modify** permits you to modify answers to previous questions; and **Don't Know** tells ADCAD that you do not have an answer to that question. You cannot respond **Don't Know** to three basic questions that the system asks: (1) The name of the brand for which you want to develop an ad, (2) The product category in which the brand competes, and (3) The segment to which you want to target the ad.

The following two screens show examples of how the system responds if you click **Why** and **What**.

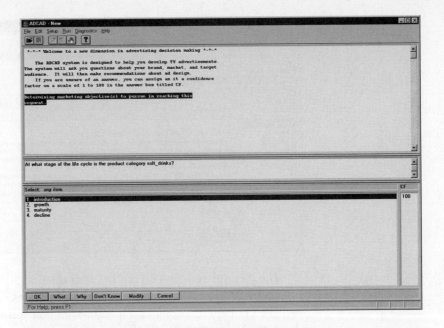

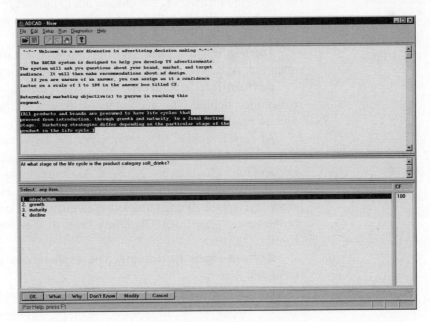

After you answer all the questions that ADCAD asks, it will give you a set of recommendations as shown in the following screen:

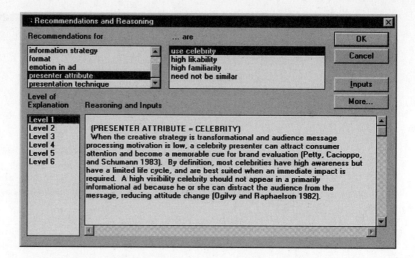

The recommendation screen has four quadrants.

Top-left quadrant. This displays categories of recommendations, such as (1) benefit presentation technique, (2) information presentation strategy, (3) format, (4) emotion in ad, (5) presenter attribute, (6) benefit to be shown in the ad, (7) overall presentation technique, and (8) overall promotion technique.

Top-right quadrant. When you click a category in the top left quadrant, ADCAD will display its recommendations for that category.

Bottom-left quadrant. ADCAD permits you to explore the reasoning behind its recommendations. It organizes the reasons hierarchically by levels.

At Level 1, ADCAD summarizes the key conclusion(s) that led to the recommendation and may cite the research literature to back up the explanation. At Level 2, ADCAD summarizes the intermediate conclusion(s) that led to the key conclusions at Level 1. Explanations at other levels identify the knowledge elements that support the conclusions at the next higher level. Click any level to view the explanation at that level.

Bottom-right quadrant. The explanations are displayed in this quadrant.

By clicking the **Inputs** button, we can view the particular set of input values (responses to questions) that were instrumental in arriving at a recommendation. The following screen shows the inputs associated with the recommendation "use celebrity" as a "presenter attribute" in the ad.

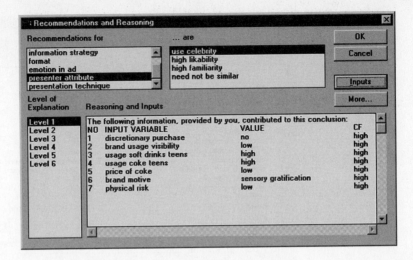

If you click the **More...** button you will see options for saving, printing, or viewing the complete set of recommendations. (Under some operating systems, the **View** window may be hidden behind the currently activated screen. You can use the ALT-TAB key sequence to bring the **View** window to the foreground.)

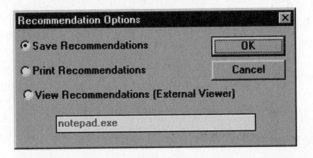

Click **Save Recommendations** to save the entire set of recommendations to a file. You will be prompted to provide a file name.

Select **Print Recommendations** to obtain a printout of the recommendations. If you want to print out any of the explanations or the inputs used to generate a report, use the Windows **Copy** command to highlight and copy text to the clipboard. You can then transfer the text to a word-processing program (e.g., Word for Windows or Notepad) using the Windows **Paste** command.

Select **View Recommendations** to view the entire set of recommendations on the screen using an external viewer, e.g., Notepad.

Once you have reviewed the recommendations and explanations, click **OK** to get back to the main screen. At this point, ADCAD will ask,

"Would you like to rerun this consultation with different input scenarios?"

If you click **Yes**, you will see the following screen displaying the inputs you provided.

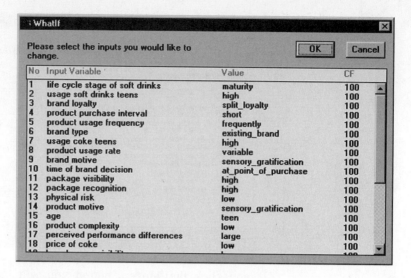

Use the mouse to select the input(s) you want to change and click **OK**. ADCAD will then ask for new answers (inputs).

> **NOTE**: *Your new answers may trigger additional questions that were not asked in the original consultation.*

By including your new answers to the questions, the system will generate new recommendations. If you make only minor changes to inputs, the recommendations may not change much. You can continue this cycle: Change inputs → Explore new recommendations → Change inputs, as many times as you wish.

Other features of ADCAD

As you respond to questions, the system keeps track of your inputs. It stores them in a "cache" in its internal memory. This mechanism allows you to store consultations and retrieve them later.

Storing inputs for future use: You can store the current set of inputs in a file at any time during a consultation by going to the **File** menu and clicking **Save Cache As**. The system will prompt you to provide a file name. If you want to retain the entire set of inputs for future reference, use the **Save Cache As** command after you have displayed all the recommendations and before you make any changes to inputs in a what-if session.

Storing inputs automatically: At the end of a consultation, the system automatically stores the most recent set of inputs in a file named STORE.CAC. After you exit from the ADCAD program, you should rename this file if you want to retain this set of inputs for future use. If you do not rename the file, ADCAD will overwrite on STORE.CAC the next time you use it.

Retrieving stored inputs: You can load a prior consultation by go-ing to the **File** menu and clicking **Load Cache**. The system will prompt you to provide the name of the file in which you stored the inputs.

Restarting a consultation: Unlike the **Start** command, the **Restart** command (on the **Run** menu) does not reset the system but continues from where you left off. Use this command to start a consultation after you retrieve stored inputs by going to the **File** menu and clicking **Load Cache**.

Confidence factors: ADCAD permits you to attach confidence levels to your answers, numbers between 1 and 100 (representing the range of certainty you feel about your answer from "know almost nothing" to "being certain"). ADCAD does not interpret confidence levels as probabilities but as subjective indices of the amount of evidence supporting a particular input value. When you are not confident of an answer you can alert ADCAD to this fact by appending a confidence factor to your answer by entering a number between 1 and 100 in the box titled **CF**. If you do not enter a confidence level with your input, ADCAD assigns by default a value of 100, indicating that you are sure of your answer. We recommend that you use this default option.

Multiple answers: For some questions, ADCAD will accept multiple answers, each with 100 percent confidence. The directions above the answer box will alert you to opportunities to enter multiple answers. However you can provide multiple answers to any question by entering a confidence factor of less than 100 for each answer. For example

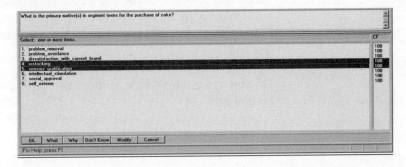

If you answer "Don't Know" or give multiple answers to many questions, ADCAD's recommendations will be correspondingly imprecise.

Reference

Burke, Raymond R.; Rangaswamy, Arvind; Eliashberg, Jehoshua; and Wind, Jerry 1990 "A knowledge-based system for advertising design," *Marketing Science*, Vol. 9, No. 3 (Summer), pp. 212-229.

EXERCISES

1. The best way to learn to use the ADCAD system is to develop the key components of a TV commercial for a familiar brand, such as Pepsi or Coke. In doing so, keep a specific target segment in mind and compare the recommendations of the system with a recent brand

commercial targeted to that segment.

2. Use the ADCAD system to develop ad-copy recommendations for Enhance instant hair conditioner (Johnson Wax Enhance (A) case, page 193 of this volume). Use as inputs to the model the data available in the case and any other input values you think are appropriate. In your report, include the inputs you provided and the recommendations made by the system.

3. Use these recommendations to develop a one-page print advertisement for Enhance. Indicate how you used the recommendations in developing your print ad.

4. Summarize the advantages and limitations of the ADCAD system for developing ad-copy-design parameters.

5. After using the ADCAD system, a senior ad agency executive commented, "This is precisely the type of systematic approach that I would like our creatives to use. They need to develop an appreciation of the strategic rationale for an ad before they let their creative juices flow." On the other hand, after using the system, an art director commented, "Developing an ad is like making an omelette. McDonald's will consistently make us a half-way decent omelette but it takes a great chef to make one that we will remember for long. I don't think creatives will accept a mechanistic approach to ad design."

Do you agree with either of these two points of view? Explain why or why not.

TUTORIAL FOR SALES RESOURCE ALLOCATION GENERALIZED SYNTEX WORKBOOK (SYNGEN)

The generalized Syntex model can be used for sales-force sizing and allocation. It uses the judgmental inputs of sales personnel regarding segment-level sales response to selling effort. It helps you to determine the optimal size for the sales force and the allocation of effort within a set of specified constraints provided by the user. It parallels the modeling approach taken in the Syntex Laboratories (A) case. While the generalized resource allocation model is flexible in its usage, the Syntex Product model and the Syntex specialty model are specifically designed to accompany the Syntex Labs (A) case. In particular, the product and specialty models are preset with the data from the Syntex case whereas the generalized model requires the user to provide all essential input data.

When you click on the **Generalized Resource Allocation Model** (Syngen.xls) under the **Sales Resource Allocation** option of the **Model** menu, you will see this message:

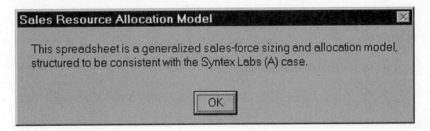

Click **OK** to get to the first of two worksheets that will prompt you for input.

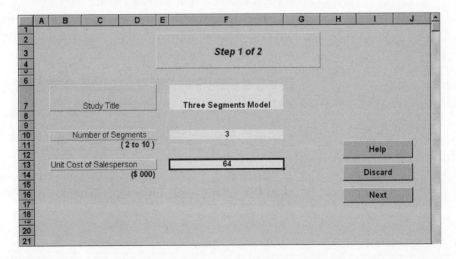

As an example, set up a simple problem consisting of three segments. Enter the requested information for the three fields and click **Next** to advance to the second step.

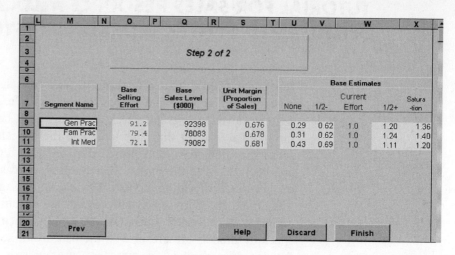

Segment Name	Base Selling Effort	Base Sales Level ($000)	Unit Margin (Proportion of Sales)	Base Estimates				
				None	1/2-	Current Effort	1/2+	Satura -tion
Gen Prac	91.2	92398	0.676	0.29	0.62	1.0	1.20	1.36
Fam Prac	79.4	78083	0.678	0.31	0.62	1.0	1.24	1.40
Int Med	72.1	79082	0.681	0.43	0.69	1.0	1.11	1.20

Next name the segments (10 characters maximum); provide baseline information about selling effort, sales level, and unit margin; and give the parameter values that will determine the shape of the initial response curve.

For example for "General Practice," you are asked what the sales level would be if there were:

- No selling effort
- Half of the current effort
- Percent more than current effort
- Unlimited selling effort

The answers to these four questions (0.29, 0.62, 1.2, 1.36 respectively) are normalized relative to base level sales ($92,398 K). Thus the value 0.29 means: "If we cut our selling effort to 0, we expect to sell 29 percent of $92,398 K or $26,795 K."

Click **Finish** and the system will quickly estimate the coefficients for the response curves and then prompt you for a file name under which to save your basic model setup.

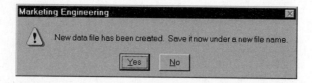

Generally it is a good idea to save your newly configured model now. Give it any name other than Syngen.

Click **OK** to get to the next screen, the main page summarizing your input information.

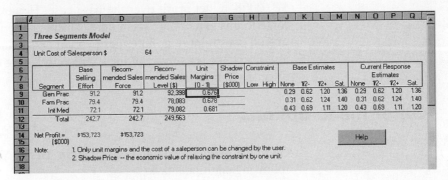

To start the optimization go to the **Model** menu and select **Main Menu**. Select **Optimization** and click **OK**.

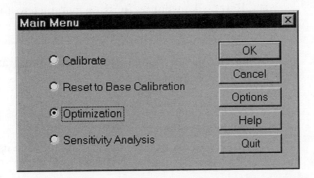

Now you have the opportunity to provide values for possible constraints. Simply clicking **OK** will initiate the optimization search process.

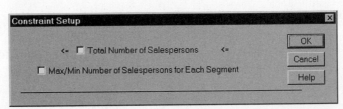

The following shows the result of the optimization run.

		Base Selling Effort	Recommended Sales Force	Recommended Sales Level ($)	Unit Margins (0 - 1)	Shadow Price ($000)	Constraint Low	Constraint High	Base Estimates None	Base Estimates 12-	Base Estimates 12+	Base Estimates Sat.	Current Response Estimates None	Current Response Estimates 12-	Current Response Estimates 12+	Current Response Estimates Sat.
Three Segments Model																
Unit Cost of Salesperson $		64														
Segment	Gen Prac	91.2	190.4	116,669	0.676		0		0.29	0.62	1.20	1.36	0.29	0.62	1.20	1.36
	Fam Prac	79.4	171.3	101,417	0.678		0		0.31	0.62	1.24	1.40	0.31	0.62	1.24	1.40
	Int Med	72.1	123.8	89,772	0.681		0		0.43	0.69	1.11	1.20	0.43	0.69	1.11	1.20
	Total	242.7	485.5	307,858			0									
Net Profit = ($000)		$153,723	$177,694													

Note: 1. Only unit margins and the cost of a salesperson can be changed by the user.
2. Shadow Price -- the economic value of relaxing the constraint by one unit.

Help

Hence in the unconstrained case the solution suggests that by nearly doubling the sales-force effort (size), you could get an increase of $20,000K in net profit over the base case. However expanding the sales force to this extent may seem unreasonable. You may wish to impose an overall constraint (e.g. 300 sales people) and rerun the analysis. You can also check the sensitivity of the solution by going to the **Main Menu** and selecting **Sensitivity**.

Other menu options

Go to the **Model** menu and select **Main Menu**. You can accomplish the following additional tasks:

- Experiment with different sales response functions by selecting **Calibrate**.
- Reset all response function parameters to the base case by selecting **Reset to Base Calibration**.

Go to the **Model** menu, select **Main Menu**, and then **Options**. You can then do the following:

- Make changes directly to sales response parameters and to the base sales levels.
- Create a new model under a separate file name.

Limitation of the software

Number of cases:　　　2-10

Reference

Harvard Business School, 1983, "Syntex Laboratories (A)," HBS Case Study #584033, 1-25.

SYNTEX LABORATORIES (A)

April 1982 found Robert Nelson, vice president of sales for Syntex Laboratories, considering the results of a sales force size and allocation study. Those results presented Nelson with a dilemma. He had previously submitted a business plan increasing the number of sales representatives from 433 to 473. By now, the corporate budget cycle of which that plan was a part was well under way. The study, however, indicated that sales and contribution to profit for fiscal 1985[*] at the 473 level would be much less than could be obtained with an optimal sales force size of over 700. Although Nelson was unsure how fast Syntex Labs could hire and train sales reps, the study clearly showed that a sales force growth rate of only 40 reps per year would severely limit both present and future profitability.

The study results had been presented by Laurence Lewis, manager of promotion research, and Syntex Labs' liaison to the consultants that had done the analysis. Following Lewis's initial presentation, Nelson arranged a second presentation for Stephen Knight, senior vice president of marketing for Human Pharmaceuticals. They had agreed that the results were so dramatic that, if they had confidence in the results, they should attempt to interrupt the corporate planning cycle and request more sales reps.

Company background

Syntex Corporation began in 1940 when Russell Marker, a steroid chemist, derived a cheap and abundant source of steroid hormones from the black, lumpy root of a vine growing wild in the jungles of the Mexican state of Veracruz. Syntex's first products were oral contraceptives and topical steroid preparations prescribed by gynecologists and dermatologists respectively. By 1982 Syntex Corporation had become an international life sciences company that developed, manufactured, and marketed a wide range of health and personal care products. Fiscal 1981 consolidated sales were $710.9 million with $98.6 million net income. Since 1971, Syntex had recorded a 23 percent compound annual growth rate.

---

[*]Syntex fiscal year ended on July 1.

This case was prepared by Associate Professor Darral G. Clarke as the basis for class discussion rather than to illustrate either effective or ineffective handling of an administrative situation.

Syntex Laboratories

Syntex Laboratories, the U.S. human pharmaceutical sales subsidiary was the largest Syntex subsidiary. During fiscal 1981, Syntex Laboratories' sales increased 35 percent to $215,451,000, and grew as a percentage of total pharmaceutical sales to 46 percent, continuing a recent upward trend. Operating profit in 1981 was 27 percent of net sales. Syntex Laboratories developed manufactured and marketed anti-inflammatories used to treat several forms of arthritis; analgesics used to treat pain; oral contraceptives; respiratory products; and topical products prescribed by dermatologists for skin diseases. Syntex emphasized pharmaceutical research in support of these existing product lines, and in several important new therapeutic areas, including immunology, viral diseases, and cardiovascular medicine.

Syntex Labs' product line

Syntex Labs' product line consisted of seven major products. Naprosyn was by far the largest and most successful, while Norinyl and the topical steroids represented Syntex's early development as a drug manufacturer. Exhibit 1 presents retail drug purchases and market shares for Syntex products.

Naprosyn

Naprosyn[*] was the third largest selling drug in the nonsteroidal anti-inflamatory (NSAI) therapeutic class[†] in the country, behind Clinoril and Motrin. NSAIs were used in the treatment of arthritis.

Major selling points for Naprosyn were its dosage flexibility (250, 375, 500 mg tablets), twice daily regimen (less frequent than for competing products), and low incidence of side effects within a wide dosage range. The NSAI market in fiscal 1980 was $478 million. Exhibit 2 has details of NSAI market trends.

The extremely competitive arthritis drug market would soon become even more competitive as other pharmaceutical firms entered the huge and fast-growing market for alternatives to aspirin in treating arthritis. According to one expert, Naprosyn would "weather the storm (of increased competition) better than any existing agent, although its share will be lower in 1985 than today."

Anaprox

Anaprox was launched in the United States early in fiscal 1981. It was initially marketed for analgesic use and for the treatment of menstrual pain. Nearly twice as many prescriptions were written for analgesics as for anti-arthritics in the U.S., making this an important, but highly competitive, market. Exhibit 2 presents details on analgesic market trends.

---

[*] All Syntex Labs product names were registered trademarks.

[†] Drugs used for similar purposes were combined for reporting purposes into groups called *therapeutic classes*.

At the end of fiscal 1981, the U.S. Food and Drug Administration approved Anaprox for the treatment of mild to moderate, acute or chronic, musculoskeletal and soft-tissue inflammation.

Topical Steroids

Lidex and Synalar were Syntex's topical steroid creams for treating skin inflammations. Fiscal 1981 sales of dermatological products, Syntex's second largest product category, were only slightly ahead of sales in 1980. United States patents on two of the active ingredients in Lidex and Synalar expired during 1981, but other Lidex ingredients continued to be protected under formulation patents. Syntex anticipated some continued growth from these two important products and new dermatological products were under development.

During fiscal 1980, Syntex was the only established company to increase total prescription volume in topical steroids, while two new entrants grew from smaller shares. Market shares of new prescriptions and total prescriptions are in Exhibit 3. Syntex had a very strong following among dermatologists—21 percent of all *new* topical steroid prescriptions written by dermatologists were for Syntex products. Topicort, a competitor's brand, had enjoyed 65 percent growth ($3.66 million to $6.02 million) as a result of successful selling to both dermatologists and general practitioners.

Norinyl

Total drug store sales for oral contraceptives (OC) in 1980 were up 23 percent over the previous year, but this dollar-volume growth was primarily the result of a price increase. Total cycle[*] sales declined by 3.5 percent. New prescriptions overall declined 1.5 percent, while new prescriptions for low dose oral contraceptives increased by 21 percent.

Syntex's oral contraceptive, Norinyl, was available in three dosages that together totaled $37 million, or 10 percent of the market. The low-dose segment was the growth segment of the OC market; 30 percent of all new prescriptions were for low-dose products. Mid-dose products accounted for 54 percent of all new prescriptions, and high-dose products, only 16 percent.

The oral contraceptive market was extremely competitive, with seven major competitors and dozens of products. Syntex's fiscal 1981 sales increase was due primarily to larger sales to the Agency for International Development than in the previous year, price increases, and the introduction of low-dose Norinyl, which was approved by the FDA in that year. Exhibit 3 contains OC market trends.

Nasalide

Nasalide was a steroid nasal spray for the treatment of hay fever and perennial allergies. It was approved for United States marketing early in fiscal 1982.

---

[*] Oral contraceptive sales were recorded by the amount of the drug used for one menstrual cycle.

The sales representative

The sales rep's job was to visit physicians and encourage them to prescribe Syntex drugs for their patients. This was usually done by providing the physician with samples and with information about the appropriate dosage for various medical uses. Performance of this task was complicated by the difficulty of getting appointments with busy physicians, obtaining and maintaining credibility as a reliable source of information on drug use, the number of competing sales reps vying for the physician's time, and the difficulty in measuring the results of the detailing effort.

Robert Nelson described the physician visit as follows:

A good sales rep will have a pretty good idea of what the physician's prescribing habits are. For example, most physicians are aware of Naprosyn by now, so our sales rep would try to find out what the physician's usage level is. If the physician was not prescribing Naprosyn, the sales rep would present clinical studies comparing Naprosyn with other drugs. probably stressing Naprosyn's lower incidence of side effects and its twice-a-day regimen and then request the physician to prescribe Naprosyn for their next six rheumatism patients. The same sort of information might be used to persuade a physician to move Naprosyn up from third choice to second or first choice. Physicians already prescribing Naprosyn could be encouraged to increase the dose for severe cases from 750 to 1000 mg per day, using recent research showing Naprosyn to be safe at those levels. New uses cleared by the FDA could also be explained, or the rep might just reinforce the physician's choice of Naprosyn and counteract competitors' claims for their drugs.

The choice of which physicians to visit, how often to visit them, and what to present was a major consideration for the individual sales rep. Though sales management might set quotas and provide guidelines, on a day-to-day basis the final choice was largely the rep's. Laurence Lewis explained:

Sales reps tend to divide the physicians in their territories into two groups: "prescription-productive" physicians and "easy-to-call-on" physicians. Suppose a company sets a minimum daily call average of seven. The sales rep tries to visit the most productive physicians first; they are busy physicians for the most part, so the rep may have to wait a while to see them. Later in the day the sales rep gets nervous about making the seven calls so he fills in with easy-to-call-on physicians that might not be terribly productive. His bonus, however, is based on quota and annual sales increase over the previous year, So he can't be totally unconcerned about the productivity of the physicians he visits.

Nelson felt that once the decision had been made about the number of sales reps and the sales territories had been defined and assigned, the limits of his organizational authority had about been reached. Decisions he might make about which physician specialties to visit and what drugs to feature would be subject to individual reps' interpretation and preferences. It would be necessary to educate and motivate the reps to act in accordance with the sales plan. If the reps didn't agree with the plan, strict quotas and overly directive policies would be counterproductive.

Sales management at Syntex Labs

Robert Nelson had been promoted to vice president of sales from director of marketing research. In his new position, he reported directly to Stephen Knight, the senior vice president of marketing for Syntex Laboratories. Reporting to Nelson through Frank Poole, the national sales manager, were 6 regional, 47 district sales managers, and 433 general sales reps. Also reporting to him separately was a group of reps that specialized in hospital sales and dermatology sales.

After some consideration, Nelson decided he had a few major decisions to make in managing the sales force that were of a relatively strategic nature: The size of the sales force and its geographic allocation were of obvious importance. Call frequency, allocation of sales calls across physician specialties, and product-featuring policies were also important decisions that were relatively difficult to change once implemented.

Sales Force Size

Data available in 1980 showed that Syntex's sales force[*] was rather small compared with those of its direct competitors:

NSAI		Oral Contraceptives		Topical Steroids	
Upjohn	930	Ortho	330	Schering	615
Merck	955	Wyeth	724	Squibb	761
McNeil	457	Searle	405	Lederle	600
Pfizer	663			Hoechst	379

It was by no means obvious to Nelson, however, how much larger the Syntex sales force needed to be. Since each competitor had a different product line that required calling on a different mix of physician specialties. it wasn't clear how the size of the Syntex sales force should compare with the others.

Call Frequency

The 433 sales reps at Syntex had been generally adequate to support a six-week call cycle (each physician was scheduled to be visited once every six weeks) with approximately 70,000 targeted physicians. Indeed. this was how the number of reps had been determined in the first place. Since many of the physicians Syntex visited were visited by other companies with four-week call cycles, Nelson had considered that possibility.

The four-week call cycle seemed attractive for at least two reasons. First, if one believed that the sales force had a positive influence on phy-

---

[*] This case deals only with the general sales force and does not include the hospital sales force. For simplicity, "sales force" will be used to mean the general sales force.

sicians' prescribing behavior, it seemed reasonable that offering less frequent positive contact than the competition had to hurt. Second. dermatologists and rheumatologists had been visited by Syntex sales reps in nearly a four-week cycle, and these were felt to be Syntex's most successful physician specialty groups.

Allocation of Sales Effort Across Products and Physician Specialties

The necessity to allocate sales force effort across various physician specialties was apparent from the number of physicians in various specialties—a total of 135,229 physicians in office-based practice. Visiting all of them in a four-week call cycle would have required at least 1,200 sales reps (assuming no geographic complications). This would have been nearly three times as large as Syntex Labs' current sales force and nearly one-third larger than its largest competitor.

The Syntex sales policy called for a rep to attempt to make seven sales calls per day, during which presentations would be made for two or three Syntex products. (The average was 2.7 presentations per sales call.) Which products would be featured depended on a number of factors, such as the physicians' specialty, the availability of new information on Syntex product efficacy and or comparative advantages, and national sales priorities

The fact that not all physicians were likely to prescribe all of Syntex's products complicated the choice of both product presentations and physician specialties. The fact that a sales rep could make an average of seven calls and 19 presentations in a day did not necessarily mean that a recommended product-featuring schedule could be followed exactly. For example, if the rep called on four dermatologists and three obstetricians in a particular day, there would be no opportunity to make Naprosyn presentations.

Geographic Allocation of Sales Force

When Robert Nelson became vice president of sales, geographic allocation of the sales force seemed to be the most critical factor, so it had received immediate attention. The problem turned out to be a reasonably tractable one, however. Gathering information about the location of physicians and competitors' sales reps was a huge data-gathering task, but as Laurence Lewis explained:

> Almost everyone deploys their sales reps based on regional physician counts. We made an effort to get away from just physician counts, and looked at market potential. I know other companies have done that. In the end, it all came down to where Lilly, Pfizer, Merck, and ourselves would all have a rep in a given geographical territory. Maybe one of the big companies would have two reps in a particular territory, but regional deployment ended up being almost standard. I don't suppose any of us have any real hope of coming up with good enough data to really override that allocation, at least at the territory level. We finally built a model at the state level which is based on six factors that are weighted differentially according to management judgment. We assumed that when we got below the state level a lot of geographical things, or whatever, would have to be taken into account. We now

have a comfortable deployment scheme at the State level. But we still have to know how many sales reps we should have in total and what specialties we are going to push.

Sales force strategy model

Nelson and Knight had observed that the rapid growth of Naprosyn was changing the balance in Syntex Laboratories. According to Knight:

> We had always been a specialty-oriented company. We began with a product for dermatologists, then followed that with an oral contraceptive, so we visited OB-GYNs[*] too, and for the first 15 years those were the main physicians we visited, along with a limited number of primary-care physicians.[†] So we've thought of ourselves as a small, specialty-oriented pharmaceutical company. Along came Naprosyn and suddenly we had the ninth largest selling drug in the U.S. and we were growing at over 25 percent a year. We were being forced to re-think just what kind of a company we were. It was this dynamic change in the nature of Syntex that led us to consider a more sophisticated analysis.

According to Nelson:

> We knew we had some opportunities to expand the sales force. We could see how rapidly Naprosyn was growing and that our detailing penetration with generalist doctors was very low compared to the big anti-arthritis competitors like Upjohn and Merck. They each had 900 sales reps, so we knew we were behind them. But we were trying to make major plans on the back of envelopes! We'd make notes like: If there are 60,000 generalist doctors and we've got this many people, how many calls can we make a year if each of them makes 1,360 calls a year? How are we going to divvy up those calls? We then realized we were saying that all these doctors respond to sales reps the same way, and yet we all knew that they didn't. But we could never make the differences explicit! We were assuming all products responded the same way, and we knew that wasn't right. Finally we asked ourselves if there wasn't some better way to do this.

In an effort to find a better way, Nelson created the position of manager of promotion research. The position was filled by Laurence Lewis, an analyst in the marketing research department who had earlier been a sales rep. Lewis's first task was to identify a method for determining the size of the sales force and allocating sales force effort across products and physician specialties. After studying the marketing research and trade literature and consulting other knowledgeable people, Lewis decided to approach Leonard Lodish, a professor at the Wharton School, whose name had surfaced repeatedly during his research.

---

[*] OB-GYN—obstetrician and gynecologist

[†] Primary-care physicians (PCP) included physicians specializing in internal medicine, general practices, and family practice.

Lodish was subsequently invited to visit Syntex and make a presentation on his approach to determining sales force size and sales effort allocation. Two aspects of his approach struck responsive chords with Knight and Nelson. Nelson stated:

> One of the attractive features of the approach was getting our sales and marketing management people together and making explicit what we believed about how each of our products responds to detailing.

Knight felt that:

> Our history had been one of increasing the sales force size in relatively small steps. I've never been really satisfied that there was any good reason why we were expanding by 30 or 50 representatives in any one year other than that was what we were able to get approved in the budget process. Over the years I'd become impatient with the process of going to the well for more people every year with no longterm view to it. I felt that if I went to upper management with a more strategic, or longer-term viewpoint, it would be a lot easier to then sell the annual increases necessary to get up to a previously established objective in sales force size and utilization.

Subsequently, a contract was signed with Management Decision Systems (MDS), a Boston area-based management consulting firm of which Lodish was a principal, to produce a sales force strategy model for Syntex. Laurence Lewis was appointed liaison with MDS.

Model Development Process

The sales force strategy model (SSM) was designed to help Syntex management deploy the sale-force strategically. The model would be used to calculate the amount of sales effort to direct to various Syntex products and physician specialties, and to maximize the net contribution for a given sales force size. Repeated applications of the model with different numbers of reps could be used to make decisions on the best totals.

The technique used in the model combined management science techniques with historical data and management judgment to calculate the incremental gain in net contribution for each additional amount of sales resource (either product presentations or physician calls).

Defining the Model Inputs

The SSM used information from various sources. The average number of presentations per sales call, the number of sales calls per day, the contribution margin for Syntex products, and the cost per sales representative were estimated from company records and syndicated data sources. (See Exhibit 4.) The current allocation of sales force effort was a key element in developing the model, since these data provided the background for Syntex managers to use in estimating the response of various Syntex products and physician groups to different levels of sales effort.

There were two separate, but similar, versions of the SSM model. One sought to allocate the number of *sales rep visits to physician specialties* to maximize contribution, while the other sought the optimal allocation of *sales presentations to Syntex products*. Each estimated the optimal sales force size independently of the other.

The judgmental estimates of response to sales effort were obtained during a series of special meetings held in conjunction with the annual marketing planning meetings. Leonard Lodish, Stephen Knight, Robert Nelson, Laurence Lewis, Frank Poole, and a few product managers and regional sales managers participated. According to Lewis:

> The meeting began with a short lecture on sales response and an exercise in which we were each asked to come up with an optimal sales plan for a sales rep who had six accounts and four products. Trying to do this led us to understand what the model would try to accomplish and demonstrated the impossibility of trying to plan by hand for more than 400 sales reps selling six or more products to 13 different physician specialties.

The main agenda of the meetings was to come to a group consensus on the likely response of each Syntex product and physician specialty to sales rep effort. On Monday, the first day of the annual meetings, worksheets were distributed to the participants on which they were asked to estimate the change in sales for each of seven Syntex Labs' products and nine physician specialties that would result from different levels of sales rep activity. Each manager responded to the following question for each product and specialty:

According to the strategic plan, if the current level of sales force effort is maintained from 1982 to 1985, sales of Naprosyn (Anaprox, etc.) could be the planned level. What would happen to Naprosyn's (Anaprox, etc.) 1985 sales (compared with present levels) if during this same time period it received:

1. no sales effort?
2. one half the current effort?
3. 50 percent greater sales effort?
4. a saturation level of sales effort?

After a summary of the participants' answers had been presented to the group and discussed, new worksheets were passed out and the process repeated. When a reasonable consensus had been obtained, the meeting was recessed.

Following this meeting, a preliminary version of the model was produced. When the group reconvened on Friday, a preliminary analysis was presented and the results were discussed. The initial analysis appeared generally reasonable to the participants and, after a final discussion and some later fine-tuning, resulted in the response estimates that appear in Exhibit 5. Commenting on the process, Knight explained:

> Of course, we knew that the responses we estimated were unlikely to be the "true responses" in some absolute knowledge sense, but we got the most knowledgeable people in the company together in what seemed to me to be a very thorough discussion and the estimates rep-

resented the best we could do at the time. We respect the model results, but we'll utilize them with cautious skepticism.

According to Poole. "We did the best we could to estimate the model. At first we were uncomfortable at having to be so specific about things we weren't too sure about. but by the end of the discussions, we were satisfied that this was the best we could do."

Model Structure

The sales force strategy model assisted a manager in determining the size of the sales force and the allocation of sales effort across products or customers by:

1. Predicting the net contribution and sales volume that would result from a particular sales force size and allocation policy; and

2. Providing an efficient means of searching over various sales force sizes to find both the optimal sales force size and the optimal allocation policy

The basic concept of the model was quite simple: each additional sales rep should be assigned to visit the specialty which. considering the allocation of the current sales force, would provide the highest incremental contribution. Consider the following example of a company that has

1. Two products—A and B
2. Three sales reps who sell only A, and two sales reps sell only B
3. The response of A and B to sales effort pictured below

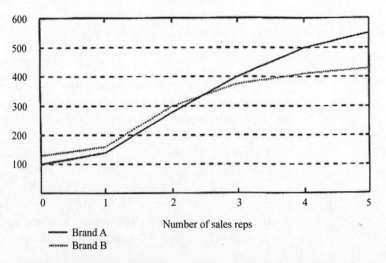

Number of sales reps

—— Brand A
········ Brand B

Suppose now that the company wants to add two sales reps. The model considers the additional reps sequentially. If the first new rep is assigned to sell product A, the result will be $100 incremental contribution ($500–400). If the first new rep is assigned to sell B, only $75 incremental contribution ($375–300) will result. Thus. the first sales rep should be assigned to sell Bell A. The company now has 4 "A sales reps," and 2 "B sales reps." If the second new rep is assigned to sell product B, he or she could still generate $75 incremental contribution. But if assigned to sell A, only $50 could be generated.[*] So the second new sales rep could be assigned to sell B.

Exhibit 6 presents a portion of the model output allocating sales representatives to specialties. At each step in the analysis, the model indicated the number of reps already allocated, the number of new reps allocated, and to which specialty. If successive additional reps were to be allocated to the same specialty, they were accumulated in a single step.

The SSM could be used to determine the optimal number of sales reps by increasing the size of the sales force and observing the net contribution to profit and incremental contribution per sales rep added. At each sales force size the sales force was optimally deployed, and the optimal sales force size was the one with maximum net contribution and incremental net contribution per added rep equal to zero.

Syntex management had estimated response functions for both products and specialties, so running the model in both modes would provide a validity check on the approach in general. The specialty-based analysis indicated an optimum sales force size of 768, and the product-based analysis 708 sales reps.

Results of the SSM Analysis

The recommended optimal sales force sizes computed on the basis of physician specialty and products were reasonably close together. The models differed considerably, however, in their estimation of incremental net contribution per added sales rep at levels between the current sales force size and 600 reps. (See Exhibit 7.)

Not only did both SSM analyses indicate that the current Syntex sales force was too small, it also showed that allocation was suboptimal. According to the specialty-based analysis, FY 1985 net contribution at the present sales force size would be more than $7.2 million less than could be obtained with an optimal deployment policy. (See Exhibit 8.)

A direct comparison of present and optimal deployment according to the product-based analysis was somewhat more difficult, since the SSM indicated that Anaprox should either receive no sales attention or the equivalent of the next 130 sales reps. Nothing in between was optimal. This resulted in reported optimal sales force sizes of 369 and 499 sales reps, but no report on the current size of 433. The SSM results were clear, however, that the current Syntex allocation of effort across products was even more suboptimal than it had been across specialists. Exhibit 9 shows that when 369 sales reps were optimally deployed across products, sales and net contribution would be $50.5 million and $45.7 million higher, respectively.

Finally, with both optimal sales force size and optimal deployment, FY 1985 sales and contribution (see Exhibit 10) would be dramatically larger than with the current sales force size and optimal deployment:

---

[*] The simplified algorithm presented here does not assure an optimal solution for S-shaped response curves. The actual SSM algorithm is the same in spirit as this example but has a refinement to assure an optimal solution for all reasonable response functions.

SSM Predicted FY 1985 Sales and Contribution from Optimal Deployment

According to	Sales Force Size	Sales ($mm)	Net Contribution
Specialty model			
(current)	434	$373.1	$220.4
429	380.1	227.6	
768	447.7	251.7	
Product Model			
(current)	430	$373.1	$218.6
369	423.6	264.2	
708	485.9	279.6	

Management implications

Robert Nelson had expected that the sales force would be found to be too small and that Naprosyn probably needed more emphasis, but no one had anticipated that the optimal sales force size would be between 700 and 800 reps. According to Laurence Lewis:

> When Len [Lodish] asked how far out he should run the thing, we were standing at 430 reps and I said. "Why don't you run it out to 550 or the maximum, whichever comes first." We knew we weren't paying enough attention to Naprosyn because our major NSAI competitors outnumbered us so far, and that's our biggest and most important market. We also knew that Naprosyn was our most important product, but we didn't really know to what *degree* it was our most important product. We had the perception that a lot of the attention given to launching three new products had been at the expense of our smaller products, but the model showed it had come out of Naprosyn and that was exactly what we hadn't wanted to happen.

When he received the SSM analyses, Lewis decided four major conclusions could be drawn from them:

1. Until the size of the sales force approaches 700 general representatives, profitability will not be a constraint to adding representatives.

2. From the FY 1981 base of roughly 430 representatives, Syntex Labs should grow to an optimal allocation of sales effort rather than by redeploying the current sales force. This could be done by devoting additional sales resources largely to the primary-care audience.

3. Naprosyn was the largest product in Syntex's product line, the most sales-responsive. and highly profitable. Thus Syntex Labs

should make it the driving force behind nearly all deployment and allocation decisions.

4. Syntex should consider itself a major generalist company, since optimal deployment would require the greatest portion of a large sales force to be devoted to the generalist physician audience.

Although enthusiastic about these conclusions, Lewis added a note of caution to their acceptance.

A significant change in the marketplace that would decrease the ability of any of our products to compete would challenge the validity of the model output. Such phenomena as a product recall or a revolutionary new competitive product might act to reduce the value of this model.

Significant error in the sales response estimates of either products or specialties could lead to reduced validity of model output. The similarity between the two model outputs derived from independent response estimates hints at the low likelihood of significant error in the sales response estimates. The model would be most sensitive to significant error in the estimate of Naprosyn's sales responsiveness.

Lewis had concluded his presentations of the study results by stating that Robert Nelson and Stephen Knight were faced with two choices if they decided not to expand the sales force to an optimal size. They could:

1. Optimize the physician sales call allocation with a smaller than optimal sales force by dramatically reducing coverage of Specialists to increase calls on primary-care physicians. This option would maximize sales for the number of sales reps by leading to large gains in Naprosyn at the expense of sales losses in oral contraceptives and topical steroids.

2. Limit Naprosyn's growth to substantially less than its potential, while maintaining the present contact levels with Syntex's traditional specialist physicians and older products.

	Retail Drug Purchases			Total RX		
	July 80–July 81	**81-82**	**%**	**80-81**	**81-82**	**%**
Therapeutic Class						
NSAI (anti-arthritics)						
Market	$477,834	$533,980	+16%	49,759	51,466	+3%
Naprosyn	90,448	114,242	+26%	6,837	7,849	+19%
Syntex share	18.92	21.42		13.7%	15.3%	
Analgesic (pain killers)						
Market	$315,324	$346,784	+1%	89,774	91,881	+2%
Anaprox	8,119	13,027	+60%	762	1,569	+106%
Syntex share	2.5%	3.8%		0.8%	1.7%	
Oral Contraceptives						
Market (all forms)	$359,942	$442,669	+23%	50,811	53,896	+6%
Syntex Total	36,925	50,726	+37%	5,636	5,865	+4%
Syntex Share	10.3%	11.42		11.1%	10.9%	
Topical Steroids (skin ointments)						
Market	$138,895	148,895	+7%	24,948	24,531	+2%
Syntex products	31,361	37,768	+20%	5,181	5,241	+1%
Syntex share	22.6%	25.4%		20.8%	21.4%	

	New RX		
	80-81	**81-82**	**%**
Therapeutic Class			
NSAI (anti-arthritics)			
Market	$23,829	24,569	+3%
Naprosyn	3,323	3,656	+10%
Syntex share	13.9%	14.9%	
Analgesic (pain killers)			
Market	65,976	67,160	+2%
Anaprox	591	1,040	+76%
Syntex share	0.9%	1.5%	
Oral Contraceptives			
Market (all forms)	13,730	13,182	-0.4%
Syntex total	1,620	1,520	-7%
Syntex share	11.8%	11.5%	
Topical Steroids (skin ointments)			
Market	15,345	15,009	-2%
Syntex products	3,044	3,103	+2%
Syntex share	19.8%	20.7%	

EXHIBIT 1

Syntex Laboratories (A) Recent Sales Trends in Syntex*

*Compiled from IMS data

EXHIBIT 2
Syntex Laboratories (A)

Nonsteroidal anti-inflammatory market trends

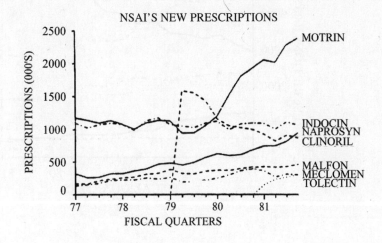

NSAI'S NEW PRESCRIPTIONS

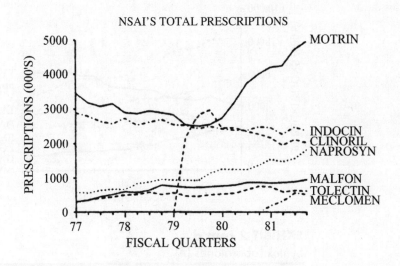

NSAI'S TOTAL PRESCRIPTIONS

Analgesic (drug store only) market trends

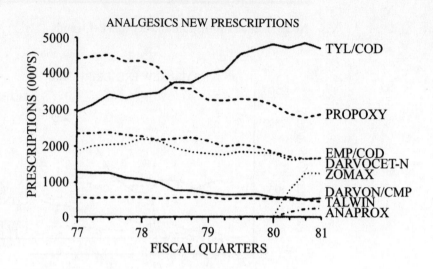

ANALGESICS NEW PRESCRIPTIONS

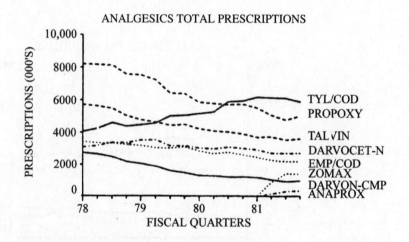

ANALGESICS TOTAL PRESCRIPTIONS

EXHIBIT 2 cont'd.
Syntex Laboratories (A)

EXHIBIT 3
Syntex Laboratories (A): Topical steriod market trends

Topical steroid market trends

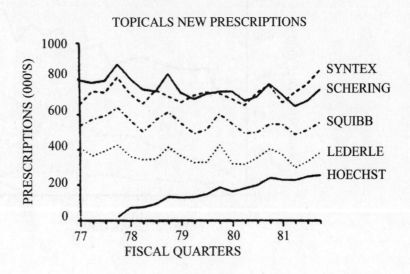

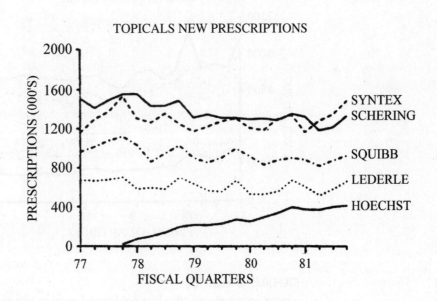

Oral contraceptive market trends

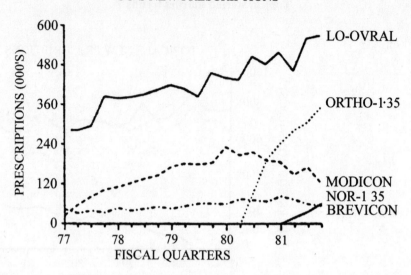

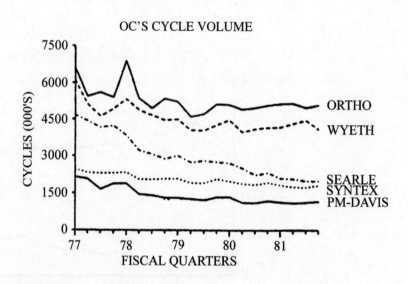

EXHIBIT 3 cont'd.
Syntex Laboratories (A): Topical steriod market trends

Normal planned 1985 calls or presentations based on FY 1981.

Products (Presentations)		Specialties (Calls)	
Naprosyn	358,000	General practice	124,000
Anaprox	527,000	Family practice	108,000
Norinyl 135	195.000	Internal medicine	98,000
Norinyl 150	89,000	Orthopedic surgeon	54,000
Lidex	101,000	Rheumatologist	13,000
Synalar	110,000	Obstetrician	
Nasalide	210,000	gynecologist	117,000
TOTAL	159,000	Dermatologist	50,000
		Allergist	14,000
Ave/rep.	3,677	Ear, nose, throat	12,000
		TOTAL	590,000
		Ave/rep.	1,360

Planned 1985 sales ($000) with present policy—(Syntex 1985 estimates by product, allocated to specialties on FY 1981 product by specialty distribution).

Product		Specialty	
Naprosyn	$214,400	General practice	$92,398
Anaprox	36,500	Family practice	78,083
Norinyl 135	21,200	Internal medicine	79,082
Norinyl 150	37,200	Orthopedic surgeon	19,671
Lidex	38,000	Rheumatologist	16,961
Synalar	14,600	Obstetrician	
Nasalide	11,200	gynecologist	51,312
		Dermatologist	26,598
TOTAL	$373,100	Allergist	3,434
		Ear, nose, throat	5,561
		TOTAL	$373,100

Contribution as percent of Factory Selling Price

Product		Speciality	
Naprosyn	70%	General practice	67.6%
Anaprox	55	Family practice	67.8
Norinyl 135	72	Internal medicine	68.1
Norinyl 150	72	Orthopedic surgeon	68.4
Lidex	62	Rheumatologist	67.5
Synalar	53	Obstetrician/	
Nasalide	52	gynecologist	66.2
		Dermatologist	55.3
		Allergist	62.5
		Ear, nose, throat	62.2

Estimated 1985 average cost per representative (excluding samples) $57,000
Estimated 1985 fixed selling overhead (present organization) $2,800,000

EXHIBIT 4
Syntex Corporation (A) Basic Model Inputs[*]
[*]1985 plans have been disguised.

Product Response Functions

	No Calls	One-Half	Present 50%		More Saturation
Naprosyn	47	68	100	126	152
Anaprox	15	48	100	120	135
Norinyl 135	31	63	100	115	125
Norinyl 150	45	70	100	105	110
Lidex	56	80	100	111	120
Synalar	59	76	100	107	111
Nasalide	15	61	100	146	176

Specialty Response Functions

	No Calls	One-Half	Present 50%		More Saturation
General practice	29	62	100	120	136
Family practice	31	62	100	124	140
Internal medicine	43	69	100	111	120
Orthopedic surgeon	34	64	100	116	130
Rheumatologist	41	70	100	107	112
Obstetrician/ gynecologist	31	70	100	110	116
Dermatologist	48	75	100	107	110
Allergist	17	60	100	114	122
Ear, nose, throat	20	59	100	117	125

EXHIBIT 5

Syntex Laboratories (A)

Step No.	No. of Reps.	Chg. n Reps	Sales (000s)	Chg. In Sales (000s)	Net Profit (000s)	Chg. In Net Profit Per Rep (000s)	Alloc. To:
26	391.8	0.9	367,818	312.4	224,144	185.7	RHEU
27	392.6	0.8	368,119	300.5	224,285	176.0	ENT
28	428.7	36.1	380,052	11,933.4	230,390	169.1	ORS
29	437.0	8.3	382,766	2,713.5	231,752	164.3	GP
30	463.7	26.7	393,586	10,820.2	235,995	158.7	DERM
31	470.9	7.2	395,871	2,285.4	237,133	157.6	FP
32	477.5	6.6	397,911	2,039.6	238,149	155.0	IM
33	480.8	3.3	399,201	1,290.2	238,646	148.7	DERM
34	481.6	0.8	399,463	262.2	238,763	146.3	ENT
35	489.4	7.8	401,814	2,350.5	239,873	142.0	OBGYN
36	493.0	3.6	402,863	1,049.4	240,385	141.9	ORS
37	493.9	0.9	403,114	251.1	240,505	138.1	RHEU
38	502.2	8.3	405,412	2,297.6	241,586	130.4	GP
39	509.7	7.5	407,603	2,191.4	242,529	125.9	ALLG
40	510.6	0.9	407,874	270.8	242,645	123.9	ALLG
41	517.8	7.2	409,787	1,913.1	243,530	122.7	FP
42	524.4	6.6	411,452	1,665.1	244,291	116.1	IM
43	525.2	0.8	411,659	206.4	244,374	103.0	ENT
44	533.5	8.3	413,610	1,951.8	245,221	102.2	GP
45	534.4	0.9	413,814	203.8	245,309	101.3	RHEU

Key:
GP   general practice
FP   family practice
IM   internal medicine
ORS   orthopedic surgeon
RHEU   rheumatologist
OBGYN   obstetrician/gynecologist
DERM   dermatologist
ALLG   allergist
ENT   ear, nose, throat

EXHIBIT 6
Syntex Laboratories (A): Syntex Laboratories Sales Force Strategy Model Specialty Allocation

Contribution to profit versus number of sales reps

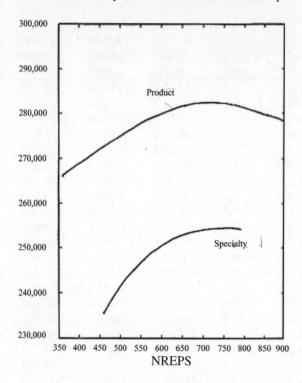

Marginal contribution versus the number of sales reps

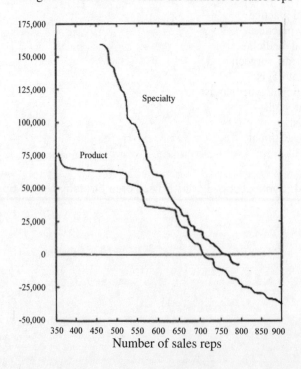

EXHIBIT 7
Syntex Laboratories (A)

Present Policy

Allocation to	Number of Reps	Sales Calls	Sales in Dollars (000s)	Gross Profit (000s)	Net Profit (000s)
GP	91.2	124,000	92,398	62,461	57,264
FP	79.4	108,000	78,083	52,940	48,414
IM	72.1	98,000	79,082	53,855	49,747
ORS	39.7	54,000	19,671	13,455	11,192
RHEU	9.6	13,000	16,961	11,449	10,904
OBGYN	86.0	117,000	51,312	33,969	29,065
DERM	36.8	50,000	26,598	14,178	12,081
ALLG	10.3	14,000	3,434	2,146	1,559
ENT	8.8	12,000	5,561	3,459	2,956
Total	433.8	590,000	373,100	247,910	220,382

SSM Recommended Policy

Allocation to	Number of Reps	Sales Calls	Sales in Dollars (000s)	Gross Profit (000s)	Net Profit (000s)
GP	116.0	157,818	103,915	70,246	63,632
FP	108.3	147,273	92,624	62,799	56,627
IM	78.6	106,909	81,586	55,560	51,079
ORS	36.1	49,091	18,622	12,737	10,680
RHEU	10.4	14,182	17,273	11,660	11,065
OBGYN	70.4	95,727	47,120	31,194	27,181
DERM	0.0	0	12,767	6,805	6,805
ALLG	0.0	0	584	365	365
ENT	8.8	12,000	5,561	3,460	2,956
Total	428.7	583,000	380,052	254,825	227,590

Key:

GP	general practice
FP	family practice
IM	internal medicine
ORS	orthopedic surgeon
RHEU	rheumatologist
OBGYN	obstetrician/gynecologist
DERM	dermatologist
ALLG	allergist
ENT	ear, nose, throat

EXHIBIT 8

Syntex Laboratories (A): Comparison of Existing Policy with Recommended Policy at Current Sales Force Levels [*] (1985)

[*] Optimal allocations are only computed for sales force sizes in a step (see Exhibit 6). A consequence of this is that allocations are not available for every sales force size and thus allocated sales force sizes don't exactly match the current level.

Present Policy

Allocation to	Number of Reps.	Presentations	Sales in Dollars (000s)	Gross Profits (000s)	Net Profit (000s)
N	96.8	358,000	214,400	150,000	144,565
A	142.4	527,000	36,500	20,075	11,956
N 135	52.7	195,000	21,200	15,264	12,260
N 150	24.1	89,000	37,200	26,784	25,413
L	27.3	101,000	38,000	20,140	18,584
S	29.7	110,000	14,600	7,738	6,043
N	56.8	210,000	11,200	5,824	2,589
Total	429.7	1,590,000.	373,100	245,905	218,610

Recommended Policy 369 Reps

Allocation to	Number of Reps.	Presentations	Sales in Dollars	Gross Profits	Net Profit
N	246.3	911,272	306,526	214,568	200,530
A	0.0	0	5,475	3,011	3,011
N 135	57.5	212,727	22,019	15,854	12,576
N 150	28.4	105,181	38,049	27,394	25,774
L	37.2	137,727	41,222	21,847	19,726
S	0.0	0	8,614	4,565	4,565
N	0.0	0	1,680	873	873
Total	369.4	1,366,909	423,585	288,115	264,257

Recommended Policy 499 Reps

Allocation to	Number of Reps.	Presentations	Sales in Dollars	Gross Profits	Net Profit
N	246.3	911,273	306,527	214,569	200,530
A	129.5	479,091	33,708	18,539	11,159
N 135	57.5	212,727	22,019	15,854	12,577
N 150	28.4	105,182	38,048	27,395	25,774
L	37.2	137,727	41,222	21,848	19,726
S	0.0	0	8,614	4,565	4,565
N	0.0	0	1,680	874	874
Total	498.9	1,846,000	451,819	303,644	272,405

EXHIBIT 9

Syntex Laboratories (A): Comparison of Existing Policy with Recommended Policy at (Near) Current Levels

Optimal Sales Force Policies

Based on Specialties

Allocation to	Number of Reps.	Sales Calls	Sales in Dollars (000s)	Gross Profit (000s)	Net Profit (000s)
GP	198.9	270,545	118,680	80,227	68,888
FP	173.3	235,636	104,067	70,558	60,682
IM	131.0	178.182	90,700	61,767	54,299
ORS	61.4	83,454	22,818	15,608	12,110
RHEU	16.5	22,454	18,327	12,371	11,430
OBGYN	117.3	159,545	55,389	36,667	29,980
DERM	43.4	59,091	27,551	14,685	12,208
ALLG	12.2	16,546	3,667	2,292	1,599
ENT	13.6	18,546	6,506	4,047	3,270
Total	767.6	1,044,000	447,706	298,221	251,665

Based on Products

Allocation to	Number of Reps	Sales Calls	Sales in Dollars (000s)	Gross Profit (000s)	Net Profit (000s).
NAPROSYN	263.9	976,363	309,379	216,565	201,524
ANAPROX	168.3	622,818	39,847	21,915	12,321
NORINYL 135	76.7	283,636	24,068	178,329	12,959
NORINYL 150	37.2	137,545	39,060	28,123	26,004
LIDEX	49.6	183,636	43,155	22,872	20,043
SYNALAR	29.7	110,000	14,600	7,738	6,043
NASALIDE	82.6	305.455	15,802	8,217	3,512
Total	708.0	2,619,454	485,911	322,761	279,606

Key:

GP	general practice
FP	family practice
IN	internal medicine
ORS	orthopedic surgeon
RHEU	rheumatologist
OBGYN	obstetrician/gynecologist
DERM	dermatologist
ALLG	allergist
ENT	ear, nose, throat

EXHIBIT 10
Syntex Laboratories (A)

TUTORIAL FOR SALES CALL PLANNING
(CALLPLAN & JFRENCH)

Callplan was developed by Lodish (1971) to help salespeople allocate their calling time to customers and prospects based on judgmental response functions.

JFrench.xls is specifically designed to accompany the Unsweetened Breakfast Cereals (UBC) exercise. This spreadsheet incorporates the Callplan model and includes data for that exercise.

On the **Model** menu, select the generalized **Callplan** model (callplan.xls) to see the **Introduction** screen.

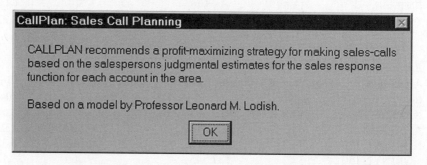

Click **OK** to go to the first of two dialog boxes, which will prompt you for your input.

As an example, we will set up a simple model for Mr. Smart Sell who serves two accounts.

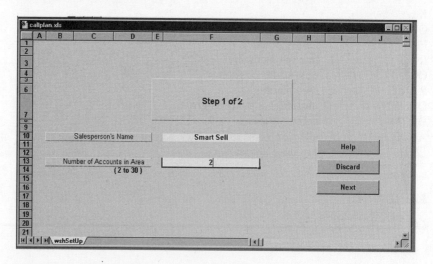

Click **Next** to go to the second setup box.

Next name the accounts, provide some baseline information about sales visits currently made during a selling period, sales levels, and sales margins, and estimate sales response to variations in sales effort to determine the shape of the initial response curves.

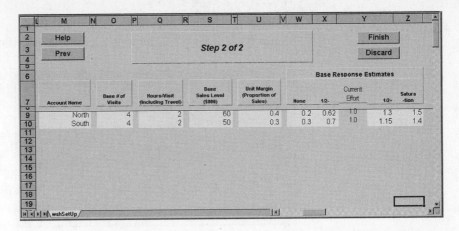

Account Name	Base # of Visits	Hours/Visit (Including Travel)	Base Sales Level ($000)	Unit Margin (Proportion of Sales)	Base Response Estimates		Current Effort		
					None	1/2-		1/2+	Satura-tion
North	4	2	60	0.4	0.2	0.62	1.0	1.3	1.5
South	4	2	50	0.3	0.3	0.7	1.0	1.15	1.4

Click **Finish** and the system estimates the coefficients for the response curves and then prompts you for a file name under which to save your basic model setup. (This can take some time on slower machines: the system must set up and run two separate estimation procedures for each account—the actual response curve and a concave envelope that is needed for optimization.)

It is a good idea to save your newly configured model now. Give it a name other than Callplan.

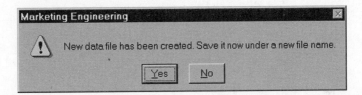

Click **Next** to see a summary of your input information.

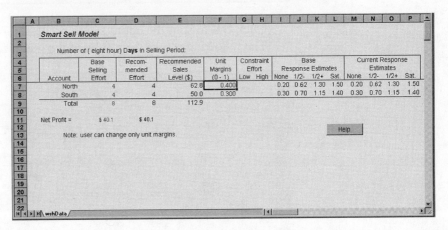

Account	Base Selling Effort	Recom-mended Effort	Recommended Sales Level ($)	Unit Margins (0 - 1)	Constraint Effort		Base Response Estimates				Current Response Estimates			
					Low	High	None	1/2-	1/2+	Sat.	None	1/2-	1/2+	Sat.
North	4	4	62.8	0.400			0.20	0.62	1.30	1.50	0.20	0.62	1.30	1.50
South	4	4	50.0	0.300			0.30	0.70	1.15	1.40	0.30	0.70	1.15	1.40
Total	8	8	112.9											

Smart Sell Model

Number of (eight hour) Days in Selling Period:

Net Profit = $ 40.1 $ 40.1

Note: user can change only unit margins.

Help

To start the optimization, go to the **Model** menu and select **Main Menu**. For this base calibration, select **Optimization**, and click **OK**.

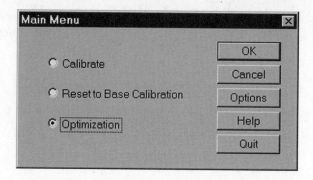

Now specify the time frame for the optimization. For this example, specify a two-day selling period for Mr. Smart Sell. In addition, you can provide constraints on the number of visits.

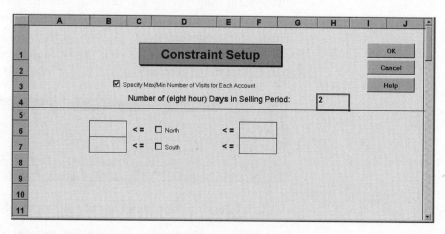

Click **OK** to start the optimization process.
The following shows the results of the optimization run.

For the unconstrained case the solution suggests that by shifting one unit of effort (for our example, two hours of selling time, including travel time) from South to North, Mr. Smart Sell could gain $1300 in net profit over the base case. You may wish to rerun the analysis and impose a new overall constraint, i.e., the number of (eight hour) days in a selling period, or change the limits for each individual account. You can also recalibrate any of the account response functions at any time.

To perform other analyses or to exit the program, go to the **Model** menu and choose **Main Menu**.

Reference

Lodish, Leonard M. 1971, "CALLPLAN: An interactive salesman's call planning system," *Management Science*, Vol. 18, No. 4, Part 2 (December), pp. 25-40.

THE JOHN FRENCH EXERCISE: SALES CALL PLANNING FOR UBC (CALLPLAN)

The Unsweetened Breakfast Cereals (UBC) division of Conglomerate, Inc. competes with Post and Kellogg but with a narrower range of products based primarily on corn. UBC estimates that it has about a five percent market share of a $9.8 billion market.

UBC has a mixed distribution system: it does mostly direct delivery to its large accounts using its own fleet of delivery trucks, but relies on distributors to deliver to small accounts. UBC account sales reps operate the trucks, restock store inventories, and interact with store managers to negotiate for shelf space, end-aisle display space, and the like. While running its own fleet is a more costly alternative than the more usual industry methods, UBC has found that it achieves a higher level of sales and a higher level of retained margins (by capturing the distributor markup), which makes it a reasonable investment.

In early 1996, corporate pressures to reduce staff and to outsource noncore functions forced UBC to carefully evaluate and document the cost-effectiveness of the operation and make sure it managed the operation in the most efficient manner possible. To help it to control and justify its costs and to conform with Conglomerate's program of sales-force automation, UBC began experimenting with a software tool called CallPlan.

CallPlan relies on a salesperson's judgmental inputs about likely customer response to calling frequency to suggest optimal allocation of that salesperson's calling time.

To test the CallPlan system, UBC management provided its Northeastern US sales force, including its sales rep for eastern and central Pennsylvania, John French, with a prototype of the software. John covers 15 Pennsylvania counties and tries to visit his key accounts at least once per month.

John chose his four accounts in State College for a test: BiLo, Weis, Giant, and O.W. Houts. He travels through Centre County every week anyway (although he does not always stop there). In planning his visits for the next quarter, he thought as follows:

"Let's see...I can visit these accounts up to 12 times a quarter or not at all. Actually, for the large retailers, like BiLo, Weis, and Giant, I wouldn't want to visit less frequently than twice a quarter, and once a quarter would be the minimum for Houts. I'll have to check my records to see what we actually sold through these retailers last quarter and how many times I actually visited them. I also need to fill in the 'judgmental calibration' form to indicate how much more or less I think we could sell if I call more or less often. I can't possibly work more hours total than I do now, so I can spend no more time with these accounts in the next quarter (5.25 days) than I did in the last."

(Those data are saved in a version of CallPlan called JFrench.xls, which you should use for this analysis. Select the John French exercise under CallPlan in the **Model** menu of *Marketing Engineering*.)

EXERCISES

1. Set up the sales-call constraints as John has specified them and run the optimization in Callplan to get a recommended calling plan. Do the results make sense? Interpret them.

2. John is thinking about putting one or more of these accounts through his distributor. (This is equivalent to removing the minimum visit restriction for each of the accounts.) How does this affect the solution in Question 1? Should he do it?

3. John is rethinking BiLo's likely response to more selling effort because its volume has grown recently. He now believes that 50 percent more effort will bring in 50 percent more sales and unlimited effort will bring in twice the current level of sales. How does this affect his calling frequency (assuming no minimum visit constraints)?

4. John's regional sales manager has suggested that he spend more time at a new Weis that has just opened in Harrisburg. According to John's best guess, if he made two additional visits to that store each quarter, he would bring in $1400 more in quarterly sales (with a margin similar to that of the store in State College). Should he do this if it means cutting the number of visits to his State College store-clients to four per quarter (again, assuming no minimum number of visits per quarter for any account and using the calibration from Question 3)?

5. How can CallPlan or a similar model be adapted to a range of products, some of which are new (whose sales will not be immediate), or to a mixture of current and prospective accounts? (Prospective accounts may or may not provide any sales at all at low levels of selling effort.) Is the model's objective the right one for these cases? What would you recommend?

TUTORIAL FOR GEODEMOGRAPHIC SITE PLANNING

A gravity model helps firms to determine where to locate a retail site (e.g., a store or a shopping mall). The model helps them to compute the probability that consumers living in any selected geographic area (e.g., a MicroGrid, a ZIP code, or any specified region) will patronize a particular retail site. They can then use these probability measures to compute the sales and market shares the retail site can attain. The model estimates market shares for competing stores based on two primary factors: (1) the overall reputation (also referred to as image or attractiveness) of the stores for fulfilling consumers' needs, and (2) ease of access to a site from a consumer's base location. To use the model, you will need data on the composition of the population in each elemental geographic unit (e.g., MicroGrid) and the distances (for determining ease of access) from each retail site to each geographic unit. The Scan/US database contains an extensive amount of geo-coded data for this purpose.

The gravity model in Scan/US uses a Microsoft Excel macro to evaluate the market shares for up to 80 sites in a single run. After you specify the location of the competing retail stores, the model can compute the required distances internally using its databases. However, you must provide an index of each store's attractiveness. Typically, people use the gross leasable area (GLA) of a site as a proxy for the store attractiveness under the assumption that the larger the store, the greater the variety of products it can offer, and therefore, the more likely it is to meet customer needs. However, one could use any index of overall store attractiveness that is appropriate for a given decision situation. Ease of access is typically measured as the inverse of the weighted distance between store locations and the areas from which customers come to a store.

Scan/US is a comprehensive software program for geodemographic analysis. It includes a detailed online help file. Here we describe only the features that you will need for the J&J Family Video exercise.

NOTE: *To view or print a copy of the complete manual, you will need the original CD on which the marketing engineering software was distributed:*

If you do not have Adobe Acrobat™ installed on your system, run ACROREAD.EXE on the Marketing Engineering CD to install it. Follow the installation instructions that you see on the screen.

*After Acrobat™ is successfully installed, start the Acrobat program. From the **File** menu, select **Open** and open the file manual.pdf from the x:\scanus\manuals directory, where x is the letter representing your CD-ROM drive. Under the **File** menu, select **Print** to print any part of the manual.*

In the J&J Family Video exercise, you will build a gravity model to locate a new video store in the Phoenix, Arizona metropolitan area. This tutorial describes the three steps that you should follow to complete the exercise:

1. Setting up the data for the gravity model
2. Using Microsoft Excel to build the gravity model
3. Mapping the results of the gravity model

Insert your Marketing Engineering CD in the CD-ROM drive. From the **Model** menu, select **Geodemographic Site Planning** to see the following screen:

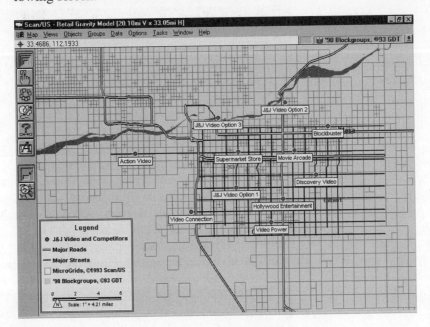

Step 1—Setting up the data for the gravity model

To set up the gravity model, you should first create or load the specific geographical area you want to work with. Next, you add various types of data, called layers, to the specified geography. You should then load a file indicating the locations of the retail sites (if it is not already loaded) as the location layer. We have completed these tasks for the J&J Family Video exercise. If this exercise is not automatically loaded when you open the program, go to the **Map** menu and **select J&J Family Video Exercise**.

NOTE: *Gain familiarity with the software before you attempt to set up your own study area and retail site options. Follow the instructions* *available. in the online **Help** menu. Briefly, the steps are: 1) Select an area of the US map for study, 2) Select the geographic features you want to include for analysis (e.g., zip centroids, major streets), 3) Indicate the location of various retail sites of interest, and 4) Create and name a new location layer.*

Specify the set of competitive sites to be used in the analysis (Location Layer): Make locations the active layer by clicking on the arrow in the upper right corner of the screen and selecting **J&J Video and Competitors.**

Next, select the set of retail sites (video stores) that you want to include in your analysis. To do this, first define a group that contains the selected stores. From the **Groups** menu, choose **New Grouping,** name the grouping, e.g., J&J Sites 1, and click **OK**. Go to the **Groups** menu, click **New Group** and name the group, e.g., All competitors. You can specify many different groups within one grouping.

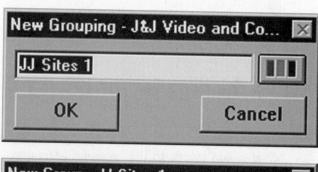

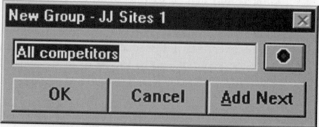

Click **OK**. This should bring you back to the original screen and in group mode (click the group mode icon [icon] on the left side of the screen, if it is not already activated). Now you are ready to specify the sites to be used for the analysis under the group name you provided. It is convenient to first activate the Group-By Polygon submode ([icon]) and draw a polygon around the selected video stores by dragging the mouse while pressing the left mouse button. (For the present, select for analysis all the stores that you see on the screen.)

Specify the geographic area you want to include for analysis (Consumer layer): Here you have two choices: You can either specify the entire geography already included in the J&J Family Video exercise, or you can select a part of this area.

Using the entire geography in the J&J Family Video exercise: (Until you become familiar with the software, we suggest that you select the entire geography for analysis). Here, simply copy the distances from the location layer (J&J Video and competitors) to the consumer layer (MicroGrid layer), which contains information about where people live in the study area. To do so, make locations (i.e., **J&J Video and Competitors**) the active layer at the right upper corner of the screen. Go to the **Objects** menu and select **Copy Distance**. You will see the following box:

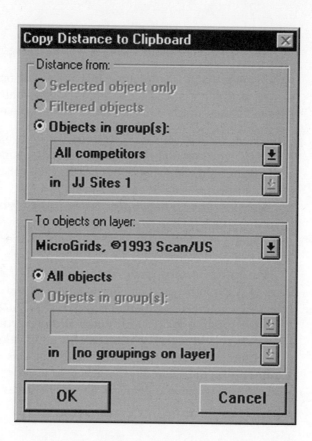

Copy the distance information from **Objects in groups** (e.g., J&J Sites) to **All objects** on the consumer layer (MicroGrid layer), by choosing **MicroGrids, ©1993 Scan/US** from the drop down menu.

Click **OK** to proceed.

Using a subset of the geography in the J&J Family Video exercise: Instead of computing distances for all geographical units in the consumer layer, you can also first create a group on the consumer layer and load the distance information from the location layer to the newly defined group on the consumer layer. To do this, click the arrow in the upper right corner of the screen and select the MicroGrid layer:

Go to the **Groups** menu and select **New Grouping** and give the MicroGrid grouping a name:

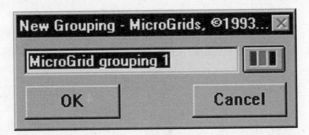

Click the **Group-By Polygon** button (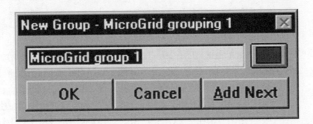) and draw a polygon around the selected geography by dragging the mouse while pressing the left mouse button. Once you have defined a closed polygon, the system will ask you to give a name to the group, for example, MicroGrid Group 001:

Click **OK**, and you will see a screen highlighting the area you selected in red:

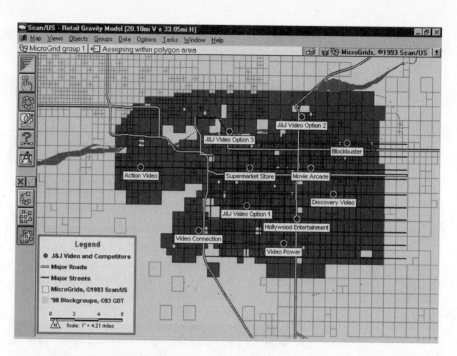

To run the gravity model, you have to copy data about distances from stores to the MicroGrids to the consumer layer (e.g., a selected group in the MicroGrids layer). You need to make sure that the location layer, i.e., J&J Video and Competitors, is activated by clicking the arrow in the right upper corner and choosing **J&J Video and Competitors**. Next, go to the **Objects** menu and choose **Copy Distance**. You will see the following box:

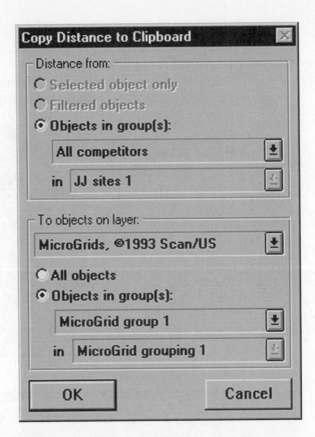

Select **Objects in group(s)** and specify the group and the grouping in the MicroGrid layer you want to include in the analysis. If you select a small geographical area as a group, the gravity model will calculate estimates only for that specific group (area), thus reducing its computation time. Click **OK**.

Step 2—Using Excel to build the Gravity Model

You build the gravity model using a Microsoft Excel macro. First, you must enter data on store attractiveness indices for each site and the attractiveness and distance impact coefficients.

The distance impact coefficient indicates how much ease of access to a store (site) would influence a consumer's decision to buy from that store. The higher this coefficient, the faster the decline in consumer's utility for a site as its distance from the consumer's home base increases. For example, in a rural area, people commonly travel five miles or more to a store; in a metropolitan area, they do not. The distance impact coefficient in a rural area might be 1.5, while in a metropolitan area it might be 2.0 or higher.

The Scan/US Gravity Model Assistant, a Microsoft Excel macro, generates a data file containing the gravity model estimates, which can then be displayed within the Scan/US program.

On **Tasks** menu, choose **Build Gravity Model.** Microsoft Excel will launch and bring up the Scan/US Gravity Model Assistant.

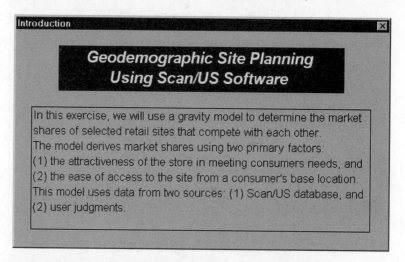

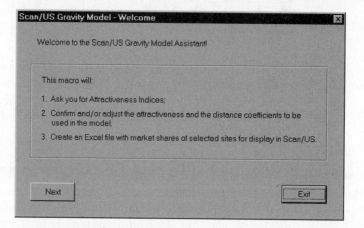

Click **Next** to see the next screen.

Fill in the attractiveness index for each store on a suitable scale (1-100 is typical, with higher numbers indicating more attractive stores) based on your best judgment about the attractiveness of each store.

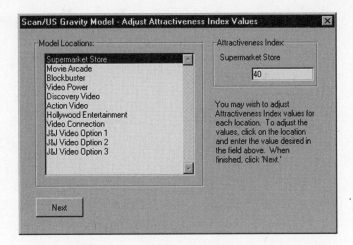

Click **Next** to get to this screen:

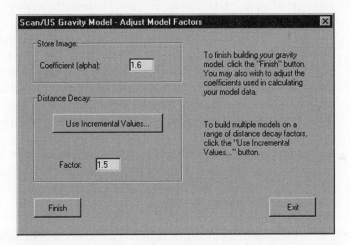

Enter your best guesses as to how store attractiveness (image) and distance influence store choice, choosing alpha and beta coefficients to reflect these influences. You can choose a single value for the beta coefficient, or choose multiple values in a selected range to represent varying degrees of influence of distance on store choice For the latter case, click **Use Incremental Values** and specify the range:

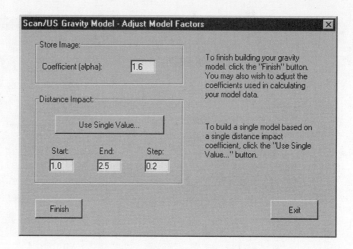

(If you choose a range of values for distance impact, save each set of results under a different Excel 4.0 file at the end of the model run).

Click **Finish** to continue.

The model now starts its computations using the distances generated by Scan/US and the attractiveness indices and the alpha and beta coefficients that you provided. Processing may take several minutes (or even hours) depending on the number of geographic entities included in the analysis. For the J&J Family Video exercise, it should take only a few minutes. The status bar at the bottom of the screen indicates the progress.

When data processing is completed, the Gravity Model Assistant prompts you to save your gravity model table. Change the path in the **Save in** box to the \mktgeng\Scanus\Userdata folder and be sure to set the **Save as Type** to Microsoft Excel 4.0 Worksheet. Enter a filename and click **Save**.

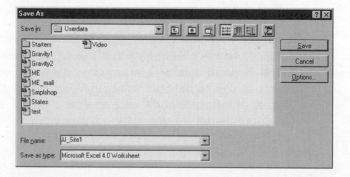

At this point, you are given the option to restart the Excel macro to obtain model results under a different set of attractiveness indices and alpha and beta parameters. To restart the excel macro, click **Back to the Beginning**. Save each run under a separate Excel 4.0 filename. For this exercise, you have to run the model at least four times, once with just the existing stores (i.e., by setting the attractiveness indices to zero for the three new sites being considered by Jack and Jeri) and once for each store location option available for J&J Family Video (i.e., by setting the attractiveness indices to zero for the two new sites not included in an analysis).

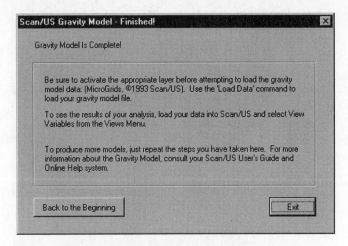

Click **Exit** to get back to Scan/US.

Step 3—Mapping the results of the Gravity Model

To view the model's market share estimates in Scan/US, you need to load the gravity model results (which are in the saved Microsoft Excel file) to the consumer layer (MicroGrids) and create a new thematic view.

1. Click the arrow in the upper right corner of the screen and choose MicroGrids (the consumer layer) from the drop down menu.

2. Go to the **Data** menu and choose **Load Data**. Switch to the Scanus\Userdata folder and select one of the gravity model files you saved in Excel. (To change directories, check the **Directories** option first). Click **OK**.

3. Go to the **Views** menu and click **New Thematic**.

NOTE: *If you grouped objects in the consumer layer when you set up the model, be sure to select **Analyze: Grouped objects in grouping** to view the selected area.*

To see how each geographical area contributes market share to a specific site location, you can stratify geographical areas using a color scheme. First select the variable whose geographic distribution you want to view—either estimated market shares for all stores, or for selected stores. In the example above, we have selected **Estimated % Market Shares** for all stores. Next, click the **Strata Manager** button.

You can change the range of values that are assigned to a particular color by dragging the appropriate black dumbbell up or down with the mouse. After you finish specifying the parameters, click **OK**.

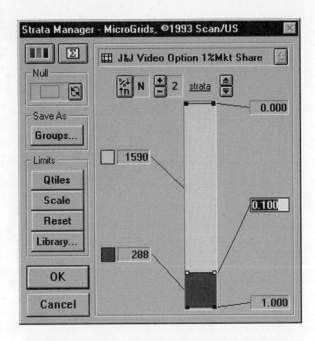

Click **Groups** and assign a name to the group.

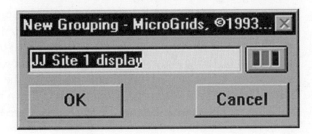

Click **OK**. You will now see the selected geography highlighted with the color scheme you specified showing how market shares for J&J video store option 1 varies by geographical units.

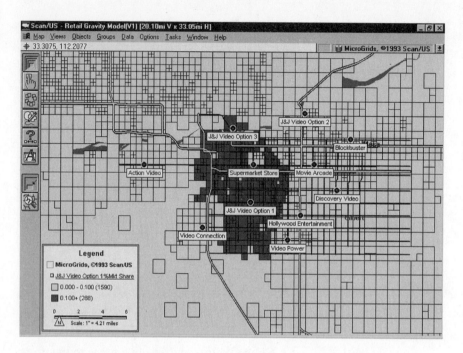

Viewing a group's data

You can also use Scan/US to automatically aggregate the data for each object in a group to create a group summary. First, ensure that the data are attached to the active layer. For example, if you want to investigate the results of the gravity model, activate the MicroGrids layer by clicking on the arrow at the upper right corner of the screen and choosing **MicroGrids, ©1993 Scan/US** from the drop down menu.

The market share estimates for each group are loaded into this layer.

Next click the group mode button: . Select an existing grouping or create a new group for which you wish to see summary information. For example, if you want to look at market share estimates for a certain area extending over many MicroGrids, you should build a group containing the MicroGrids that lie in the area of interest. Next, go to the **Views** menu and click **QuickLook** to see the active group's data.

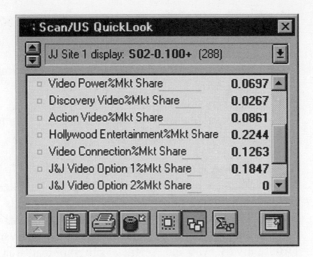

(**Estimated %Market Shares** gives the value for the primary contours, i.e., here 0.2546 is the highest market share estimate reached by any of the competitors in the set.)

You can switch between viewing the data for the active group or of an object (e.g., a selected MicroGrid) by clicking on the "Show Group" button ( ) or "Show Object" button (left).

Advanced analyses: Customizing your data in Excel

You can get further insights about the sales potential of a site if you index the estimated choice probabilities from the gravity model with demographic information available in the from the Scan/US database. For instance, for the J&J Video exercise, you can index your probability estimates by taking into account the density of family households with children. You can also calculate potential sales using the probability values and data from the Scan/US retail potential database. To conduct these analyses, use Microsoft Excel to create your own customized data set or to merge your data with the data provided by Scan/US.

NOTE: *There are various databases commercially available that offer information—beyond that contained in the Scan/US BasePak—that can aid your analyses, e.g., data about household expenditures by product category. Some of these databases (e.g., Scan/US retail potential database), come with this educational version of Scan/US but are restricted to the Washington DC and Phoenix, AZ areas.*

In the following section, we explain how to combine data from a Scan/US application with your own data. Principally, you need to know:

1. How to group a subset of the Scan/US product databases and export it to Excel for further manipulation

2. How to prepare your own Excel data for import into the Scan/US program

3. How to display your data by creating a thematic view (see previous sections)

1. Specifying data for export to Excel

First, you need to indicate which data to include in the analysis. The following example considers only the MicroGrids that have probability values of more than 10 percent for patronizing J&J Video Option 1. You can limit the amount of data to use in an analysis by "hiding strata." (Alternatively, you can select a geographical area by grouping objects (e.g., MicroGrids) as we described earlier.)

"Hiding strata" is a useful way of focusing an analysis on a specific set of objects. You can hide strata only when a variable's strata, instead of data values, are being rendered by the thematic presentation. To prepare your data, go to the **Views** menu and click **View Variables**. Select **J&J Video Option1%Mkt Share** as the layer variable to be displayed.

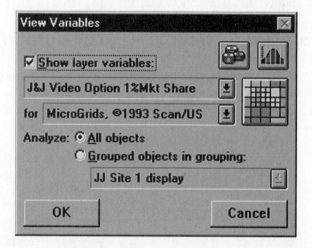

To open the dialog box shown below, click the "Strata Manager" button: . Click the presentation icon next to the desired stratum, and a window shade will replace the color icon for the stratum (i.e., a hidden stratum has been created).

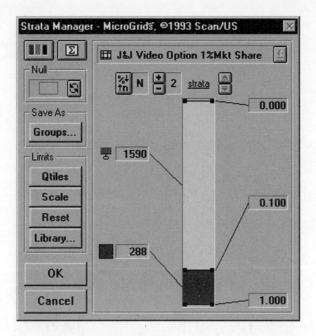

Click on **Groups** button and save your data as a new grouping.

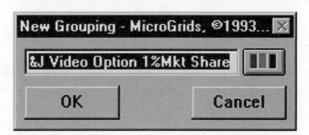

Click **OK** (on several open windows). Next, from the **Data** menu, click **Copy Data** and copy the data to the Windows clipboard for **Objects in groups**.

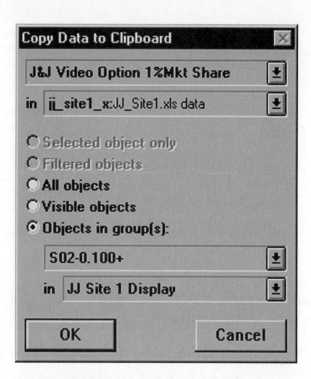

Click **OK**. Now open Excel and paste the data into a spreadsheet (use the Windows copy command or the key combination Ctrl+V).

Exporting Scan/US demographic data

As an example, we will copy the "Average annual expenditure per household for videos, tapes, disks" variable from the Home Electronics datalist and the "Total Households (hh90)" variable from the data in the BasePak and paste the data into the spreadsheet shown above.

For these tasks, the relevant data need to be available to the consumer layer. Several data lists can be loaded onto a layer (although only one can be active at a time). In this example, we use information from the Scan/US data lists on home electronics and key demographics, as well as the probability estimates from the gravity model. To load the home electronics data list, go to the **Data** menu in the Scan/US program, choose **Data Center,** select **'93 Home Electronics**, and click the **Load** button (if the data is not already loaded).

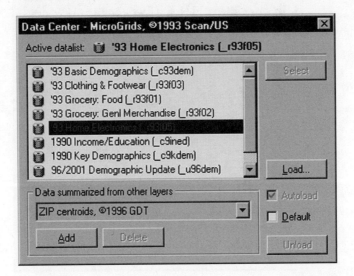

Next, go to the **Data** menu and click **Copy Data.** Choose Home Electronics as your database in the drop down menu and select the variables that you want to copy into your spreadsheet. In this example, restrict the demographic data to be copied to the strata group that you specified earlier (e.g., J&J Video Option1%Mkt Share) or simply choose **Filtered Objects**. This ensures that only data for the microgrids that obtained choice probability values of more than 50 percent for J&J Video Option 1 will be copied.

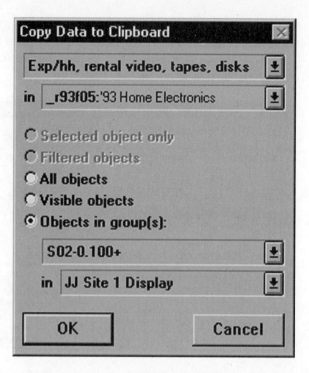

Go back to Excel and paste the data into the spreadsheet.

Similarly, copy the Total Households variable from the data in your BasePak, and paste the data into the spreadsheet.

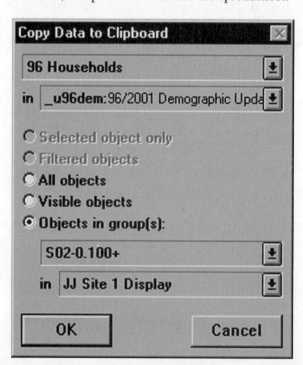

Now you can create variables that combine demographic information and choice probabilities from the gravity model. To compute potential sales for J&J Video Option 1 for the "filtered" area (assuming that this is the primary trade area), multiply the column containing the probability values (the variable is called huffprob9 on the spreadsheet) by the Total Households and by Average Annual Expenditure per Household for Video rentals, disks, and tapes. You can then total the potential sales across MicroGrids to derive an estimate for the total potential sales for the retail site under consideration.

2. Prepare your own Excel data for import into Scan/US

	A	B	C	D	E	F	G	H	I	J	K
1	[data]	288		1	1	1 jj_site1_x:	1	1	MG90	M-grid	JJ Site 1
2	Key	Group	Name	huffprob9:J&J Video Option 1%Mkt Share							
3	#33111/1658.0	2	Grid 33111/1658.0	0.10448							
4	#33111/1754.0	2	Grid 33111/1754.0	0.11534							
5	#33111/1755.4	2	Grid 33111/1755.4	0.13601							
6	#33111/1756.2	2	Grid 33111/1756.2	0.13075							
7	#33111/1756.3	2	Grid 33111/1756.3	0.14079							
8	#33111/1756.4	2	Grid 33111/1756.4	0.14426							
9	#33111/1757.3	2	Grid 33111/1757.3	0.12213							
10	#33111/1757.4	2	Grid 33111/1757.4	0.1332							
11	#33111/1853.3	2	Grid 33111/1853.3	0.10559							
12	#33111/1854.0	2	Grid 33111/1854.0	0.1405							
13	#33111/1855.1	2	Grid 33111/1855.1	0.16271							
14	#33111/1855.21	2	Grid 33111/1855.21	0.1548							
15	#33111/1855.22	2	Grid 33111/1855.22	0.14808							
16	#33111/1855.23	2	Grid 33111/1855.23	0.16808							
17	#33111/1855.24	2	Grid 33111/1855.24	0.16064							
18	#33111/1855.3	2	Grid 33111/1855.3	0.19468							
19	#33111/1855.41	2	Grid 33111/1855.41	0.18505							
20	#33111/1855.42	2	Grid 33111/1855.42	0.17578							
21	#33111/1855.43	2	Grid 33111/1855.43	0.20647							
22	#33111/1855.44	2	Grid 33111/1855.44	0.19616							
23	#33111/1856.0	2	Grid 33111/1856.0	0.15672							
24	#33111/1857.1	2	Grid 33111/1857.1	0.12629							
25	#33111/1857.2	2	Grid 33111/1857.2	0.144							
26	#33111/1857.3	2	Grid 33111/1857.3	0.13257							
27	#33111/1857.4	2	Grid 33111/1857.4	0.16002							

When preparing your own Excel data for input to Scan/US, you need to ensure that your Excel data file meets the following specifications to make it readable by the Scan/US software:

- Put your object keys in column A. An object key is a unique identifier for each record that matches the data with the geographic object to which it pertains. These keys must be in text format. A pound sign (#) in front of numeric keys makes them "text." (For best performance, sort your object keys in ascending order.)
- Your data columns must have column headings without any numbers in their names.
- You must define a named range called "**database**" that includes all the cells containing the column names, object keys, and data.

You must complete this step, or Scan/US may not read your data correctly. If you modify the number of rows and columns in your data file, you must redefine the range of "**database**".

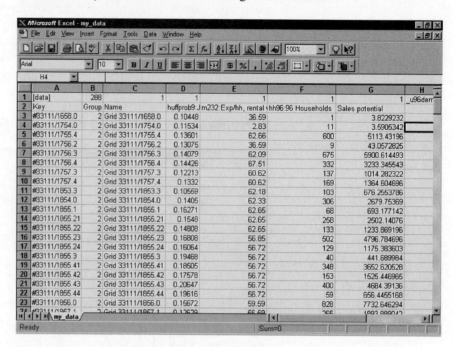

- You must save your spreadsheet in Excel 4.0 format. For convenience, save it in the Scanus\userdata folder. Close the file before trying to import it into Scan/US.

3. Display imported data within Scan/US

Now you can load your data into Scan/US, more specifically, to the layer that contains your objects codes. In this example, make sure that MicroGrids is the active layer. Next, go to the **Data** menu and choose **Load Data**. You may then create thematic views to visualize your data and conduct further analyses.

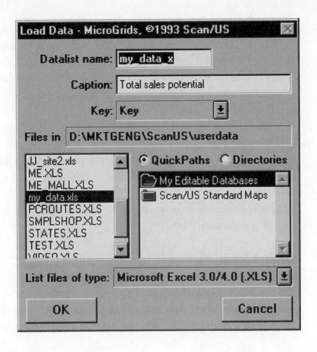

Glossary

Data: Scan/US provides census-based demographic data with most geographic features in the BasePak. Data are automatically loaded with each feature in a study area.

Groups: By creating groups, you can classify objects on a layer into distinct and unique subsets. In general, you can select any group to operate on as a unit. For instance, you can copy, paste, hide, or show groups on a layer.

A classification of objects into groups is called a grouping. A grouping can consist of a number of groups. Because objects can be classified in any number of ways, you can define any number of groupings on the layer. You can create as many groupings as you like, limited only by the amount of memory on your computer. However, only one grouping can be active at a time on any given layer.

Grouping objects is a powerful feature in Scan/US. As a fundamental tool for handling multiple objects, grouping is a first step in analyzing a territory, or in limiting an analysis to a specific region. For example, you can examine sales across territories by creating a group for each territory, such as California, Washington, and Oregon in the western region/group, and then look at the group's data in "QuickLook."

Layers: Geographic features, such as states, counties, roads, or geology, are loaded as layers into the study area, each feature on its own layer. In the gravity model application, there are special names for two of those layers: the consumer layer and the location layer. The *consumer layer* contains (demographic) geo-coded information about your clientele -- at the level of detail needed for your analysis (e.g., mostly data provided by Scan/US such as MicroGrids or block-level census data) . The *location layer* contains information about the location of the sites that you wish to consider in your analysis.

Each item of a feature on a layer is called an *object*. For example, California is an object on the Places 500T+ layer. Although several features or layers are present in a study area, only one layer can be active at a time. The terms *feature* and *layer* are often used interchangeably.

Object: A set of points, lines, or polygons in a spatial database that represent a real-world entity.

Object key: An object key is a unique identifier for each record. This key matches the data with the geographic object to which it pertains. You have object keys that match your data to standard geographical units, such as zip codes or census tracts. Or you can have your own unique keys that identify your store or branch office locations.

References

Scan/US Basic Skills, 4th edition. June 1996.
Scan/US User's Guide, 1st edition, December 1994.

J&J Family Video[*]

Jack and Jerilyn Rodeman are longtime residents of Scottsdale, Arizona. Jack recently took early retirement from the aviation division of a leading firm in electronic instrumentation and controls after several years of successfully managing its manufacturing operations. Jeri is currently working part-time as an independent software consultant to small businesses in the Phoenix area. As Jack and Jeri planned the next phase of their life, they decided to open a small service business, such as a cybercafe, a restaurant, or a video store. After discussions with their children and friends, they decided to explore the feasibility of opening a video store close to their home.

Over 85 percent of U.S. households have a VCR and about 50 percent of American households rent a video at least once a month. A "VCR household" had an average of 47 rentals per year at an average price of $2.50 per rental. In 1996, video rentals and sales were estimated to be around $18 billion, with rentals representing about half the industry revenues, and the rest attributed to sales of used video tapes (at around $10 per tape) and other related products. Nationally, there were about 27,500 video stores, but this number had declined from a high of 31,500 in 1990. Although some industry observers believed further consolidation would lead to fewer video stores, others, like Bob Finlayson of the Video Software Dealers Association, believed that consumers will drive only a short distance (three or four miles) to rent a video rental, and that the number of video outlets would actually increase over the next few years. In fact, a recent trend has been the growth of video rental and sales through supermarkets ($1.9 billion in 1996), mass merchandisers such as K-Mart ($200 million in 1996), and even gasoline stations.

Industry leader, Blockbuster Entertainment Group, operated 14 percent of all stores and had an over 20 percent share of the revenues. Other large companies included Portland-based Hollywood Entertainment and Philadelphia-based West-Coast Entertainment. Blockbuster competed by offering consumers a large selection with an emphasis on recent releases, with stores carrying over 40 copies of some new releases. Blockbuster had a number of large stores that were over 6000 square feet in size, and had over 20,000 rental units under 5000 or more titles. Smaller video stores were typically less than 2000 square feet and carried fewer than 6000 rental units. Video rental prices varied greatly with new releases, renting for about $3.50 for two nights at Blockbuster and $3 for a single night at Hollywood Entertainment. Older movies rented for about $1.50 to $2.00 for three nights, and "family movies" rented for as little as 99 cents for two nights. Video stores often had ongoing promotions, such as

---

[*] This exercise describes a hypothetical situation. It was developed by Arvind Rangaswamy and Katrin Starke using publicly available information.

half-price rentals during "happy hours" (e.g., 9 am to 10 am), or special pricing on selected days (e.g., Tuesdays), and senior citizens discounts.

Jack and Jeri determined that site location would be the primary factor that determined the competitive environment the new store would face and therefore its long-term viability. They hired a consultant friend, Ruby Jackson, to do preliminary research to assess the competitive environment in the catchment area within which they planned to locate their new store. Based on her experience, Ms. Jackson concluded that several factors influence what video stores consumers patronize: (1) the distance of the store from their homes, and (2) overall attractiveness of each store, which could depend on such factors as proximity to other shops, variety of videos for rent, service quality, average price, and size of the store. She identified eight existing stores with which the proposed new store would compete in the geographical area of interest and gathered preliminary information about these stores. She organized the information into the following table:

Store	Proximity to Other General Shops (1 poor to 7 good)	Estimated Number of Titles Carried	Service Quality (1 good to 7 excellent)	Estimated Average price per Rental	Size (Square feet)	Estimated Percent Unit Market Share in Study Area (from Traffic Counts)
Discovery Video	2	2,000	6	1.95	1,200	5
Blockbuster Entertainment	6	4,000	3	2.30	4,400	25
Video Connection	2	800	6	1.70	1,000	5
Video Power	5	2,500	4	2.10	1,800	12
Hollywood Entertainment	3	3,500	5	2.20	3,000	20
Movie Arcade	7	1,500	5	1.75	1,000	10
Local Supermarket	7	300	1	2.40	200	5
Action Video	2	1,300	7	2.85	1,400	18

While Blockbuster and Hollywood offered wide variety, such stores as Action Video focused on the latest releases, adult video, and suspense and adventure titles. Video Connection and Movie Arcade focused on older movies and "seconds" of recent releases. Ruby guessed the combined annual sales of these video stores to be around $8 million per year (including sales to people outside the study area).

Jack and Jeri wanted their video store to carry only family-oriented and children's videos (PG or G ratings). They planned to carry a maximum of 1600 titles, including new releases, and they hoped to realize an average rental rate of $2.10. Jeri had access to a software program called Scan/US which she used in her work helping small businesses to develop direct marketing programs. She decided to use this software to evaluate three alternative sites where space was currently available. The table below shows the characteristics of these sites:

Location	Proximity to Other General Shops (1 poor to 7 good)	Estimated Number of Titles	Service Quality (1 good to 7 excellent)	Estimated Average Price Per Rental	Size (Square feet)
Option 1	2	1,200	6	2.10	1,200
Option 2	4	1,600	5	2.10	2,500
Option 3	3	1,200	6	2.10	1,200

EXERCISES

1. Using the tabular data, develop and justify an overall measure of store attractiveness for each existing store and for the three potential sites.

   To answer the following questions, you will need to build a gravity model using Scan/US and Microsoft Excel. Select **J&J Video and Competitors** as your location layer.

2. Insert the overall index of store attractiveness for each store into the gravity model and evaluate which of the three locations that Jack and Jeri are considering would achieve the highest market share. (To evaluate one site at a time, choose a store attractiveness index value of zero for sites not under consideration.)

3. Jeri estimated that the total annual operating costs of an established video store would be roughly $300,000 for a 1200 square-foot store and about $450,000 for a 2500 square-foot store at all three locations. She also estimated that the cost of opening a new store would be between $250,000 and $300,000, depending on its size. These initial costs cover purchasing such items as tapes, furniture and fittings, and computer equipment and software. Are any of the proposed store locations a good business proposition given this cost structure? Why or why not?

4. Jack and Jeri are also concerned about the long-term viability of video stores in view of the growth of direct TV broadcasts and the expansion of cable offerings. They wondered whether the gravity model could be modified in some way to take into account the potential threats posed by these developments.

TUTORIAL FOR LEARNING CURVE PRICING (LEARNER)

The Learning Curve Pricing spreadsheet helps firms to price strategically in markets with experience-curve cost effects. It simulates a simple (noncompetitive) market situation and explores how the optimal short-term and long-term pricing policies depend on the experience-curve phenomenon.

From the **Model** menu, select **Learning Curve Pricing** (Learner.xls) to see the **Introduction** screen.

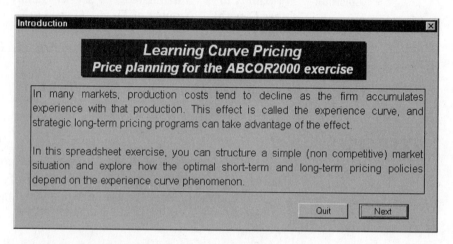

Click **Next** to get to the Analysis Area.

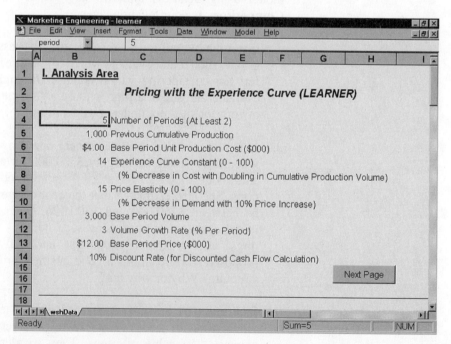

Here you should provide estimates of the main characteristics of the market (cumulative production, current cost, experience curve constant, and the like) and the other parameters needed to produce the analysis.

Click **Next Page** to go to the Optimization Area.

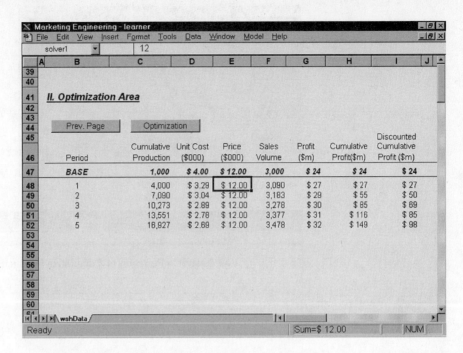

Here you can enter prices to indicate a pricing policy and examine the effect of that policy on profit.

Click **Optimization** to invoke Solver. Set the Target Cell (e.g., profit in a certain period, cumulative profit, discounted profit), indicate which prices in which periods are subject to optimization, and set any appropriate constraints on those prices.

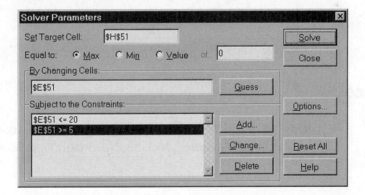

On the **Model** menu, click **Main Menu**, and choose among three graphing options. For example the graph of the Unit Cost as a function of Cumulative Production here shows the experience-curve effect.

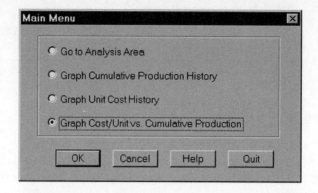

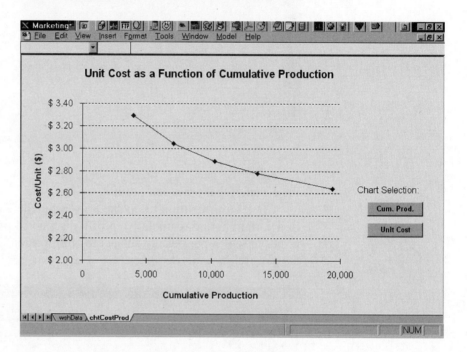

Reference

Alberts, William W. 1989, "The experience curve doctrine reconsidered," *Journal of Marketing*, Vol. 53, No. 3 (July), pp. 36-49.

PRICE PLANNING FOR THE ABCOR2000

Abcor Industries, a wholly owned subsidiary of Conglomerate Inc., is one of the largest sellers of engraving plate material and plate-making equipment in the U.S.

In 1996, Abcor introduced new equipment that uses a proprietary process developed in Conglomerate's engineering polymers division—a polymer plate and associated plate-making equipment. It has named the first generation of this equipment the ABCOR2000; it is costlier than its metal-alloy equipment (the ABCOR1000 line), but it produces plates that are much less expensive than metal plates. (For more background on Abcor and the ABCOR2000 see the Value-in-use pricing exercise "Account pricing for the ABCOR2000.")

Abcor had developed a software tool called VALUE to support its sales force in selling the ABCOR2000. Initial use of the VALUE model was quite successful. Salespeoples' evaluations included the following comments:

- "The VALUE software helped me close two sales in half the time."
- "I finally felt I was in control of the sales negotiation."
- "I felt comfortable making on-the-spot offers for equipment and for contracts on plates."
- "I could sell quite a few more of these machines with more aggressive pricing!"

This last comment struck Fran Collins, marketing manager for the ABCOR2000 line. Fran's background was in equipment and tool manufacture, and she felt that as Abcor gained experience producing the ABCOR2000 line it could reduce its production costs. She also felt that a coherent long-term pricing strategy would give structure to Abcor's overall marketing program.

Fran had worked with the ABCOR1000 (predecessor to the ABCOR2000), and she had noticed that costs of manufacture for that equipment seemed to drop 13 to 15 percent every time production doubled (after the first thousand machines or so). This learning-curve or experience-curve effect in manufacture was something that Abcor managers had noted in other products as well. Fran developed a simple spreadsheet model (Learner) to study the learning-curve effect on short- and long-term pricing.

To address the pricing question, Fran needed to make some assumptions about the future of the product and its production costs:

- Experience-curve effect = 14 percent. (Manufacturing and related costs decrease 15 percent when production volume doubles.)
- Previous production experience = 1000 units.
- Initial production cost = $4000.
- Initial market price = $12,000.

- Sales forecast (at $12,000) = 3000 units.
- Price elasticity = 15 percent (defined as percent decrease in demand with a 10 percent increase in price).
- Growth rate = 3 percent. (The underlying market demand at the current price is growing at this annual rate.)

The problem

Fran then faced the issue of recommending a pricing policy for the ABCOR2000. To define the problem, Fran noted that although the anticipated life cycle of the ABCOR2000 is about five years, Abcor managers were split over whether to make short-term (annual) or long-term (five-year) profits their major goal. Hence Fran ran a number of analyses for comparison, seeking

- The short-term profit-maximizing price
- The single price fixed over five years that maximizes discounted five-year cumulative profit (Hint: set all cells below E47 equal to E47 and use Solver to optimize profit by changing cell E47.)
- The price policy that maximizes discounted five-year cumulative profit, with prices that can vary year by year
- The sensitivity of the above to possible changes in price elasticity (12 percent? 18 percent?) and the learning curve constant (10 percent? 20 percent?)

The baseline for comparison for the pricing program was an anticipated three percent annual price increase from the current price of $12,000.

What pricing policy do you recommend for Abcor and why?

NOTE: *These are the key spreadsheet relationships:*

Learning curve effect:

$$C = C_0 Q^r$$

where

C = unit production cost,
C_0 = constant,
Q = cumulative production,
r = learning curve exponent (derived from the input data).

Demand/price relationship:

$$V = kP^e$$

where

V = current volume,
k = constant,
P = current price,
e = price elasticity (as a negative number).

TUTORIAL FOR VALUE-IN-USE PRICING (VALUE)

The Value spreadsheet runs a pricing analysis based on customer value (value-in-use). It is based on the idea that organizations should base their pricing on a careful understanding of what a product is worth economically to a specific customer as well as what it costs the organization to produce the product. The spreadsheet is designed to accompany the exercise "Account Pricing for the ABCOR2000."

From the **Model** menu select **Value-in-use Pricing** (value.xls) to see the **Introduction** screen.

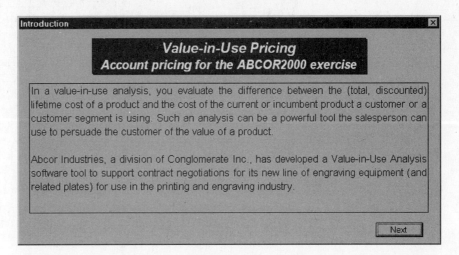

Clicking **Next** brings you to the Input/Analysis Area.

You can set parameters for analyses on such key inputs as initial annual number of plates, price per plate, machine price, and use growth.

The graphing parameters set the origin (start) and the increment size (step) for graphs—the x-axis on the graph begins with the starting value and includes 10 increments of the step size.

Click **Next Page** to see the resulting cash flows.

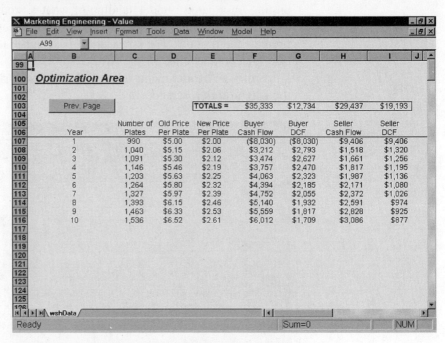

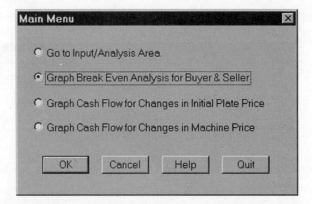

Go to the **Model** menu and choose **Main Menu** to choose among a number of forms of graphical output.

If you select **Graph Breakeven Analysis for Buyer & Seller**, you will see the range of machine and plate prices that are economically attractive to the buyer and to the seller. Any point at which discounted cash flow (DCF) is positive for both buyer and seller could be an acceptable contract arrangement.

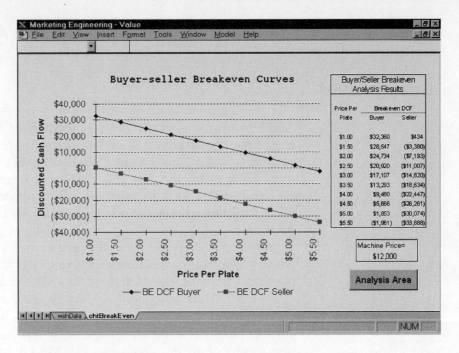

Other graphs provide additional information. You can return to the analysis area to reset parameters by clicking **Analysis Area**.

Reference

Lee, Donald D. 1978, *Industrial Marketing Research*, Technomic Publishing, Westport, Connecticut.

ACCOUNT PRICING FOR THE ABCOR2000

Background

Abcor Industries, a wholly owned subsidiary of Conglomerate Inc., is one of the largest sellers of engraving-plate material and plate-making equipment in the United States. While engraving equipment is used to make brass plates for gifts and ceremonial items (plates on pictures, statuettes, and the like), its oldest and most traditional use is in engraving plates for printing business cards, high quality stationery, invitations, and informals.

Major customers are specialty printers nationwide. Most of these printers own their own plate-making equipment and typically buy their plate stock from the manufacturer of their plate-making equipment.

In 1996, Abcor introduced new equipment using a proprietary process developed in Conglomerate's engineering polymers division—a polymer plate and associated plate-making equipment. It has named the first generation of this equipment the ABCOR2000; the plate-making equipment is more costly than the metal-alloy equipment (the ABCOR1000 line), but it produces plates that are considerably less expensive than metal plates but of comparable quality. (When purchased in lots of 500 or more, metal plates range from $4.78 to $4.92 each, with prices about 10 percent higher for smaller volumes.)

With the introduction of the ABCOR2000, Abcor's support staff in sales has developed a software tool called Value. Initial discussions with some of Abcor's prospective customers suggest that these unsophisticated small manufacturers do not fully understand how the lower cost of materials (the plates) will compensate over time for the higher cost of the plate-making equipment. The software is designed to help the sales force (which is given price discretion) to bid on contracts and to negotiate pricing arrangements with customers.

In introducing Value to the sales force, Abcor has identified three typical prospect-accounts for a training exercise: Longform Printing of Medford, Massachusetts; Smithfields Quality Printers of Wilmington, Delaware; and Franklin Printers of Fort Lauderdale, Florida. The training exercise requires salespeople to make an initial bid (and justify it) to each of these accounts.

EXERCISES

As an ABCOR salesperson, you are to prepare a bid for each of these customers as well as a justification. (You may decide that it is not in ABCOR's best interest to bid on some or all of these contracts.) Salespeople at ABCOR are salaried, and they are given a small bonus based on customer satisfaction measurements.

In each case, assume the following:

- Our machine costs $3980 to produce and ship
- The list price for our machine is $12,000. (Salespeople can generally discount up to 20 percent below list without sales management approval; larger discounts are subject to written review.)
- Metal plate prices will continue to rise three percent per year
- The (marginal) production cost per plate (including delivery) is $0.60
- Our machines depreciate 25 percent per year (for salvage value calculation)
- We expect to increase prices at about the same rate as metal prices

Prepare and justify bids for these three accounts:

1. Longform Printing of Medford, Massachusetts.

   - Formed in 1947 and client of ours since the mid-1950s. 15 employees.
   - Usage: 990 plates; 1994 usage: 940 plates.
   - Three-year-old ABCOR1000 (Initial price: $4000).
   - Highly conservative firm: Looking at a 10-year time horizon and a 15 percent cost of capital.

2. Smithfields Quality Printers of Wilmington, Delaware.

   - Relatively new prospect, using competitor's equipment and material.
   - Demand is uncertain (between 250 and 500 plates per year) but appears to be growing at about 11 percent per year.
   - Old equipment worth about $3000 on market.
   - Conservative investor: Looking at a 20 percent cost of capital. Appears to like to evaluate investments over a five-year lifetime.

3. Franklin Printers of Fort Lauderdale, Florida.

   - A small, general commercial printer that does a small amount of engraving on the side. Its business is stable.
   - Has bought 200 to 250 plates from us per year over the last four years.
   - Has an old machine of ours (an ABCOR 11), bought about 15 years ago and which is fully depreciated.
   - Evaluates investments based on a five-year payback period—i.e., it expects that (with no discounting) the sum of the simple cash flow from the investment will become positive after a maximum of five years for it to consider the investment.

The value spreadsheet

The spreadsheet contains the following relationships:

Buyer Cash Flow = Col C × (Col D - Col E)+ Old Machine Salvage Machine Price in Year 1

= Col C × (Col D - Col E) in intermediate years

= Col C × (Col D - Col E) + New Machine Salvage in final year

Seller Cash Flow = Col C × (Col E - Plate Cost) + Machine Price - Machine Cost in Year 1

= Col C × (Col E - Plate Cost) in Other Years.

The discounted cash flow (DCF) columns simply discount the simple cash flow columns.

The graphing parameters allow one to plot discounted and undiscounted cash flows for a range of price possibilities.

TUTORIAL FOR COMPETITIVE BIDDING (BID)

The BID spreadsheet has two elements. The first part calculates the probability of winning a bid against a known number of competitors whose bids follow the probability distribution you specify, and it then develops the optimal bidding strategy in such a situation with known costs. The second part of the spreadsheet is designed to accompany the Paving I-99 exercise; it simulates the results of a bidding competition with an unknown number of competitors and uncertain costs.

On the **Model** menu, select **Competitive Bidding** (bid.xls) to see the **Introduction** screen.

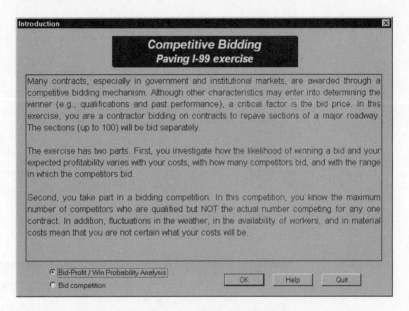

Select **Bid Profit/Win Probability Analysis** and click **OK** to get the following dialog box for specifying the parameters of the probability graph.

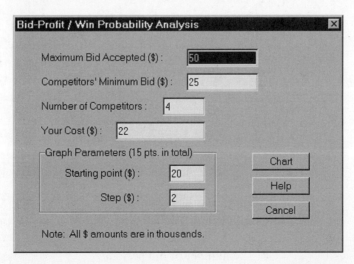

You must specify the characteristics of the bidding competition (maximum allowable bid, minimum competitive bid, number of competitors, and your costs). You also set the starting point and the step size for your graph. Click **Chart** to see a chart showing your probability of winning the first bid.

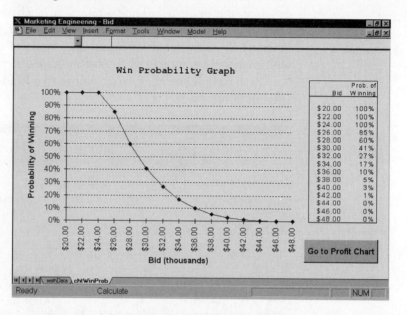

Click **Go To Profit Chart** to see how your expected profit varies with your bid.

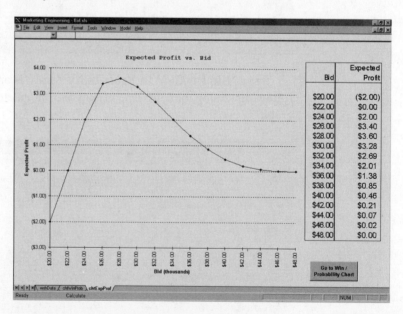

To go to the bid competition, select **Model, Main Menu**, and then **Bid Competition**. The bid competition dialog box asks for

- The number of bid periods
- The maximum number of competitors
- Your bid (your decision variable set at the same level each period)

- Your cost-range (minimum to maximum to complete the contract)
- Valid bid range (minimum to maximum) for you and for your competition

When you have entered those inputs, click **Run** to run the competition and see the results for each of the periods. You will also see how many times you win, your total profit across all competitors and your average profit (total profit divided by number of times you won) and your expected profit (total profit divided by number of bid periods).

NOTE: *The models in both parts of this software assume that the likelihood of a competitor bidding a specific value is uniformly distributed between U (the upper bid limit) and L (the lower bid limit).*

Your probability of winning a competition with *n* competitors when bidding *b* is

$$[(U - b) / (U - L)]^n$$

Your expected profit with a bid of *b* is equal to

win probability $\times$ *(b - cost).*

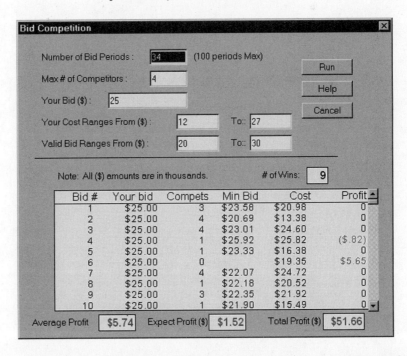

Clicking **Cancel** at any time will send you back to the Main Menu.

Because the bid competition is a simulation, you can click **Run** repeatedly to get different results (costs and actual number of competitors vary with each simulation).

References

Monroe, K. B. 1990, *Pricing: Making Profitable Decisions*, second edition, McGraw-Hill, New York.

Rothkopf, Michael H. and Harstad, Ronald M. 1994, "Modeling competitive bidding: A critical essay," *Management Science*, Vol. 40, No. 3 (March), pp. 364-384.

PAVING I-99 EXERCISE:
BIDDING FOR PAVEMENT CONTRACTS BY
CONGLOMERATE INC.

Background

Many contracts, especially those for government and institutional markets, are awarded through competitive bidding mechanisms. Although issues other than price, such as degree of qualification and past performance level, are important, the bid price is often the critical factor with the low bid winning. (Remember: When the seller—contractor here—bids, low bid wins; when the buyer bids, high price wins.)

The construction division of Conglomerate, Inc. is bidding on a series of construction contracts to pave strips of Pennsylvania Route I-99. Thirty-four such contracts are up for bid, and they are essentially designed to be approximately equivalent in cost to pave.

The actual bidding-exercise simulation is part 2 of this exercise. In part 1, we will attempt to convey how the likelihood of winning a bidding competition varies depending on the firm's cost to complete the contract, the number of competitors who bid, and the range of those competitive bids.

In part 2 of the exercise, you are to simulate the effect of different bidding strategies under different competitive scenarios. As this is a public bid, the names of the firms who requested the RFQ (request for quote or bid) are public knowledge. However, all of those who requested the RFQ may not bid, so you generally know the maximum number of possible competitive bidders but not the actual number.

The best bidding strategy balances the opportunity cost of losing profitable business to a competitor (because the bid is too high) against the lost profits (or actual losses) associated with bidding too low. (The "winner's curse" is an expression that describes the theoretical and empirical finding that when costs are not known for sure but must be estimated as here, the competitor most likely to win a contract is the one who most underestimates its costs!) Note that fluctuations in the weather, in the availability and productivity of workers, in material costs, and the like make it uncertain just what actual costs are likely to be even if you have had considerable experience in similar projects.

In this market, after you specify an upper and lower bound either for costs or for competitors' bids, the actual costs and bids are about equally likely to be found anywhere in those ranges. (They are uniformly distributed in those ranges.)

The training exercise

Use part 1 of the exercise to prepare for the competition.

1. Set up the "Bid Profit/Win Probability" so that you can see what the probability of winning the competition is when (a) your costs will be $25,000; (b) bids will be disqualified if outside the range of $25,000 to $50,000 and we are expecting: one, three or six competitors. How does the number of competitors affect your probability of winning, the best bid, and your expected profit?

2. Assume you know that there are three competitors but that the upper bid limit is $40,000 rather than $50,000. How does this affect your bid in Q1? What if the upper limit was $50,000, but you were able to get your costs down to $20,000 in the three-competitor case. What would your optimal bid be in this case?

The bid-competition simulation

The bid simulator allows you to study the effect on the results above when the actual number of competitors is unknown (although the maximum number is known) as well as when your own costs are known. The government is asking for bids on all 34 road segments to be submitted simultaneously (that is, not sequentially).

Your information from the state government is that four competitors (besides you) have asked for the RFQ. In addition, you have been told that the government has set a "quality floor" (lowest acceptable price) of $20,000 per strip and a maximum price of $50,000. (Bids outside these ranges will be declared nonresponsive; strips of road where there are no responsive bids will be rebid.)

Your past experience with this type of business has shown that your costs can range anywhere from $12,000 to $25,000. And you do not have the capacity to fulfill more than 10 of the contracts. (Assume that you lose $2,000 in subcontracting costs for every contract you win over your capacity.)

Conglomerate, Inc. needs guidance on the following decisions:

1. What should we bid on the contracts? Should we bid on all of them or on just a portion?

2. Arthur Anderson, our accounting firm, has sent us a proposal that it claims will reduce the range of variation in our cost estimates. It is (conservatively) estimating that it can identify the causes of cost overruns and reduce the upper cost-estimate bound from $25,000 to $21,000. It is asking for $10,000 to do this work. Should we hire the firm?

3. The government is considering splitting the bidding competition into two competitions of 17 contracts each. Suppose you win three, six, or eight segments in the first round. What is your best bid for the remaining 17 segments?

TUTORIAL FOR YIELD MANAGEMENT FOR HOTELS (YIELD)

Yield management or revenue management models are intended to optimize the pricing of hotel rooms, airline seats, and other "perishable" commodities for a given duration by taking into account demand variability over time and capacity constraints. Our Yield Management system for the hotel industry runs on the Excel spreadsheet. The task is to price hotel rooms and set capacities for various room classes.

From the **Model** menu, select **Yield Management for Hotels** and then the **Generalized Yield Model** (Yield.xls) to see this introduction:

Click **OK** to continue.

Phase 1—Designing the hotel

In phase 1, you outline the characteristics of the hotel. As an example follow the simple hotel setup that consists of two classes. Provide the requested information for the three fields and click **Next** to advance to the second step of this phase.

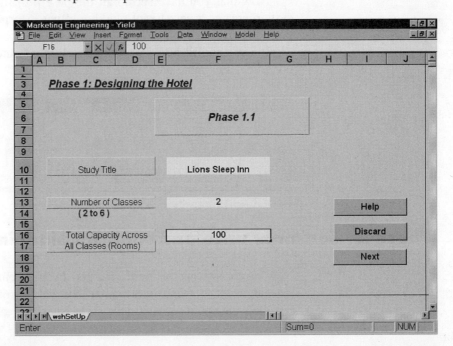

Next, name the classes (15 characters maximum), provide some baseline information about the prices and the expected demand at these prices, and finally give demand elasticity estimates for each of the classes. (Elasticity is the percentage decrease in demand with a one-percent increase in price.) The model assumes constant elasticity coefficients in each class. Click **Finish** to proceed.

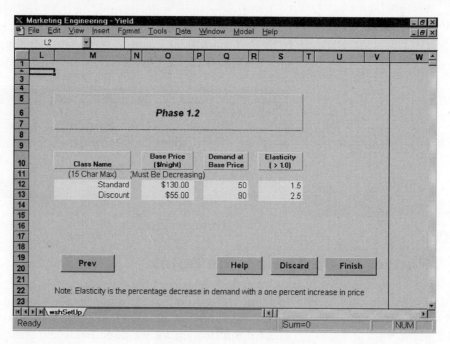

Now that you have set up all the base properties for the model, the system creates a new Excel workbook that incorporates the information provided up to now.

It is a good idea to save your newly configured model now. If you do, give it any name other than Yield or Forteyld.

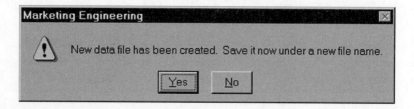

Phase 2—Seasonal price and capacity planning

Now customize all the fields marked by blue entries, i.e., target date, marginal cost, demand information, and values for seasonal multipliers. See the explanations given in the spreadsheet for each table column.

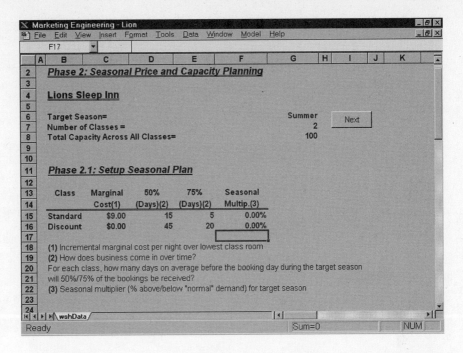

The target season, e.g., summer, serves as a reference for the demand function specification. The way demand generally arrives over time for each class is specified in columns 3 and 4. For instance, for the "standard" class in the example, 15 "days on average before the arrival date during the target season" (target date), the hotel will have bookings for approximately half of its Standard rooms and five days before the target date it will have bookings for about 75 percent of its Standard rooms. The class segments are assumed to be distinct, so no one switches class if the price differential changes in the optimization process.

Instead of setting up the demand function specific to the target season, you can specify an "average" time-demand relationship for each of the classes and make seasonal adjustments: the seasonal multipliers are the percentage deviations from the normal demand.

Click **Next** to go to the next screen:

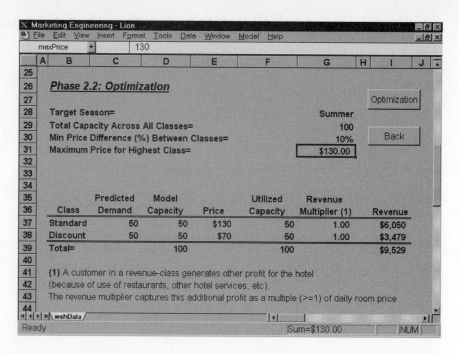

Click **Optimization,** and the model will calculate optimal capacities and prices for each of the classes. For instance, the optimization results show that a profit-maximizing pricing strategy implies a room price of $130 for the Standard class and $70 for the Discount class.

NOTE*: Excel's Solver sometimes requires numerous iterations to arrive at the revenue maximizing solution.*

Go to the **Model** menu and select **Main Menu** to access the previous setup screens to modify the parameter estimates you provided earlier or to access other functions of the Generalized Yield model, such as **View Demand Curves** and **Set Daily Capacity**.

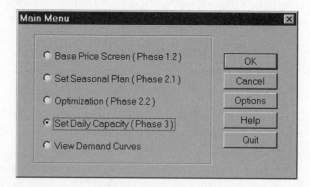

Phase 3—Set daily capacity

If you select **Set Daily Capacity (Phase 3)**, you can determine how many rooms to set up for each class given the prices you determined in phase 2. To do so, customize all the fields marked by blue entries, i.e., provide a target date, the number of days before the target date, and indicate how many rooms are booked so far.

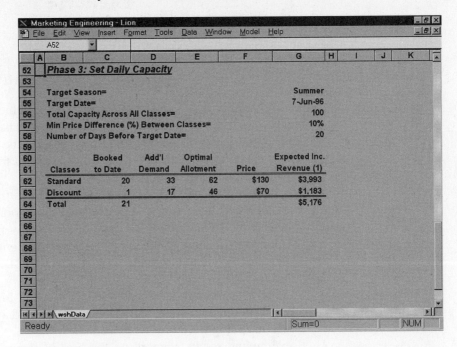

Given the "optimal" pricing scheme and the number of rooms booked by the current date (that is May 18), the model computes the additional demand for the remaining days until the target date and determines the optimal capacity for each class. The "Optimal Capacity" column suggests how many of the unbooked rooms should be allocated to each of the classes. In the example, 20 days are left until the target date.

NOTE: *The Yield Management Model refers only to a single specified day for which hotel rooms are booked and does not deal with carryover effects and the like.*

Limitations of the software

Maximum number of classes: 6

Reference

Smith, Barry C. 1992, "Yield management at American Airlines," *Interfaces*, Vol. 22, No. 1 (January-February), pp. 8-31.

FORTE HOTEL YIELD MANAGEMENT EXERCISE

NOTE: *A version of Generalized Yield Model called Forte Hotel Yield management Exercise includes the data for this exercise.*

Having recently engaged L&R Planning, Inc. to apply conjoint analysis to aid in the design of their new hotel chain, the Forte Hotels, Ltd. board, headed by Charles Long, engaged the same consultants to apply the important concept of yield management to set prices and room allocations for these new hotels.

A unique aspect of the new Forte design was that the three types of rooms (which they were calling Premiere, Superior, and Standard) had the same physical design. The main differences were the floor level and on-floor and in-room amenities. Thus Standard rooms were on the lowest floors and included the standard-room characteristics that emerged from the conjoint analysis.

Superior rooms added bathrobes, an iron and ironing board, free use of an in-room exercycle, shoe-shine service, and twice daily room refresh (including fresh towels, if needed).

Premium rooms were all on the highest floors of the hotel and included Superior room amenities. In addition, Premium rooms offered on-floor concierge service, access to the Premiere Club rooftop lounge, which offered complimentary continental breakfast and free cocktails and hors d'oeuvres during the 5 p.m. to 7 p.m. happy hour.

These different room types tend to attract different types of customers:

Premiere-room customers are typically upscale business travelers, who are not very price sensitive and want the best the hotel has to offer. They tend to use room service quite a bit, often buy personal items and family gifts in the hotel shops, and book meeting rooms and order catering at the hotel.

Superior-room customers include upscale pleasure travelers as well as business travelers with budget constraints. These customers plan somewhat farther in advance than the Premiere room customers.

Standard room customers are a mixture of budget-conscious business travelers and family vacationers. The latter group, in particular, is generally on the lookout for deals and tends to plan well in advance.

As a test application, Mr. Long gave L&R the task of developing and applying a prototype of the system to their first hotel in the chain, located in Arlington, Virginia. This small hotel (consistent with Forte's plan for intimacy) has only 100 rooms and was opened in January 1996. After a year of operation, Mr. Long thought that he and his staff had a reasonable understanding of the flow of room demand during the year and how that room demand reacted to price changes. Forte's policy is to adjust prices and capacities by season, four times a year, and the first task it assigned L&R was to suggest prices (and capacities) for the three room classes for summer 1997.

The model that L&R put together required answers to a number of questions:

- What is the "price elasticity" (percent decrease in demand for each one-percent increase in price) for each room type?
- What is the expected demand level at some base price for each room type?

Because the idea was to use this model regularly, the model also asked the following questions:

- How much does this demand vary (up or down) from an annual average? (For the summer season Forte expected more pleasure travelers and fewer upscale business travelers than during the winter months, for example.)
- How does room booking come in over time? The way the model specified this was by asking, for each room type: "How many days in advance of a date of stay would 50 percent (75 percent) of the ultimate bookings be on hand?"

Thus Forte management had to supply two such estimates for each room type.

Other management inputs included these:

- An estimate of incremental cost per room type: How much more the amenities and services for each room type cost the hotel as compared to the lowest-priced classes;
- An estimate of incremental revenue (multiplier): How much money above the price of the room the average customer brought into the hotel (input as a multiple of the room price).
- The maximum room price (the "rack rate" for the highest price room) and the minimal incremental price difference between room rates for adjacent price classes.

L&R's first task was to provide Mr. Long with an initial price and allocation of rooms to the three classes for summer of 1997. The tool it developed, called Generalized Yield Model, was designed to support this decision. (A version of the model, saved as ForteYld.xls, includes the data for this application.)

How the Generalized Yield Model works

The spreadsheet is based on the following idea: demand for each class of service can be characterized by a total demand function of the following form:

$$D(p) = k\,p^{-e}$$

where

D = demand,
p = price,
e = price elasticity,
k = constant,

and where k and e are determined by the user input in phase 1 of the program.

In addition, booking takes place over time. We assume that we can approximate that process with a log-normal distribution of booking arrivals. That distribution has two parameters, and in phase 2, we ask how many days in advance of the service date will 50 percent of bookings (Cell D14 for class1) and 75 percent of bookings (Cell E15 for class 1) arrive. To get the parameters of the log-normal distribution, we set ln(D15) as the mean and ln[(D15-E15)/3.92] as the standard deviation.

In cell S13, we have the booking date. According to these three inputs, if the booking date is 20 days in advance of the service date, the 50 percent days are 15 and the 75 percent days are five (i.e., D15 = 15 and E15 = 5), then we expect that log-normal (20, 2.7, 2.4) = 62 percent, or 38 percent of the ultimate demand for this date is yet to be realized. We must factor this into our original demand estimate in C38 to account for what we have observed thus far. If 20 people have booked in this class thus far, we can expect that 20/(1-62) = 53 will be the total demand we can expect and that we can expect 33 more people to book for that date.

(If demand is "bumpy," such as when a special group books a number of rooms on a given date, users of yield management systems remove that demand (and the associated booked capacity) from the system and rerun the analysis without that unusual demand spike.)

We apply a greedy rule to allocate remaining unbooked space as we get closer to the booking date: any slack capacity is first allocated to the highest (most profitable) class of service up to the amount of remaining expected demand. If slack capacity remains, it is then allocated to the next highest class, etc. Thus, depending on how demand arrives, a low class of service may be fully booked 30 days in advance of the service date, but because expected demand for higher classes of service did not materialize, the yield management model may release additional space for assignment to a lower class as the booking date approaches.

EXERCISES

1. Using the Forte Hotel version of the model, suggest the number of rooms and the prices for those rooms for the June 1 through August 31 1997 summer season.

2. How would your recommendation change if Forte management set a maximum room price of $180?

3. What if there were a 15 percent minimum increment between room classes?

4. Do the recommendations make sense? (What are the limitations and shortcomings of this analysis from Forte management's perspective?)

The next use of the model is for daily reservations. Local management at the hotel has to decide the number of rooms of each class to book on each day. (With very rare exceptions, customers booked into a lower class who are given a "free upgrade" are happy; hence booking upward is feasible. Booking downward—giving someone who requested a Premiere room a Standard room—is not.)

It is May 23, and the following two reservation requests have come in. Would you accept either or both of these reservations?

5. For June 7, a request from Centre For Travel, a Pennsylvania travel agency that is a steady customer, for a block of 12 Standard rooms for a Washington museum tour group:

   Booked to date:

   > Premiere: 6   rooms
   > Superior: 11   rooms
   > Standard: 59   rooms

6. For May 28, a request for 20 Standard rooms for a foreign delegation visiting the Department of Commerce:

   Booked to date:
   > Premiere: 9   rooms
   > Superior: 25   rooms
   > Standard: 44   rooms

   As a consultant to Mr. Long you have been asked to help him evaluate L&R's work. Comment on the appropriateness of these prototype models—specifically

7. Should they be implemented as is? (If not, what changes would you require?)

8. Particularly for daily reservation requests, what discretion should be given to the local hotel management in taking bookings? The reservations clerk? Why?

TUTORIAL FOR PROMOTIONAL SPENDING ANALYSIS
(MASSMART)

Retailers can use Promotional Spending Analysis to develop optimal promotion policies to maximize their total profits from selling brands in a product category. Samples, manufacturer-price-off offers, coupons and in-store displays are examples of promotions that retail outlets commonly run. Sometimes it may be more profitable to give large discounts on just one or two brands than to give small discounts on all the brands in a product category. Promotional Spending Analysis helps retailers to evaluate such alternatives and to develop brand-promotion schemes that will maximize a retail outlet's profits.

This spreadsheet exercise implements the model for MassMart, Inc., a big mass merchandiser. Your task is to analyze and improve the promotional activities of the company's store in State College, Pennsylvania. The software includes three models for analyzing the store's promotional activities: the Choice Model, the Quantity Model and the Promotion Model.

NOTE: *The Promotional Spending Analysis Excel spreadsheet relies on the Analysis Toolpak add-in to run a regression analysis. If this add-in is not already loaded, you should load it manually. To do so, go to the* **Tools** *menu, then* **Add-Ins**, *and choose* **Analysis ToolPak**. *If this option is not in the list, you will have to install it via the setup program in Excel (or MS Office).*

From the **Model** menu select **Promotional Spending Analysis** (Promote.xls) to see the **Introduction**.

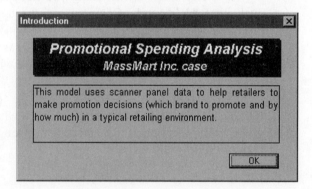

From the **Model** menu, choose **Main Menu**. The **Main Menu** dialog box looks like this:

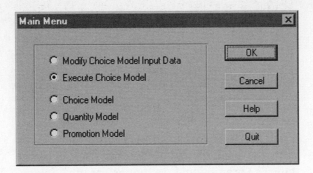

Choice model

From the **Main Menu** dialog box select **Execute Choice Model** and click **OK**. The Choice Model uses information on the quantity purchased and on retailer promotion activities at the time of purchase, such as discounts, feature ads, and displays. MassMart obtains this information from its scanner-panel data. The model assesses the likelihood that a consumer will choose a particular brand based on the promotional activities directed at all the brands. After the model executes it will display a spreadsheet that includes coefficients of each variable and the associated t-statistics. The coefficient of each variable indicates the magnitude of that variable's impact on a consumer's probability of choosing a brand. The t-statistics indicate the statistical significance of the coefficients.

The Choice Model output screen looks like this :

| | | | | | | **PROMOTIONAL SPENDING ANALYSIS** | | | | | | |
| | | | | | | **Which and How Much?** | | | | | | |

Case Name: MassMart

					Coefficients	8.0	-3.1	8.9	1.4	1.4	0.0	0.0	-0.4
Choice Model					T stats	3.9	-2.3	3.7	2.6	2.3	0.1	0.0	-0.5
Customer	Month	Brands	Quantity	Choice	Loyalty	List Price	Discount	Display	Feature	Wisk	All	Tide
1	1	Wisk	0	0	0.07	3.25	0.63	0	0	1	0	0
		All	0	0	0.07	3.10	0.71	0	0	0	1	0
		Tide	1	1	0.80	3.30	0.82	1	1	0	0	1
		Yes	0	0	0.07	2.95	0.86	0	0	0	0	0
	2	Wisk	0	0	0.05	3.25	0.63	0	0	1	0	0
		All	0	0	0.05	3.10	0.71	0	0	0	1	0
		Tide	0	0	0.64	3.67	0.82	0	0	0	0	1
		Yes	1	1	0.25	2.95	0.60	0	1	0	0	0
	3	Wisk	0	0	0.04	3.32	0.12	0	0	1	0	0
		All	0	0	0.04	3.05	0.33	0	0	0	1	0
		Tide	0	0	0.51	3.55	0.12	0	0	0	0	1
		Yes	1	1	0.40	2.90	0.42	0	1	0	0	0

Quantity model

From the **Model** menu, select **Main Menu** to get the **Main Menu** dialog box. Select **Quantity Model** and click **OK** to see the Quantity Model output.

> **NOTE**: *Sometimes when **Quantity Model** is chosen from the **Main Menu** dialog box, Excel displays an error message, either **Analysis Toolpak Absent** or **Add-in Absent**. In this case you need to install the Analysis Toolpak: from the **Tools** menu, select **Add-Ins**. Excel will display the **Add-Ins** dialog box. Check **Analysis Toolpak**. The program will then be able to run the **Quantity Model**.*

The Quantity Model uses the Choice Model's output as its input. It uses the quantity of the product each consumer consumed and the retailer's promotional activities as its inputs. The Quantity Model calculates the responsiveness of the quantity each consumer consumes as a function of several variables (e.g., regular list price and excess inventory at the consumer's home).

The Quantity Model output looks like this:

	Customer	Month	Quantity	Constant	List Price	Discount	Lag Inv
PROMOTIONAL SPENDING ANALYSIS Which and How Much?							
Case Name: MassMart							
Quantity Model Coefficients			1.36	-0.12	1.21	-0.15	
T-Stats			1.42	-0.40	3.71	-2.49	
	1	1	1	1	3.30	0.82	1.00
		2	1	1	2.95	0.60	0.71
		3	1	1	2.90	0.42	0.43
		4	1	1	3.30	0.26	0.14
		5	3	1	3.05	0.70	0.00
		6	1	1	2.99	0.43	1.71
		7	1	1	3.38	0.49	1.43
		8	1	1	2.91	0.45	1.14
		9	1	1	2.99	0.30	0.85
		10	2	1	2.95	0.70	0.56
	2	1	1	1	3.10	0.49	1.28
		2	1	1	2.95	0.20	0.99
		3	2	1	3.15	0.41	0.70
		4	1	1	3.40	0.29	1.41
		5	1	1	3.21	0.17	1.13

Promotion model

Using the Promotion Model, you can develop recommendations for the promotional activities of a retail outlet. It allows you to:

- Select the brands for which it is profitable to run promotional activities, and
- Select the ideal promotional vehicles (discount, displays, or features) for each brand.

From the **Model** menu, select **Main Menu** to see the **Main Menu** dialog box. Select **Promotion Model**. Click **OK**. The Promotion Model's analysis area will be displayed:

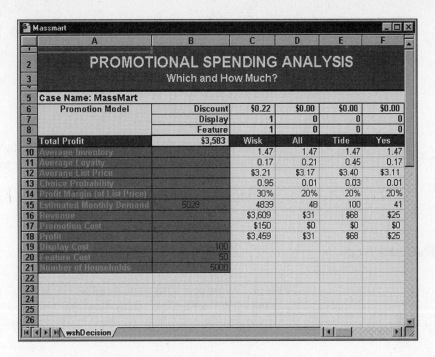

You can use Excel's Solver tool to select a set of promotional activities to maximize Total Profit.

1. From the **Tools** menu, select **Solver** to see the **Solver Parameters** dialog box, which looks like this:

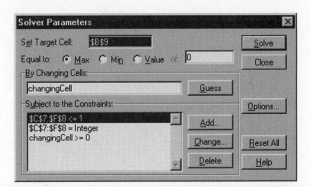

2. In the **Set Target Cell** area, enter the cell number that contains the Total Profit amount (e.g., $B$9).

3. In the **By Changing Cells** area, enter the range of cells that contain the amount of discount and the display and feature variables (e.g., $C$6:$F$8).

4. In the **Subject to Constraints** area, enter constraints that ensure that

   a. the display and feature variables are equal to either 1 or 0,

   b. the discount amounts are greater than or equal to 0.

The following equations are just one way of achieving the above constraints:

$C$7:$F$8 < = 1
$C$7:$F$8 = Integer
$C$6:$F$8 > = 0.

5. Click **Solve**. The Promotion Model displays the optimal promotional activities to maximize the retailer's total profit.

6. Use Solver in a similar manner to answer the questions at the end of the MassMart case.

Reference

Tellis, J. Gerard and Zufryden, Fred S. 1995, "Tackling the retailer decision maze: Which brands to discount, how much, when and why?," *Marketing Science*, Vol. 14, No. 3, pp. 271-299.

MASSMART INC. CASE*

It was Friday, February 23, 1997. Donna Sullivan, marketing manager for MassMart for the central Pennsylvania region, was in her office. She was writing a report for her boss, Jack Chen, vice president of marketing for the company. In January, Jack had asked her to do a preliminary strategic review of the company's promotion programs for its store in State College, Pennsylvania. MassMart is a leading mass merchandiser with over 80 stores in Pennsylvania, Ohio, and Maryland. The company has had a strong presence in central Pennsylvania for over 25 years. Competition has, however, increased recently with two WalMart stores and one Sam's Club outlet established in State College in the last five years.

In preparing her report, Donna spent one morning at the local university library reading articles about in-store sales promotions. One article (by Gerard Tellis and Fred Zufryden in *Marketing Science*) in particular caught her eye. The authors described how to plan sales promotions in retail stores using scanner-panel data (individual-level purchase data collected by the scanner at the checkout counter). Using these data, analysts can track the purchases made by a selected sample of consumers. She knew that the State College MassMart collected this kind of data and used these data to identify trends and plan inventory.

The ideas in the article impressed her because they suggested an approach that was different from what she had been doing. She became increasingly skeptical about the current promotion strategy and excited by the prospect of developing a new promotion strategy.

Background

MassMart established its store in downtown State College in 1975 and it was the first mass merchandiser in State College, a college town that is the home of Penn State University. The company had established relationships with several wholesalers and brokers on the east coast from whom it purchased products for sale to local residents and students. Between 1984 and 1994, as the university and the town expanded, sales at MassMart had grown over 500 percent. Its main competitors during this decade were a Sears and a J.C. Penney store located in a mall a few miles out of town. However, in the past two years, there had been increasing pressure on sales from the two WalMarts and the Sam's Club, also located a few miles from the town center.

Donna thought that the past increases in sales at the MassMart store in State College were in large part caused by the company's promotional policy of always passing on the trade discounts it received from wholesalers to its consumers. The logic behind this policy was simple: Those discounts caused no incremental costs to MassMart but helped attract

---

* This case was developed by Jianan Wu under the guidance of Professor Arvind Rangaswamy. The case describes a hypothetical situation.

new consumers from nearby communities, some of whom would keep coming back to buy other merchandise, thereby contributing to growth in sales and profits.

When Donna met with Jack in January to review 1996's promotional activities, both thought that they needed some fresh ideas for a more intelligent strategy for promoting sales. The tougher competition had led to thinner profit margins and anything they could do to increase profitability would help them compete better.

Scanner-panel data

MassMart had installed an optical scanner system in its State College store in 1988, with the primary objective of improving checkout service and the store's accounting and inventory systems. This investment paid off: The store inventory was better monitored than ever before; price changes have been easier to implement; and check out time decreased by an average of 40 percent. To keep better track of consumer needs and trends, MassMart developed its own "scanner panel," consisting of a representative sample of consumers from the shopping areas of its key stores. Panel members get a five percent discount for shopping at MassMart when they show their membership cards at checkout. Data on their purchases go into a database maintained by the company. Separately MassMart also kept records on prices, in-store promotions, special store displays, and newspaper inserts featuring specials at these stores. The complete scanner-panel database could provide all of the following data:

- The regular prices of all brands at the time of purchase
- The identification numbers of the panel members (to protect their privacy, the company did not store members' names directly in the database)
- The dates each panel member made purchases
- The product category and brands purchased
- The quantity of each item purchased
- Temporary price cuts (if any) for all the brands in a category at the time of purchase
- Whether each item purchased was part of an in-store display
- Whether each item purchased was featured in the local newspaper

(Exhibit 1 shows a sample of scanner-panel data for the liquid-laundry-detergent product category.)

Donna talked to Jack Chen about some of the ideas she had for using scanner data in planning promotions: "Jack, I think we should revamp our promotion program. The more I think about our current promotion strategy, the more I am convinced that we need to do something very different. You know, we simply pass on trade deals directly to consumers, but we have never looked at whether this is a good strategy. These trade deals are designed by our wholesalers and the packaged-goods companies. I am not sure these discounts really serve our interests here in

State College. We really have no idea what discount levels would increase our sales and profitability most."

"Donna, I guess you're right. Go on."

"We often give discounts on several brands at the same time just because we have gotten trade discounts on all of them. Our sales for all the discounted brands increase, but I wonder whether this makes sense. It might be better sometimes to combine what we get in trade deals so that we can give a larger discount on the brand WalMart is promoting. Loyal consumers of the nondiscounted brands will still buy that brand."

"But Donna, won't our profits go down if we discount just the brand WalMart discounts?"

"Not necessarily! According to an article I read, when two brands are on discount fewer people switch brands than when only one is discounted. If we discount both brands our opportunity costs are higher. Loyal consumers of both brands who would purchase the brand anyway without a discount are just subsidized by the discount. Of course the opportunity costs depend on the number of loyal consumers of each brand. But I think offering simultaneous discounts on two brands is likely to be less profitable than discounting just one brand."

"Donna, I think you have something. But we often get trade deals simultaneously for several brands from our wholesalers. How would we know which brand to discount and how much to discount?"

"To figure that out, I think we need to look at our promotions from the point of view of our consumers. That article I read said that the key is to understand consumer responses to price-cuts, displays, and features. Response will of course vary for different brands and product categories. I think looking at our scanner-panel data may give us some insights."

"Donna, if the best discounts to offer vary by brand and category, won't we have to continuously monitor the effectiveness of our promotions and the promotions of other stores and change our discounts to suit each specific situation? If so, won't we need to use this database on an ongoing basis? All this seems so much more complicated than the simple policy we have now."

"It is! But we already have the data. The MIS department told me that it wouldn't be hard to put together a database, at least as an experiment for one or two categories. In fact, they got us some data on the liquid-detergent category last week. I also got some software from a professor in the business school so that we can build a computer model to evaluate promotion effectiveness. Let me try it out with the detergent category, and we can take it from there."

"Good idea, Donna! Let me know what you find out. I don't want to do anything new without testing it out carefully. I am also concerned about whether managers at our 79 other stores, who are not fans of all this computer stuff, will adopt your approach. What we have now is so easy for them to follow."

"I know, but easier may not be better."

The promotion model

The software Donna got from her professor friend builds a choice model of consumers using the scanner-panel data and a profit model for the retailer that is based on the consumer-choice model. Together the two models incorporate three components:

Consumer-brand-choice component: This component assesses the likelihood (P) that consumers will purchase a specific brand in response to retail promotion variables, such as price discount, in-store display, and newspaper feature. The model captures consumers' loyalty to certain brands through a loyalty index that it derives from panel members' histories of past purchases of alternative brands.

Purchase-quantity component: This component of the model determines how many units of a brand a consumer will purchase once he or she decides to buy a particular brand. The quantity purchased (Q) will depend on the price cut, the consumer's current inventory of that product category, and the consumption rate of the product. The model estimates household inventory and consumption rates by examining the panel member's past purchase history.

Retailer-promotion component: The third component of the model computes retailer profits based on the brand discounted and the size of the discount. The retailer's profit function is constructed as follows:

$$Profit = \sum \; profit\, margin \times P \times Q$$

where P and Q together provide an estimate of the demand for a brand in a period, and the summation is over all the brands in the category. The model assumes that the retailer seeks an optimal promotion scheme to maximize profits over a planning period.

Although MassMart carries 11 brands of liquid laundry detergent, the four most popular brands are Tide, Wisk, All, and Yes, which account for more than 80 percent of the sales in the category. Donna decided to use these four brands to conduct her experiment.

With all this preliminary work behind her, Donna Sullivan pulled up this new software and began her analysis.

Customer ID	Date	Brand Purchased	Quantity	Regular Price	Discount	Display	Feature
1001	03/01/95	Tide	50 Oz	$ 3.55	$ 0.43	No	No
1001	03/29/95	Tide	64 Oz	$ 3.99	$ 0.54	Yes	Yes
1001	04/25/95	Tide	50 Oz	$ 3.55	$ 0.45	No	No
1001	05/28/95	All	50 Oz	$ 2.99	$ 0.50	Yes	No
1001	06/27/95	Tide	50 Oz	$ 3.60	$ 0.45	No	No
1001	07/22/95	Tide	50 Oz	$ 3.60	$ 0.20	No	No
1001	08/29/95	All	64 Oz	$ 3.15	$ 0.60	Yes	Yes
1001	09/24/95	Tide	50 Oz	$ 3.65	$ 0.42	No	No
1001	10/28/95	All	100 Oz	$ 4.99	$ 1.00	Yes	Yes
1001	11/25/95	Tide	50 Oz	$ 3.99	$ 0.50	No	No

EXHIBIT 1

A segment of the scanner-panel database for liquid laundry detergent shows the purchases made by a single individual over 10 periods along with the store-environment information (e.g., regular price, display) at the time of purchase.

EXERCISES

NOTE: This exercise is based on a small data set to facilitate analysis in Excel. It consists of data for eight consumers over 10 periods in which they choose from four brands (providing a total of 320 data points).

1. Summarize the important factors that influence consumer brand choice within the detergent category. If a consumer chooses a particular brand, what other factors will influence the quantity that consumer will purchase?

2. Based on the sample input data, what is the best promotion strategy? Explain why you think that strategy will work. For the promotion strategy that you recommend, what will be the composition of sales? What proportion of sales comes from brand switchers, and what proportion comes from consumers stocking up (i.e., purchase acceleration)?

3. Does promoting two brands simultaneously make sense? Why or why not?

4. How do the trade deals (profit margins) affect retailers' promotion decisions (which brand and how much)? Should trade deals always be passed on to the store consumers? Why or why not?

5. Should Jack Chen adopt this approach for all MassMart stores? Why or why not?

INDEX